The Selected Letters of Anton Chekhov

edited and with an
introduction by
Lillian Hellman

PICADOR *Classics*

published by Pan Book

First published in Great Britain 1955 by Hamish
Hamilton Ltd
This Picador Classics edition published 1988 by
Pan Books Ltd, Cavaye Place, London SW10 9PG
9 8 7 6 5 4 3 2
© Lillian Hellman 1955
© renewed Lillian Hellman 1984
ISBN 0 330 28538 6
Printed and bound in Great Britain by
Richard Clay Ltd, Bungay, Suffolk

Anton Chekhov

Born the son of a former serf in the port of Taganrog in 1860, Chekhov went to Moscow to study medicine in 1879. His studies were handicapped by financial pressures and he had to write comic stories to pay for his education. Chekhov qualified as a doctor in 1884 and soon devoted himself to literature. His first book – *Motley Stories* – appeared in 1886 and his play *The Seagull* was produced ten years later. By then Chekhov had fallen victim to the tuberculosis which caused his tragically early death in 1904. His plays are undoubtedly masterworks of modern Russian literature. *The Seagull, Uncle Vanya, The Cherry Orchard* and *The Three Sisters* stand with the finest plays of Shaw, Ibsen and Strindberg in the first rank of twentieth century dramatic writing.

'So rich in atmosphere, so revealing and subtle, so funny and sad, so wise and tender . . . his plays sink deep roots into the Russia of his time. They make us feel with out hearts, not merely understand with our heads' J. B. PRIESTLEY

PICADOR *Classics*

Portrait of Anton Chekhov, by I. Braz (State Tretyakov Art Gallery)

TRANSLATOR'S NOTE

For the most part the translator has used the excellent and definitive text of the new edition of Chekhov's works, in twenty volumes, published in the USSR from 1944 to 1951, of which volumes 13 through 20 are devoted to his letters. These eight volumes contain 4,200 communications (mostly letters, plus a few postcards and telegrams), a number of which are published here for the first time in English, along with many previously known letters that contain passages not previously printed.

In a few letters appearing in the Soviet edition, certain passages found in earlier editions have been deleted; in such cases the translator has, of course, used the older edition and has restored the omitted words. On the whole, however, the new Soviet edition returns to the letters much that older texts had left out. Where brackets occur, they contain explanatory remarks on the part of the editor, or indicate by [. . .] omissions common to both old and new texts. Sometimes, from their context, it is plain that these brackets refer to deletions of "four letter" words; at other times it is not possible to determine whether words, sentences or even paragraphs have been suppressed.

CONTENTS

INTRODUCTION

WHEN I was young we used to play a game called what-famous-writer-would-you-most-like-to-have-dinner-with? and a lot of our choices seem surprising to me now, though we stuck pretty close to serious writers as a rule and had sense enough to limit our visiting time to the dinner table. Maybe we knew even then that writers are often difficult people and a Tolstoy—on too big a scale—might become tiresome, and a Dickens unpleasant, and a Stendhal—with his nervous posturing—hard to stand, and a Proust too special, and a Dostoevski too complex. You can argue that greatness and simplicity often go hand in hand, but simple people can be difficult too and by and large the quality of a man's work seems to have little to do with the pleasure of his company. There are exceptions to this—thank God—and Anton Chekhov seems to have been one of them. I'd like to think I had picked him for dinner back in those young days. Or, better still, for many, many dinners.

Chekhov was a pleasant man, witty and wise and tolerant and kind, with nothing wishywashy in his kindness nor self righteous in his tolerance, and his wit was not ill-humored. He would have seen through you, of course, as he did through everybody, but being seen through doesn't hurt too much if it's done with affection. He was neurotic, but unlike most neurotic men he had few crotchets and no nuisance irritabilities, nor pride, nor side, nor aimless vanity, was unlikely to mistake scorched potatoes for high tragedy, didn't boast, had fine manners and was generous and gay. It is true that he complained a lot about his ailments and his lack of money, but if you had laughed at

[ix]

him he would have laughed with you. Such a nature is rare at all times, but it is particularly remarkable in a period when maudlin soul-searching was the intellectual fashion. Chekhov lived in the time that gave us our comic-strip picture of the Russian. While many of his contemporaries were jabbering out the dark days and boozing away the white nights, turning revolutionary for Christmas and police spy for Easter, attacking too loudly here and worshiping too loudly there, wasting youth and talent in futile revolt against anything and everything with little thought and no selection, Anton Chekhov was a man of balance, a man of sense.

This is probably the most important thing to know about √ Chekhov. He was a man of sense, of common sense, in a place and time where only the bourgeoisie were proud of having common sense, and they, of course, for the wrong reasons. To them √ the words meant the sense to conform, the sense to concur, the sense to reject all other ways of thinking as inferior or comic or dangerous. This wasn't Chekhov's kind of common sense— he tried to see things as they were and to deal with them as he saw them—but it was the kind of common sense that most nineteenth century intellectuals were in revolt against, and in revolting they did a lot of good. In Russia they helped get rid of serfdom and in America of slavery, in England they were changing life and laws and in France they were coping with a more difficult enemy than their eighteenth century parents had had to face. They were valuable men and fools; heroes and clowns; for every five sincere competent idealists there were five incompetent sick children. Together, good and bad, they floundered through the heavy seas they themselves had helped stir up, sometimes trying to meet new waves with a new twist of the body, sometimes deciding the waves had become too dangerous and it was time to make for shore. Conscience was their only guide and conscience is not a scientific instrument, at least not in the hands of intellectuals who are inclined to think their own consciences superior to others. The high-minded are often admirable people but they are too often messy and noisy and confused, and this was their big day: a day of noble acts and silly high jinks, all at once, in the same group, in the same man.

The winds and waters of the nineteenth century social hurricane blew especially high in Russia and the scenery had gone hog wild. There was the magnificent side where the cliffs rose straight to Tolstoy and there were ugly places where men lay preaching gibberish to each other in the mud. Men screamed men down in Moscow and St. Petersburg with anti-Orthodox reason that sounded very like Orthodox prayers. Students were in an uproar, society in a dither, dandies contradicted each other in French so elegant that it would not have been understood in the Boulevard St. Germain. Priests led their villages in angry revolt, rich young men gave their property to the poor, men threw bombs in the belief that murder solved tyranny. The reaction was as violent as the uproar: universities cruelly punished their students, the government sent even the mildest protestants into exile and penal colonies.

It is not easy to understand nineteenth century Russia. Few of us know the language or have roots in it. Nor do many of us know much Russian history, and our schools teach us very little. There were few good observers or critics or historians; and few casual travelers, like a grandmother who might have visited Florence or Athens, or been born in Frankfort or Dublin, and lived to tell us a little of what she saw. Even late in the century —a period close to us everywhere else in the Western world— Russian life and Russian thought seemed to spring from sources more mysterious than seventeenth century England or France or Italy. Hamlet is closer to us than Papa Karamazov. We walk through the doors of Elsinore, but we have to be shoved into the Karamazov house, even though the doors were put into place by a man no older than our own grandfather. The agony of Othello could be our agony, but the agony of Raskolnikov is not ours and we give ourselves over to it with an effort. The space between America-Europe and Russia has always been wide. It is probably no wider now than it was seventy-five years ago.

The histories of Western Europe and Russia have seldom run parallel: similar things don't seem to have happened at the same time. Our society in the last half of the nineteenth century had finished with its revolutions and was entering upon the fattest and smuggest period of modern times. It was a secure and neat world for the Western middle and upper classes and they settled back to enjoy it. In many places the social and cultural standards were high, in many places the breeding and the manners were good, and sometimes even taste. There were new standards of living for large numbers of people, and science was making life easier. But this was not true in Russia. Royal money and trading money were there in great quantities, and sugar money and cotton money, but Russian culture, great as it had been in many places, was spotty now, and the ancient culture of Kiev was almost as unknown to St. Petersburg as it was to us. Great feudal landlords and princes and upper-class sons were learning the refinements of the West—they admired and envied them at the same time that they patriotically rejected them—but they were mixing the good things up and tossing them about. No sooner had the aristocracy learned to play a pretty waltz than the new merchant gentry bought the piano from under them. Fine linens were sent off to Holland to be cleaned, but the owner of the linen forgot to bathe. Wine was Western-fashionable, but all-night vodka was still preferred. It was not enough to be religious, it was necessary to be priest-ridden. Intellectuals bewailed the lot of the peasant, and cried over the filth of his village, his house, his life, and they cried so hard that they couldn't see the cockroaches above their own beds. There was no ordinary youthful mooning about life: there were great inner storms that left men broken or dead, or just too tired. "There's hardly a single Russian landowner or University man who doesn't brag about his past. The present is always worse than the past. Why? Because Russian excitability quickly gives way to fatigue . . .

before he has left his school bench, a man picks up a load he can't carry, takes up schools, the peasant and rational agriculture . . . makes speeches, writes to ministers, battles with evil, applauds good, falls in love not simply or any old way . . . it must be a blue stocking or a neurotic or a Jewess or even a prostitute, whom he rescues. . . . He's hardly reached the age of thirty or thirty-five when he starts feeling fatigue and boredom." So Chekhov wrote of his Ivan in *Ivanov* and it was so accurate a picture of the Russian estate gentleman that the play has been called a "medical tragedy." (It is not a tragedy. It is not even a good play, but it is a remarkable picture of upper-class nineteenth century society).

In some strange way—in whatever manner it is that unrest and excitement communicate themselves from one layer of society to another, so that what is felt in one place is mysteriously transmitted to another two thousand miles away—a whole people were on the go. But it is doubtful that the unrest started with the intellectual or the educated rich. It is more likely that the liberalism of nineteenth century Russia came sweeping, incoherent and unformed, from below. Perhaps the Russian intellectual whirled in so many directions just because the pressure did come from a direction that was strange to him and from a class that was seldom his own class. Whatever the cause, men were thinking in the light and acting in the dark. But the confusion worked a kind of catharsis, and from it came a few artists of the very first rank, and many of the second rank, and the second rank in art is a high rank indeed.

Chekhov wrote: "A reasoned life without a definite outlook is not a life, but a burden and a horror." This was a strange idea for the day it was written and "a reasoned life" were words that had not been heard for a long time. But they are the key words to Chekhov's life and work. They would not have been surprising words from a man of Bernard Shaw's background, but they are startling from a nineteenth century Russian intellectual, born in the middle of social uproar. Chekhov was out of line with his time and his country. It is true that he kept the almost religious kindness of most Russians, the forgiving nature that so often comes with oppression and poverty, the humor of a people who are used to trouble. But he brought to these inherited gifts a toughness of mind and spirit that was new to his world and his time. We can account for some of the forces that made the man, and give them names.

Chekhov's birth certificate reads: "January 17th, 1860 born and January 27th baptized, boy Antonius. His parents: the Taganrog merchant of the third guild Pavel Yegorovich Chekhov and his lawful wife Evgenia Yakovlevna, both of the Orthodox faith. . . ." Merchant of the third guild was a fancy way of saying that Pavel Chekhov owned a miserable grocery store which he had been able to buy after marrying Evgenia Morozov. (Morozov is a common name in Russia and Anton Chekhov's mother was no relation to the fabulously rich Moscow merchant family.) Pavel's father had been a serf who, by terrible labor and deprivation, had bought the freedom of his family in 1841, twenty years before the abolition of serfdom, in a period when such families found their new freedom almost as hard as their old slavery.

Six children were born to Pavel and Evgenia, of whom Anton was the third. Life was hard, money was short, and Pavel Chekhov was a man far more devoted to Orthodox ritual and church music than he was to his family or to his business. He was more than a devout Christian: he was a fanatic whose ambition was to have the finest family choir in Taganrog. Anton and his brothers worked long hours in the store after school and were then made to serve in the choir. The Greek Orthodox Church has a strange ritual, long services often occur late at night or very early in the morning, and this meant that the boys led a weary life of too little sleep and too much prayer. It was not unusual for the Chekhov boys to rise at three in the morning to be hustled off to an unheated church in the miserable cold of a Russian winter. Pavel was, indeed, a strange fellow: a good ikon painter, a good violinist, a genial host, and a man of terrifying temper who believed in the whip when he couldn't drive his children fast enough without it. He was also a schlemiel, which is not true of most terrifying men, and it was probably the schlemiel side of his nature that made it possible to live around him at all. Evgenia Chekhova was a kind woman who did her best to alter the iron discipline of the household and to stand between the children and their father. Many biographers have accepted a conventional picture of a sweet, uneducated and simple woman. Evgenia must have been more than that, although she does not come clear. And her relationship with Anton must have been more complex than Anton realized, or, realizing, than he was willing to talk or write about. Anton was devoted to her—or so it seems. Most certainly he was always very good to her. But there are many contradictions in the story of Evgenia and Anton Chehkov. A loving son, long after he is able to live alone, stays on with his family and, almost at the end of his life, plans a house with an eye to pleasing his mother. And yet when he does marry—an important step in his life because he waited so long to take it—he does not consult her, or even tell her of the ceremony until after it is over. Whatever the relationship was between Anton and Evgenia Chekhova —and we do not know much about it—it does not bear the sometimes ugly signs of over-devoted son to over-devoted mother.

Other pieces of the Chekhov family record are missing. Evgenia Chekhova is not the only member of Anton's family who does not come out clearly in his letters or reminiscences. The formal history of the Chekhov brothers and sister is there, but somehow they are not there as people. They lived close to Anton, but they are less close to us than many of the characters in his stories and plays. Perhaps he accepted his family without any of that romanticism that makes so many creative people either hate their background with a hate that is destructive, or cling to their parents and their past with a love so little different from hate that its destructiveness is only of another nature.

By 1876, Pavel Chekhov, merchant of the third guild, was bankrupt and lost his grocery store for good. There was nothing more to hope for in Taganrog and so he decided to move his family to Moscow. The family picked up and pushed on, leaving Anton behind to earn his own way through school by tutoring other boys. He was lonely and he was very poor, but life was better without Pavel and choir practice. Now there was time for fishing and bathing and an occasional cheap ticket to the local theatre, and sometimes there were nice visits to his grandfather who was the overseer of a large country estate. Pavel's father was as vigorous and cheerful a man as his son was mean and narrow: he was a good fellow for a boy to spend time with. These three years of being entirely on his own were important years to Anton Chekhov. He came out of them a young man equipped to deal with a tough world, and unfrightened by it.

In 1879 he left Taganrog to join his family and to enter the University of Moscow as a medical student. He arrived in Moscow knowing, of course, that things had not gone well with his father, and that his family had, as always, been having a tough time. But he was shocked to find that they were living in a filthy basement in the brothel section of the city. City poverty had made its usual ugly marks on lower middle-class provincial people. Pavel, the menacing figure of Anton's childhood, was not even living in the family basement. He had a thirty-ruble-a-month job and he mushed out his lonely life on the other side of town. Anton's older brothers, Alexander and Nikolai, were interesting and talented young men. In revolt, perhaps, against the misery in which they lived, they were, by the time of Anton's arrival, involved in the shabbiest, talkiest, hardest-drinking side of Moscow Bohemia. Chekhov's lifelong contempt for wasters and boasters, his occasional bitter preachiness to his brothers, came from this period of watching Alexander and Nikolai and their friends. He felt affection for his brothers, he was good to them all his life, but it was here he took their measure and there was never, unfortunately, any need to alter it.

The money for Chekhov's university scholarship went to pay the family debts. Supporting himself through medical school would have been hard enough, but it was now obvious that the whole family had to be supported, and he sat down to do it. In 1880 his first piece for a humorous magazine was accepted. In the next seven years Chekhov wrote more than four hundred short stories, sketches, novels, one-act plays, fillers, jokes, law reports, picture captions, one-line puns and half-page tales. The days were medical school, the nights were work, and work that had to be done in an apartment filled with a large family, noisy neighbors and casual guests. It was not easy then, as it is not easy now, to earn a living as a free lance writer. Chekhov was pushed around and cheated by editors, made to beg for the few rubles they owed him. He had to pay ten visits to one editor to collect three rubles, and another editor offered him a pair of pants in exchange for a short story. Hack literary work is very hard work, and the study of medicine is very hard work, but hack literary work, the study of medicine, and the support of a large family can be killing. Men who take on such burdens are never the men who write easy checks for the family food and rent and think their responsibility finished. Men like Chekhov take on as well the moral and spiritual burdens of the people around them, and those are the heavy burdens and take the largest due. Chekhov, from his days as a student, became the father of his family and remained their father for the rest of his life. In time, with success, the burdens became easier, but this period, this very young man period, in which terrible work had to be done against terrible odds, deprived him forever of much that he wanted:

"A young man, the son of a serf, who had worked in a shop, been a choir boy . . . was brought up to defer to rank, to kiss the hands of priests and to submit to other people's ideas; who was thankful for every bite of food, was often beaten . . . who fought, tormented animals, liked to have dinner with his rich relations; who played the hypocrite before God and man without needing to do so . . . this young man squeezed the slave out of himself, drop by drop, and woke up one fine morning to realize that it was not the blood of a slave, but real human blood, that ran through his veins." Again, in contrasting his background with Tolstoy's and Turgenev's, he wrote: "They receive as a gift what we lower-class writers buy with our youth." He bought it high: he had his first hemorrhage at the age of twenty-four.

And at twenty-four he graduated from the medical college of Moscow University. He says that he thought of medicine as his wife and literature as his mistress, but that could not have been so because he acted the other way round. By the time he graduated, he was earning money as a writer and he was a fairly well known name to Moscow magazines. He did work in a hospital the first summer after he left the university, but after that we hear less and less of medicine and nothing of the practice of medicine as we know it. It is doubtful if he ever amounted to much as a doctor although many times throughout his life he speaks of treating his neighbors or the peasants or prescribing for his friends. But one suspects that it wasn't much more than a well-trained pharmacist might have done. His relations with medicine were courtesy relations: he acted toward medicine as if it were a famous and distinguished cousin, a kind of hero he didn't get to see as often as he would have liked.

But the study of medicine was of great importance to Chekhov and perhaps that is what he meant when he spoke of medicine as his wife. Chekhov is a special kind of creative artist, a writer who finds no conflict between the imagination and the scientific fact, who sees the one as part of the other in a dependent and happy brotherhood. He said: "Science and letters should go hand in hand. Anatomy and elegant letters have the same enemy—the devil. . . . In Goethe the naturalist lived in harmony with the poet." Of course many writers think they feel that way but literary people often resent science as if science were a gruff Philistine intruder in a meeting of cultured men, an aggressive guest who says the things that nobody wants to hear. In Chekhov science not only lived in harmony with literature, but it was the very point of the writer, the taking-off place, the color of the eye, the meat, the marrow, the blood. It is everywhere in Chekhov's work and in his life: in his dislike of theorizing, his impatience with metaphysical or religious generalizations, his dislike of 4 A.M. philosophy. (He rejected high-sounding emptiness even when it came from a man he loved and respected: he said of a new Tolstoy theory, "To hell with the philosophy of the great of this world.") It is in his contempt for self-deception and hypocrisy: "You hold that I am intelligent. Yes, I am intelligent in that I . . . don't lie to myself and don't cover my own emptiness with other people's intellectual rags." He was intelligent, he believed in intelligence, and intelligence for Chekhov meant that you called a spade a spade: laziness was simply not working; too much drink was drunkenness; whoring had nothing to do with love; health was when you felt good and brocaded words could not cover emptiness or pretensions or waste. He was determined to see life as it was.

Was he this kind of a man because he was a doctor? Or had he become a doctor because he was this kind of a man? It doesn't matter. We only need to know that as a writer he was a good doctor, a sort of family physician to his characters. An honest physician tries hard to make a correct diagnosis: his whole being depends upon his ability to recognize the symptoms and name the disease. Such men are not necessarily more dedicated to the truth than the rest of us but their profession requires that they bear it more closely in mind. Chekhov bore it close.

There is no work of Chekhov's that better illustrates his determination to see things as they are than the short story, "A Tiresome Tale." A famous and distinguished scientist, knowing that he is soon to die, takes a long last look at his family, his pupils, his assistants. He had lived in the hope of leaving something behind: it is now clear to him that his career has been a waste and all his official medals cannot cover the waste. "A Tiresome Tale" is not only a wonderful short story but, coming in 1889, it was a clear, fresh statement of life. The story has in it most of Chekhov, good and bad. Dr. Stepanovich is a new figure in Russian literature: a man who must see the world for what it is, without tears, without turmoil, because he believes that only truth can bring hope for the future. But Katya, the romantic young actress of the story, is a literary throwback. She seeks the answer to the meaning of life in the same tiresome way that so many like her have sought it before. Katya is, of course, Nina in *The Seagull*. The characters in "A Tiresome Tale" appear over and over again in the stories and plays. It has been said that while Chekhov was sorry for the Ninas of the world, he was also making fun of them, and never meant their troubles to be mistaken for lofty tragedy. That is true, but it is more likely that writers who walk fast always have twigs from dead wood on their clothes, always have old stones, like Katya, in their shoes. But the twigs and the stones are of no importance to the creative artist: it's the length and speed of his journey that counts. He has very little time, no matter how fast he runs, and he cannot stop along the way to sort out the good merchandise from the bad, the old from the new, as if he were a peddler.

In Chekhov, the conflicts and contradictions of the old with the new have led to an unusual number of opinions about the man himself and to many different interpretations of his plays. People see in him what they wish to see, even if they have to ignore his words; or, more frequently, they ignore the dates on which the words were written. Some critics see Chekhov as a political radical, a man who desired the overthrow of a rotting society. Other critics see him as a non-political man, an observer of the scene, a writer who presented the problem but refused to give the answer. Still others see a man who, far from criticizing anything or anybody, was only saddened by a world that destroyed the delicate and punished the finely made. None of these points of view is the truth, although each has in it something of the truth. But the truth about Chekhov, if you keep prejudiced hands off, is not hard to find. The words are there and they are dated.

Chekhov, like all men who grow, sometimes changed his mind. He had grown up in a time of social unrest. He was a student when student riots broke out all over the land and he saw many of the boys he knew carted off to jail or banished to Siberia. His school was rigidly controlled by the Czar's representatives and his writing was rigidly censored by the Czar's literary bureaucrats. It was a time of revolt and feelings ran high on both sides. Chekhov took little part in the revolt—of that there can be no question—and many Russian intellectuals criticized him for what he didn't do or say. But he went his own way, he took his own method. In a time when it was dangerous to hint that Russia was not the most blessed of lands he was sharply critical, in his stories, of the society around him. He condemned the rotten life of the peasant, the filth and squalor of village life, the meanness of the bureaucracy, the empty pretensions of the landed gentry, the lack of any true spiritual guidance from the church, the cruelty and degradation that were implicit in poverty. He needed no political party, no group, no platform to dictate these themes. As a young man he felt the needle of his more radical friends, and he answered them: "I should like to be a free artist and that is all. . . . I consider a label or a trademark to be a prejudice." But when, two years later, a Moscow magazine took him too literally and called him a "writer without principles," he got into one of the few angry passions of his life. The letter to Lavrov, the editor of the magazine, has a kind of illogic, and a pettish, defensive quality which is unlike Chekhov. Magarshack, in his good book, *Chekhov the Dramatist,* says: "This letter is important in that it reveals the inner conflict that was going on in Chekhov's mind at that particular time. Indeed, his defense against Lavrov's criticism is rather lame, and the fury of the letter must be ascribed to his own realization of its lameness. Chekhov defends himself against an accusation which obviously hurt him to the quick . . . and he advanced the curious plea that he was really a doctor and not a writer at all, and that even as a writer he had so far got along excellently with his friends." Lavrov's charge struck something painful. The youthful "I should like to be a free artist" was no longer true, but he didn't know how to say so. The desire to be a free artist was always to be with him, but the "that is all" period was over forever. At the age of thirty-two he wrote to Suvorin that the Russian artist lacked something. "Writers who are immortal or just plain good . . . have one very important trait in common: they are going somewhere and they call you with them. . . . Some of them, according to how great they are, have aims that concern their own times more closely, such as the abolition of serfdom, the liberation of their country, politics, beauty, or simply vodka. Others have more remote aims, such as God, life beyond the grave, human happiness and so on. (In) the best of them . . . every line is permeated, as with juice, by a consciousness of an aim, you feel in addition to life as it is, also life as it should be. . . . But what about us? We have neither near nor remote aims and our souls are as flat and bare as a billiard table. We have no politics, we do not believe in revolution, we deny the existence of God. . . . But he who wants nothing, hopes for nothing and fears nothing cannot be an artist."

These two letters are so far apart in feeling because the times had changed. Now, in the 1890's, the intellectuals were disillusioned and resigned. Chekhov disliked these men and disapproved of their cowardice and their callous social irresponsibility. He was growing older and his requirements for himself and for others hung on a higher peg, and were of a different nature. (It is not a disgrace in Europe to grow older, and the

European artist need not cling to the ideas and ideals of his youth.) Truth was still the goal, but now Chekhov knew it could be bare and impotent standing by itself. He had found out that the writer must not only find the truth but he must wrap it up and take it somewhere. Chekhov, like most natural writers, never knew how he got it there, nor why, nor what made him take it in a given direction. Nor did he ever bother to find out. But somewhere he was taking his own kind of truth, and the somewhere was increasingly good.

There can be no doubt, on the evidence, that Chekhov was a man of deep social ideals and an uncommon sense of social responsibility. This has been true of almost every good writer who ever lived and it does not matter that the ideal sometimes seems to be a denial of ideal, or that it springs from hate, or has roots in snobbishness, or insanity, or alcohol, or just plain meanness. What comes out in the work is all that matters. The great work of art has always had what Chekhov called the aim, the ideal, and none of us coming after the artist has the right to define or limit his ideal by imposing upon him the moral and political standards of our time. We have the right to find in books what we need to find, but certainly we have no right to refashion the writer's beliefs to suit our own. This happens too often with us, and is a form of vanity.

If Chekhov had written only short stories or novels or poetry the opinions of his critics and his interpreters wouldn't matter very much. The printed work would be there and nobody could stand between it and us unless we allowed them to. It would be interesting to know that Mr. X. from Moscow disagreed with Mr. Y. from New York, but, in the end, the biographer, the critic, the teacher, and those who write such introductions as this, cannot do permanent harm to a printed work.

But this is not true of plays. People do read plays, but not very much, and most of us judge them by what we see on the stage. If the literary world has a handful of interpreters who mistake themselves for the author, the theatrical world has only a handful who do not mistake themselves for the playwright. We all need to see ourselves as a little more important than we are, but people in the theatre need to see themselves as a lot more important than anybody else.

Stanislavski, a great director, is probably most responsible for the frequent misinterpretations of the Chekhov plays. We have taken his prompt scripts for the Moscow Art Theatre productions and used them as our bible, adding our own misinterpretations, of course, until now we seldom see a Chekhov play that is pure Chekhov. Most of us, therefore, do not know the plays. We know only something that we call "Chekhovian," and by that we mean a stage filled with sweet, soupy, frustrated people, created by a man who wept for their fate. This interpretation holds very little of the truth: it is based on the common assumption that the writer shares the viewpoint of those he writes about. One forgives the dinner-party ladies and gentlemen who say, "You must think people terribly evil or you wouldn't write about villains," or, "I am sure you are an awfully nice person because you write about such nice people," but it is hard to forgive the serious critic or reader, or the teacher, or Stanislavski, or the followers of Stanislavski, for this kind of foolishness.

Chekhov fought long and hard against this interpretation of his plays. He lost the battle and he knew it, but, fortunately, he could not have known that it would still be lost fifty years later. Stanislavski was a theatre king by divine right, his actors children of the line, and it is always hard to convince royalty. Chekhov did argue over the plays, but he was a sick man and he was living in Yalta, far away from the theatre world of Moscow and St. Petersburg. He admired the Moscow Art Theatre and felt close to it, though he was critical of it, and sometimes sharp and bitter. He was tied to Stanislavski and Nemirovich-Danchenko by affection and gratitude but Chekhov acted like a father who is forced to sit in impotent disapproval of his child's adopted home lest if he take the child away a new set of foster parents might prove worse than the old.

Stanislavski was a man of intelligence and great ability, and one can wonder why he did not present the plays as Chekhov wished them to be presented. The answer is simple: Stanislavski's interpretation had made the plays popular. What Stanislavski put upon the stage was what the public wanted, or at least what the *avant-garde* section of the public wanted. It was their mood, the state of their disillusioned lives, their lack of hope, their tragic reading of life that was responsible for the popular conception of Chekhov as a playwright. Chekhovian came to mean something drear and wintry, a world filled with puff-ball people lying on a dusty table waiting for a wind to roll them off.

It has been forgotten that Chekhov said *The Seagull* and *The Cherry Orchard* were comedies. Trigorin, in *The Seagull,* has been interpreted in many ways, but he has almost never been played as he was intended: a third-rate writer, a man who was neither good nor bad, an aging and disappointed fellow who floundered around hoping that the next small selfish act would bring him pleasure. Nina is usually played with a certain high-minded foolishness, a virgin with her head in the air, too simple to understand the worldliness of the man who seduces her. Certainly Chekhov meant her to be a sweet and charming young woman, but the head that was in the air was not meant to be too bright, and it was filled with nonsense. She is a sad, lost, hopeless girl whose punishment springs from her own second-rate standards of life. She could never have been intended as the tragic figure that actresses and directors prefer.

And it is so with *The Cherry Orchard.* One of Chekhov's favorite themes is the need that shallow people have for emotional fancy dress, their desire to deck out ordinary trouble in gaudy colors, and to teeter around life like children in their mother's high-heeled shoes. Chekhov makes it very clear that the lovable fools in *The Cherry Orchard* are not even worth the trees that are the symbol of their end. But the play is usually presented as a drama of delicate, charming, improvident aristocrats pushed around by a vulgar, new-risen bourgeoisie. (Chekhov took great pains to point out that Lophakin was *not* a vulgar man and should *not* be played like a lout.) Mme. Ranevskaya is a woman who has dribbled away her life on trifles. Chekhov pitied her and liked her—it still seems to be news to most people that writers end up liking all their characters—but he was making fun of her. In real life it is possible to like a foolish woman, but this viewpoint is frowned upon in the theatre: it allows for no bravura, gets no sympathy for the actress, and is complex because foolishness is complex. It is thus easier, in such cases, to ignore the author's aim, or to change it. *The Cherry Orchard* is sharp comedy. Nowhere else does Chekhov say so clearly that the world these people made for themselves would have to end in a whimper.

He foresaw the end of their world, but he had the artist-scientist hope for a better world. He says so over and over again. It is doubtful, however, that he would have liked or would have fitted into the social revolution that was so shortly to follow him. It is one thing to know what is wrong with the old order, it is another to be comfortable in the new. But human personality is extraordinarily complex and is dependent upon so many factors and grows from so many different roots that one such guess is as worthless as the next. And the roots from which Chekhov grew were very special: his place of birth, his education, his family, his religion, his sexual nature, the whole *niveau* of his life was very different from ours.

Then, too, Chekhov was not a simple man and much of his life is still not known to us and much of what is known is not understood. He was a nineteenth century man and he shared with the intellectuals of his time and his country a kind of Christian ideal of life, although he divorced the ideal from the church he was born into. Human life was of very great importance to these men: they were, in the deepest sense, reformers, and they wished to reform not from busybody zeal, but from their anguish that the individual human being cease to suffer hunger and disease. It was easy for such men to become sentimentalists, and many of them did. Chekhov was a sweet man, a generous man, a tolerant man, and he gave pity where it was due, but he was a tough, unsentimental man with a tough mind, and thus he had tough tools to write with.

His friend Tolstoy, comparing him to Shakespeare, said: "Chekhov doesn't have the real nerve of a dramatist." In the end, Tolstoy is probably right, although the comparison is harsh and hasn't much point.

But then I am not a critic of writers, nor do I wish to be. Chekhov said: "When people talk to me of what is artistic or inartistic . . . I am at my wit's end. I divide all productions into two categories: those I like and those I don't like." I like Chekhov, I like these letters, and I hope you will, too.

BIOGRAPHICAL NOTES

SHOLOM ALEICHEM (1859-1916) was the pseudonym of Solomon Rabinowitz, a humorous writer who emigrated to the United States in 1906.

MARIA ANDREYEVA (? -1953) was an actress in the Moscow Art Theatre. She played Irina in the first performances of "The Three Sisters."

LYDIA AVILOVA (1865-1943) was a writer. The nature of her relationship to Chekhov is unknown. They were probably in love, and Chekhov's friends believed that one of his reasons for going to Sakhalin was to break off with Avilova. In 1947 her memoirs were published in the Soviet Union, and were translated into English as "Chekhov in My Life."

FYODOR BATUSHKOV (1857-1920) was a teacher and an authority on Western European literature, and editor of several magazines to which Chekhov contributed. After Chekhov's death, Batushkov wrote his memoirs of Chekhov and a great number of critical articles on the stories and plays.

PYOTR BYKOV (1843-1930) was a magazine writer.

ALEXANDER CHEKHOV (1855-1913) was the oldest of Chekhov's brothers. He studied mathematics and physics at Moscow University and, while still a student, began writing humorous pieces for magazines and newspapers. He started out as a brilliant and talented young man and ended as a hack writer. Chekhov's letters to Alexander were often written in a kind of teasing, insulting tone, but he had great affection for Alexander and often used him as a business agent.

EVGENIA CHEKHOVA (1835-1919), Chekhov's mother, was born Morozova. It is almost impossible to find any reliable material on her family. Her grandfather was a serf who managed to buy his own freedom and the freedom of her father, Yakov. They were peddlers and small merchants who eventually settled in Taganrog.

IVAN CHEKHOV (1861-1922), the fourth Chekhov brother, was a teacher. He taught for many years in Moscow at a city school. He was a hard-working, conscientious man.

MARIA CHEKHOVA (1863-1957) was Chekhov's only sister. The family managed, somehow, to find enough money to give her a good education. She became a teacher of history and geography in a private school for girls. She was deeply devoted to Anton and was closer to him than any other member of the family. Her whole life was given over to him and, after his death, she became his literary executor and editor.

MIKHAIL CHEKHOV (1865-1936) was Chekhov's youngest brother. He translated Upton Sinclair and Jack London into Russian.

NIKOLAI CHEKHOV (1858-1889), the second Chekhov brother, was a gifted artist. During the 1880's Nikolai did a great deal of work for humorous magazines, often in illustration of Anton's sketches and stories. He died of tuberculosis.

OLGA HERMANOVNA CHEKHOVA (no dates) was the wife of Mikhail.

ALEXANDER ERTEL (1855-1908), a writer, was a good friend of Chekhov's. As a young man he had been banished from St. Petersburg for revolutionary activities.

MAXIM GORKI (1868-1936) was born in Nizhni-Novgorod as Alexei Pyeshkov. His famous autobiography opens with a description of his mother preparing the body of his father for the burial services. Gorki went to work when he was nine years old and, for the next fifteen years, travelled around southern Russia taking any job he could get and educating himself with books borrowed from everywhere. In 1895 a St. Petersburg magazine published one of his short stories: fame and success came fast. Within two years he became a great literary figure, not only in Russia, but in Europe as well. His early romantic stories of hoboes and tramps made Gorki a hero to the working class; his persecution by the Czarist police made him an idol to most of

Russia. After the failure of the 1905 revolution, in which he played an active part, Gorki left the country and continued his political activities from Capri. In 1917, although he had not previously been a member of the party, he gave his support to Lenin and the Bolsheviks. After the revolution he became a kind of cultural arbiter for the new regime. His best known books and plays are "Twenty-six Men and a Girl," "Mother," "The Lower Depths," and "Yegor Bulichev." Gorki's reminiscences of Tolstoy, Chekhov and Andreyev are wonderful records of the three men.

DMITRI GRIGOROVICH (1822-1899) was a popular and respected Russian novelist. Chekhov dedicated his collected stories, "In the Twilight," to Grigorovich in 1887. In 1889, Chekhov received the Pushkin Prize for Literature largely through Grigorovich's efforts.

MARIA KISELEVA (? -1922) was a member of a distinguished family and the wife of a rich and cultured country gentleman. In the 1880's the Chekhovs rented a cottage on the Kiselev estate. Chekhov and the Kiselevs were close friends, but many years later Chekhov said that Mme. Kiselev had become old and reactionary and that he was sick of her.

OLGA KNIPPER (1870-1959) came from an Alsatian family of German background who had settled in Russia. Her father died young and her mother earned a living as a music teacher. Knipper grew up on the fringes of the cultural high-life of Moscow. She was a talented young actress with the Moscow Art Theatre when Chekhov fell in love with her. She was known as the unofficial hostess of his house in Yalta long before their marriage in 1901. In 1904 she played Madame Ranevskaya in "The Cherry Orchard"; in 1943, at the 300th anniversary performance of the play, she was still at it.

ANATOLI KONI (1844-1927) was a liberal lawyer, public official, and an old admirer of Chekhov's.

VLADIMIR KOROLENKO (1853-1921) was a popular novelist. He was a left wing liberal who defended the peasant against the landowner and took a courageous stand against anti-Semitism. He and Chekhov were elected honorary academicians in 1900, but in 1902 they both resigned in protest over the Academy's refusal of Gorki.

Gorki's reminiscences contain a warm and charming picture of Korolenko.

PYOTR KURKIN (1858-1934) was a doctor and an old friend of Chekhov's.

VUKOL LAVROV (1852-1912) was one of the editors of a high-brow magazine, "Russian Thought." He called Chekhov an "un-principled" writer and Chekhov answered with a famous, angry letter. But, a few years later, they patched up the fight and became good friends.

NIKOLAI LEIKIN (1841-1906) was a writer who lived in St. Petersburg. He was the editor of the humorous magazine, "Fragments."

IVAN LEONTIEV (1856-1911) was a playwright and novelist who used the pen name of Shcheglov.

MARIA LILINA (Mme. Alexeyeva) (1866-1923), Stanislavski's wife, was a talented actress of the Moscow Art Theatre.

MARIA MALKIEL (no dates) was the daughter of a rich Moscow family. She and her sister were close friends of Maria Chekhova's and she was a frequent guest at Melikhovo.

ADOLF MARX (1838-1904) was a prominent publisher in St. Petersburg. He put out the first complete edition of Chekhov's works. He was also the publisher of Turgenev, Dostoyevski and Korolenko.

MIKHAIL MENSHIKOV (1859-1919) was a sailor who became a journalist and editor of "This Week." He started out in life as a liberal and ended up as a reactionary. He wrote constantly to Chekhov, but Chekhov in the last three years of his life never answered the letters.

VICTOR MIROLUBOV (MIROV) (1860-1939) was the editor and publisher of a popular monthly, "Everybody's Magazine."

LYDIA MIZINOVA (1870-1937) was a good friend of Chekhov's sister. She was an interesting and attractive young woman who was in love with Chekhov. Chekhov liked her and liked to flirt with her, but there is no evidence that he loved her.

VLADIMIR NEMIROVICH-DANCHENKO (1858-1943) was a well known novelist and playwright long before he and Stanislavski founded the Moscow Art Theatre. He was a brilliant and highly cultivated man and, although his name has never been as

[xxxii]

famous as Stanislavski's, it is possible that he most deserves credit for the high quality of the plays produced by the theatre. It was he who recognized the talents of Chekhov as a playwright and it was he who insisted upon the production of "The Seagull." After the revolution, while the Moscow Art Theatre was making a European tour, Nemirovich-Danchenko established a famous musical studio where he developed a new style for the production of opera and operetta. In 1942, shortly before his death, he received a Stalin award for "Kremlin Chimes," a play about Lenin. The Chekhov-Nemirovich-Danchenko friendship went back to the 1880's, when they were both grinding out a living as writers of jokes and humorous pieces. Chekhov was always closer to Nemirovich-Danchenko than he was to Stanislavski and, over the years, they wrote many letters to each other. Unfortunately, much of the correspondence has been lost or destroyed.

IVAN ORLOV (1851-1917) was a doctor. He and Chekhov became friends in the Melikhovo period.

ALEXEI PLESHCHEYEV (1825-1893) was a poet and essayist. He was an early admirer of Chekhov's. He started out as a radical, inherited a fortune and moved to Paris.

GRIGORI ROSSOLIMO (1860-1928), a fellow student of Chekhov's at medical school, was a neuropathologist who taught at Moscow University. Chekhov had great respect for him as a scientist and great affection for him as a man.

PYOTR SERGEYENKO (1854-1930) is best known for his book on Tolstoy. He went to school with Chekhov in Taganrog.

ELENA SHAVROVA (1874-1937), Mme. Just, was a writer and an actress. She met Chekhov at a picnic in 1889 and asked him to read a story she had written. Chekhov sent the story to Suvorin, who printed it in "New Times."

VASILI SOBOLEVSKI (1846-1913) was the author of a number of articles on finance, economics and diplomacy. His common-law wife was the millionaire patroness of the arts, Varvara Morozova.

KONSTANTIN STANISLAVSKI (1863-1938) was born Konstantin Alexeyev. (The Russians were great name changers.) His father, and his father's friends, were the rich upper class Muscovites who were rapidly taking over the prerogatives of the

Russian aristocracy. The Alexeyevs were theatre and opera patrons—one grandmother had been the famous French actress, Varley—and Stanislavski made his first appearance at the age of three in family theatricals. He organized his brothers and sisters into an acting group of rather extraordinary standards: when, for example, they planned to produce "The Mikado," Japanese acrobats were invited to live on the family estate and give instruction in military drill, Japanese dancing, proper use of the fan, etc. Stanislavski was deeply influenced, as was most of Europe, by the Meiningen court theatre and, shortly after the Russian tour of that great company, he and Nemirovich-Danchenko founded the Moscow Art Theatre ". . . against bathos, overacting . . . the star system . . . the farcical repertoire which was . . . the Russian stage." The brilliance of the Moscow Art Theatre's productions of Chekhov, Tolstoy, Gorki, Shakespeare, Ibsen and Hauptmann changed the modern theatre. The revolution they brought about in acting, stage lighting, stage music and stage designing is the proof that Stanislavski and Nemirovich-Danchenko were the two great theatre men of modern times. On the night of the Kazanski Square massacre in St. Petersburg, Stanislavski was playing Dr. Stockman in "The Enemy of the People." He was so convincing an actor that when he reached the famous line, "You can't put on a new coat when you go out to fight for freedom and truth," the entire audience rose from their seats and rushed upon the stage to thank him for his bravery.

LEOPOLD (LEV) SULERJITSKI (1872-1916) was an artist and writer. He was thrown out of the Academy for revolutionary speeches. He was sent to an insane asylum for refusing to take the oath of allegiance to the Czar, and was then exiled to Central Asia. He organized, with Tolstoy, the emigration of the Dukhobors to Canada.

ALEXEI SUVORIN (1834-1912) was the editor of the powerful, conservative, St. Petersburg newspaper, "New Times." He was an interesting, worldly man, a close friend of Chekhov's, although Chekhov never seemed to have any illusions about Suvorin's love of money and power. The friendship broke up in a fight over Zola and the Dreyfus case.

ANNA SUVORINA (no dates), Suvorin's second wife, was a lively and imaginative woman. She wrote a book about Chekhov.

MODEST TCHAIKOVSKI (1850-1916), brother of the composer, wrote librettos. He was a great admirer of Chekhov's and called himself a "Chekhist."

JOASAPH TIKHOMIROV (? -1908) was an actor in the Moscow Art Theatre.

VLADIMIR TIKHONOV (1857-1914) was a dramatist, fiction writer, and editor of several literary magazines.

ALEXANDER VISHNEVSKI (1863-1943) was an actor in the Moscow Art Theatre. He was a schoolmate of Chekhov's in the early Taganrog days.

VLADIMIR YAKOVENKO (1857-1923) was a distinguished psychiatrist. He and Chekhov were very much interested in local government councils (zemstvos).

YEVGRAF YEGOROV (no dates) was the leader of a community in the Nizhni-Novgorod district.

THE SELECTED LETTERS OF
ANTON CHEKHOV

ANTON CHEKHOV

I

1885-1890

THIS collection of letters begins in 1885 when Chekhov was twenty-five years old. His literary output was already enormous and while the early work cannot be compared with what came later, many of the early stories are very good and all of them are interesting comments on Russian life.

Chekhov had been doing every kind of grubby literary work to support his family. He had even been writing a kind of gossip column. But in 1885 he began to move away from hack work. He gave up the pseudonym of Antosha Chekhonte with which he had signed the early humorous stories and came forth as Anton Chekhov, a modest and earnest young man who was about to take his first steps as a serious writer.

St. Petersburg was the cultural center of Russia—Moscow was the merchants' city—and to be published in St. Petersburg was of great importance to a young writer. Chekhov was already known to the St. Petersburg magazines by his humorous stories, but now the serious stories began to be commented on and praised. Chekhov, on his first visit to St. Petersburg in 1885, was surprised to find himself the literary toast of the town. It was on this visit that Alexei Suvorin, editor of the powerful, conservative, pro-government *New Times,* invited Chekhov to become a regular contributor. The newspaper was important, the pay was better than Chekhov had ever had before and his new friend, Suvorin, was a man of great prestige and influence.

The year 1885 marked other changes in his life. Financially, things were a little easier and his social life was pleasanter. He liked his friends, the Kiselevs, and when they offered to rent him a small house on their beautiful estate at Babkino he jumped at the chance. The Kiselevs were cultured people and they kept open house for the most interesting intellectuals in Russia. The summer guests came and went through days and evenings of charming picnics and brilliant talk and excellent music. Life on the Kiselev estate was on a far higher level than Chekhov had ever known before and he flourished in it.

The years 1885 to 1890 were probably the most important of Chekhov's life. They do not include his most important work, but they lay the pattern for everything that was to come. It was in these years that the stones of the character were set into place, the design of the man took shape. The future was in these years, the good and the bad of it. The first signs of tuberculosis appeared, he became a serious writer and a serious man, and he became famous. The extravagant early praise of the critics and the literary public turned, as it usually does, into extravagant attack. Now they said that he had no philosophy, that he reported life without interpreting it. A critic of great importance, Mikhailovsky, accused him of aimlessness. His connection with Suvorin and the reactionary, anti-Semitic *New Times* was looked upon with suspicion and distaste.

But nobody had taken the measure of the man as well as the man himself. Chekhov looked at his work with clarity and humility. He was on his way to himself, so to speak, and because he knew he would find himself, he was not to be hurried or pushed or bullied. True, the charge of aimlessness bit deep and he turned this way and that, smarting under it.

One of the ways he turned—and then turned back again—was toward Tolstoyism. Chekhov was never a member of the Tolstoy inner circle and even in his most enthusiastic period he disliked the ascetic side of Tolstoy's teachings, but many of the stories written at this time are under the influence of the Master: the vanity-of-earthly-goods theme in "The Bet," and the non-resistance-to-evil theme in "The Meeting." These were also the years of his first full-length play. The short plays, the vaudevilles, were already popular—they showed the great instinctive knowledge he had for theatre technique—but *Ivanov* was his first attempt at a large work for the stage. Much of *Ivanov* is interesting, particularly the first half of the play, but most of it is muddled and overstated and repetitive. It was written by a man who thought clearly, but the play is without clarity. Chekhov discovered—his later plays show how well he learned from the mistakes of *Ivanov*—that characters in a play cannot be written as if they were characters in a story or a novel. He learned, too, that writing for the stage is primarily the technique of paring down.

The Chekhov controversy, the Chekhov legend, roughly dates from *Ivanov*. "For a long time," Bunin wrote many years later, "nobody called Chekhov anything but a 'gloomy' writer . . . a man who looked at everything with hopelessness and indifference. . . . Now they've gone to the opposite extreme . . . they've been going on about Chekhov's 'tenderness and warmth,' 'Chekhov's love of humanity. . . .' All this makes intolerable reading. What would he have felt if he had read about his 'tenderness'? This is a word which one must use very rarely and very carefully about Chekhov." And Hingley in his biography makes it simple: he says that those who are pessimists think Chekhov is a pessimist and those who are optimists think he is an optimist.

I do not understand the pessimist theory. I know of no writer who ever made it more clear that he believed in the future. There is every difference between sadness and despair. Chekhov was often sad but basically he was a gay and cheerful man, calm, pleasant, full of fun. He liked pretty women, he liked wine and a party, he kept open house for his friends, he enjoyed music and fishing and bathing and gardening and money and fame. He took the good with the bad.

In 1889 Chekhov's brother, Nikolai, died of tuberculosis. Chekhov was deeply depressed by his brother's death and his great short story, "A Tiresome Tale," was written immediately afterward. Then, as if to break with the past, he began to prepare for a long and dangerous journey.

To NIKOLAI LEIKIN

October 12, 1885, Moscow

Dear Nikolai Alexandrovich,

Your letter found me in my new apartment. It is near the Moscow River and in real country: clean, quiet, cheap and— dullish. The massacre of the latest issue of "Fragments"[1] struck me like a bolt from the blue. On the one hand I regret all the work I put in, on the other hand, I feel a kind of frustration and disgust. Of course, you are right: it is better to tone down gradually and eat humble pie than to imperil the future of the magazine by getting on your high horse. One must wait and be patient. But I think you will have to tone down continually. What is permitted today will be subjected to the censorship of the committee tomorrow, and the time is near at hand when even the rank of "merchant" will constitute forbidden fruit. Yes indeed, literature supplies a thin crust of bread, and you did a clever thing in being born before me, when both breathing and writing were easier. . . .

You advise me to take the trip to St. Pete . . . and you tell me that St. Pete is not China. I myself know that it isn't, and, as you are aware, have long realized the usefulness of such a journey, but what am I to do? Living as I do in a large family

[1] The censor came down heavily on this issue of *Fragments*, tossing out, among other pieces, two sketches by Chekhov. Leikin was told that he must stop publishing satirical articles or the magazine would be banned from the newsstands.

group I can never expect to have a ten-ruble note to spare, and even the most uncomfortable and beggarly trip would stand me a minimum of fifty rubles. Where can I get that kind of money? I just can't squeeze it out of my family and I ought not. If I were to cut down on food, I would pine away from pangs of conscience. I had earlier hoped it would be possible to snatch enough for the trip out of the payment received from the "St. Petersburg Gazette"; now it turns out that in starting work for this paper I will not earn a bit more than I had previously, and that I will be giving the aforementioned gazette all that I formerly gave to "Diversion," "Alarm Clock" and the others. Allah alone knows how hard it is to maintain my equilibrium, and how easy to slip and lose my balance. Just let me earn twenty or thirty rubles less during the coming month and my balance, it seems to me, will go to the devil and I'll find myself in a mess. Financially I am terribly timid, and as a result of this financial, totally uncommercial cowardice I avoid loans and advances. It is not hard to move me to action. If I had any money I would fly continually from city to city.

I received payment from the "St. Petersburg Gazette" two weeks after I sent the bill.

If you are in Moscow in October, I will manage to pull myself together and leave with you. Money for the Petersburg trip will turn up somehow, and for the return trip I can get funds (earned) from Khudekov.

It is not possible for me to write more than I do at present, for medicine is not like the bar: if you don't practice you cool off. Accordingly, my literary earnings are a constant quantity; they can diminish but not increase.

... Tuesday evenings we have parties with girls, music, singing and literature. I want to take our poet out into the world, or he'll sour on it.

Yours,
A. Chekhov

To DMITRI GRIGOROVICH

March 28, 1886, Moscow

Your letter, my kind, warmly loved bearer of good tidings, struck me like a bolt of lightning. I was deeply moved, almost to tears, and now feel it has left a deep imprint on my soul. May God bestow the same kind serenity upon your old age as you have lavished on my youth. I can really find neither words nor deeds to thank you. You know how ordinary people look upon such a member of the elite as you; you may therefore judge what your letter means to me. It means more than any diploma, and for a beginning writer it is a reward both for now and the future. I am in a daze, as it were. I lack the ability to judge whether I deserve this high award or not. I can only repeat that it has overwhelmed me.

If I do have a gift to be respected, I can confess to you who have a pure heart that I have hitherto not given it any respect. I felt I had some talent, but had fallen into the habit of considering it trifling. Reasons of a purely external character suffice to render one unjust, extremely distrustful and suspicious toward oneself. And, as I now recollect, I have had plenty of such reasons. All my intimates have always referred condescendingly to my writing and have kept advising me in friendly fashion not to change a genuine profession for mere scribbling. I have hundreds of friends in Moscow, among them a score of writers, and I cannot recall one who would read me or consider me a talented writer. There is a so-called "literary circle" in Moscow; talents and mediocrities of all ages and kinds gather together once a week in the private room of a restaurant and give their tongues a good workout. If I were to go there and read just a short excerpt from your letter, they would laugh in my face. During the five years of my roving from paper to paper I have adopted this general view of my own literary insignificance, have quickly got used to regarding my own labors condescendingly, and consider writing a minor matter. That is the first reason. The second is that I am a physician and have been sucked into medicine up to my neck, so that the saying about hunting two rabbits at one time never could have worried anybody more than it worries me.

I am writing all of this in an attempt to justify, in some small degree, my faults. Hitherto my attitude toward my literary work has been extremely frivolous, negligent, and casual. I don't recall a *single* story upon which I have spent more than twenty-five hours; I wrote "The Huntsman," which you liked, in a bath house! I have composed my stories as reporters write their accounts of fires, mechanically, half unconsciously, with no concern either for the reader or myself. In doing so I tried in every possible way not to expend on the story those images and scenes which I held dear and which, God knows why, I have set aside and carefully hidden away.

The first impulse toward self-criticism came from Suvorin's kind, and as far as I can judge, sincere letter. I began gathering my energies to write something purposeful, but I still had no faith in my own power to guide myself.

But then your unexpected, undreamed-of letter arrived. Forgive me the comparison, but it affected me like a governor's order to leave town in twenty-four hours! i.e., I suddenly felt an impelling obligation to make haste and tear myself free as soon as I could from the rut I was in.

I am in agreement with you on all points. The cynicisms which you point out to me I myself felt when I saw "The Witch" in print. They would not have been there had I taken three or four days to write this story, instead of one.

I am going to stop doing work that must be done in a hurry, but not just yet. There is no possibility of my getting out of the routine I have been following. I am not averse to going hungry, an experience I have already had, but this is not a matter concerning me alone. I give to writing my leisure hours—two or three during the day and a small part of the night, i.e., hours suited only for minor efforts. In the summer, when I have more spare time and living costs are lower, I shall take up serious work.

I cannot put my real name on the book because it is too late: the cover design is ready and the book printed. Even before you said so, many Petersburgers advised me not to hurt the book with a pen name, but I paid no attention, probably out of vanity. I do not like my little book at all. It is a hotchpotch, a disorderly ragbag of feeble essays written at the university, slashed by the censors and editors of humorous publications. I believe many people will be disappointed after they read it. Had I known that people were reading me and that you were following my career I would not have had the book published.

All hope is for the future. I am still only 26. Perhaps I shall manage to accomplish something, although time does run out fast.

Excuse my long letter and do not hold it against a man for daring to indulge himself for the first time in his life in such a delight as writing to Grigorovich.

Please send me your photograph, if possible. I have been so flattered and stimulated by your letter that I seem to want to write you not a sheet, but a whole ream. God grant you health and happiness. Please believe in the sincerity of your deeply respectful and grateful

A. Chekhov

To NIKOLAI CHEKHOV

March 1886, Moscow

Dear young Zabelin[1]

I hear that remarks passed by Schechtel and me have offended you. . . . The capacity for taking offense is a quality confined to elevated minds, yet if Ivanenko, Misha, Nelly and I are fit

---

[1] Zabelin was a Zvenigorod landowner. He was an alcoholic. Chekhov used him as the character Bortsov in *On the High Road* (1885).

subjects for laughter, why can't we make fun of you? It wouldn't be fair otherwise. . . . However, if you aren't joking and really think you've been insulted, I hasten to beg your pardon.

People make fun of what is funny, or of what they don't understand. Choose your own interpretation.

The second is more flattering, but alas! you are no riddle to me. It isn't hard to understand a person with whom one has shared the sweet delights of childhood . . . Latin classes and, last but not least, life together in Moscow. Besides, your life happens to be so uncomplicated psychologically that it would even be comprehensible to simple souls who had never so much as seen the inside of a seminary. Out of respect for you I shall be frank. You are angry and insulted . . . but not because of my gibes. . . . The fact of the matter is that you yourself, as a fundamentally decent person, feel you are living a lie; and he who has a guilty feeling always seeks justification outside of himself. The drunkard attributes everything to some tragedy in his life, Putyata blames it on the censor, the individual running away from Yakimanki out of sheer lechery pleads the coldness of his quarters, the sneering attitude of his acquaintances and so on. . . . If I were now to cast my family upon the mercy of fate, I would try to find justification for my act in my mother's character, my blood-spitting and so forth. That is natural and excusable. Such is the quality of human nature. I know that you sense the falsity of your position, for otherwise I would not have called you a decent person. Were that decency to depart, the matter would stand differently, for then you would make your peace with yourself and cease to be aware of the falsity. . . .

Besides being no mystery to me, it is true, too, that sometimes you are rather barbarously funny. You are just a plain human being, and all of us humans are puzzles only when we are stupid, and funny for forty-eight weeks of the year. Am I right?

You have often complained that you are "not understood."

Not even Goethe or Newton did that. . . . It was only Christ who complained, and then he did not allude to himself personally, but rather to his teachings. You are easy enough to understand. . . . Others are not to blame if you do not understand yourself. . . .

I assure you, as your brother and as one who has close ties with you, that I understand and sympathize with all my heart. . . . I know all your good qualities as well as my own five fingers, I value those qualities and regard them with the very deepest respect. If you want proof that I understand you, I can even enumerate them. In my estimation you are good to a fault, generous, not an egoist; you will share your last kopek with others, you are sincere; you are free from envy and hatred, open-hearted, have pity on men and beasts, are not malicious or spiteful, are trusting. . . . You have been gifted from above with something most others lack: you have talent. That talent sets you above millions of people, for here on earth there is only one artist to every two million men. . . . That talent puts you on a plane apart, and even if you were a toad or a tarantula you would still be respected, for all is forgiven to talent.

You have only one failing. But in it lies the source of your false position, your misery, and even of your intestinal catarrh. That failing is your utter lack of culture. Do excuse me—but veritas magis amicitiae. . . . For life imposes certain conditions. . . . To feel at ease among intelligent folk, not to be out of place in such company, and not to feel this atmosphere to be a burden upon oneself, one must be cultured in a particular way. . . . Your talent has thrust you into this charmed circle, you belong to it, but . . . you are impelled away from it and find yourself forced to waver between these cultured people and your neighbors. The vulgar flesh cries out in you, that flesh raised on the birch rod, in the beer cellar, on free meals. . . . To overcome this background is difficult—terribly difficult.

In my opinion people of culture must meet the following requisites:

1. They respect the human personality and are therefore always forbearing, gentle, courteous and compliant. . . . They don't rise up in arms over a misplaced hammer or a lost rubber band; they do not consider they are conferring a favor upon the person they may be living with, and when they leave that person they don't say, "You're impossible to get along with!" They will overlook noise, and cold, and overdone meat, and witticisms, and the presence of strangers in their houses. . . .

2. They sympathize not only with beggars and stray cats; they are also sick at heart with what is not visible to the naked eye. Thus, for instance, if Peter knows his father and mother are haggard with care and do not sleep nights because they see him so seldom (and then, only in a drunken state), Peter will spurn the vodka bottle and hasten to them. They themselves do not sleep nights because they want to . . . pay for their brother's upkeep at college and keep their mother properly clothed.

3. They respect the property of others and therefore pay their debts.

4. They are sincere and fear untruth like the very devil. They will not lie even in small matters. A lie is insulting to the one who hears it and cheapens the speaker in the latter's eyes. They do not pose, they behave on the street as they would at home and do not throw dust in the eyes of their humbler brethren. . . . They are not garrulous and don't intrude their confidences where they are not sought. . . . Out of respect for people's ears they are more often silent than not.

5. They do not make fools of themselves in order to arouse sympathy. They do not play upon the heartstrings of people so that these will have pity and make a fuss over them. They don't say, "I am misunderstood!" or "I've made a mess of everything!" because all this is striving after cheap effect, vulgar, stale, false. . . .

6. They are not vain. They don't traffic in such imitation diamonds as pursuing acquaintance with celebrities . . . listening to the raptures of a casual spectator at the Salon, earning

notoriety in the taverns of the town. . . . If they accomplish a kopek's worth of good work they don't make a hundred rubles' worth of fuss over it and don't boast they can get into places from which others are excluded. . . . The truly gifted always remain in obscurity amongst the crowd and shun as much as possible the display of their talents. . . . Even Krylov[2] said that an empty barrel makes more noise than a full one. . . .

7. If they have talent, they regard it with respect. To it they will sacrifice their repose, women, wine and vanity. . . . They are proud of that talent. Because of it they won't go on drunken sprees with superintendents of low-class buildings and with Skvortsov's guests, for they are aware that they aren't called upon to associate with them, but rather to influence them to a higher cultural level. Besides, they are fastidious. . . .

8. They develop an aesthetic sense. They cannot bring themselves to go to sleep in their clothes, to look with indifference upon bugs crawling from cracks in the wall, to breathe foul air, or step upon a floor covered with spit, or feed themselves off a kerosene stove. They try as best they can to subdue and ennoble the sexual instinct. . . . Truly cultured people don't cheapen themselves. What they need from a woman is not just pleasure in bed, not horse sweat . . . not the kind of cleverness that consists in pretending to be pregnant and in constant lying. . . . Artists in particular require from their women companions freshness, elegance, humanity; not a whore, but a woman who can be a mother. . . . They don't swill vodka all the time, or sniff cupboards—because they realize they are not pigs. They drink only when they are free, on some special occasion . . . for they need to have mens sana in corpore sano.

And so on. Such are cultured people. To educate yourself not to fall below the level of your environment, it is not enough to have read the "Pickwick Papers" or to have memorized the monologue from Faust. . . .

2 Krylov was the famous writer of fables.

To MARIA KISELEVA [*1886*]

What you need is constant work, day and night, eternal reading, study, will power. . . . Every hour is precious.

. . . You must spurn this way of life once and for all, tear yourself away with a wrench. . . . Come to us, smash the vodka decanter and lie down with a book. . . . Turgenev, if you will, whom you haven't read. . . .

. . . you must rid yourself of vanity, for you are no longer a child. You are getting close to thirty. Time to make a change! I'm expecting you—so are we all.

Yours,
A. Chekhov

To MARIA KISELEVA

September 21, 1886, Moscow

. . . To begin with, thank you very much for the passages copied out of "Russian Thought." I kept thinking as I read: "I thank thee, God, that the great writers have not yet been translated in Mother Russia!" Yes indeed, our homeland is still rich on its own. From your letter to my sister I see that you too are trying to be a celebrity. (I am speaking of St. Pete and the samples of mythology stories I have seen.) Good Lord, literature is not a fish, and so I am not envious.

By the way, being an eminent author is not so great a delight. For one thing, it's a gloomy life. Work from morning to night, and not much sense to it. . . . Money—as scarce as hen's teeth. I don't know how things are with Zola and Schedrin,[1] but my place is smoky and cold. I get cigarettes, as before, only on holidays. And impossible cigarettes! They are tough and damp, like little sausages. Before smoking I turn up the lamp wick, dry the cigarette over it and only then light it; while the lamp sputters and reeks, the cigarette cracks and darkens, and I scorch my fingers. . . . you feel that death might be a welcome release.

1 Schedrin was a famous satirist.

Let me repeat, money is scarcer than poetic talent. My receipts don't start coming in until the first of October and in the meantime I stand at the church doors and beg for alms. I work, expressing myself in Sergey's words, terr-rr-ibly hard—honest to God cross my heart—very hard! I'm writing a play for Korsh (hm!), a long story for "Russian Thought," tales for "New Times," the "St. Petersburg Gazette," "Fragments," "The Alarm Clock" and similar organs of the press. I write a great deal and at great length, but I run around in circles, starting one thing before I've finished another. . . . Since I've begun, I haven't allowed my doctor's shingle to be put up, but just the same I've got to continue my practice! Br-r-r!

I'm scared of typhus!

I am never quite well and little by little am turning into a mummified insect. If I die before you, be so good as to give the cupboard to my direct descendants, who will be putting their dentures on its shelves.

I'm quite the rage now, but, judging from the critical glances of the lady cashier in "The Alarm Clock" office, my clothes are not of the latest cut and are not spotless. I don't travel by cab, but on the trolley cars.

However, the writing business has its good points too. First, according to the latest information, my book is not going badly; second, I'll be getting some money in October; third, I am already beginning to reap some laurels: people point me out in restaurants, pursue me just the least little bit and treat me to sandwiches. Korsh nabbed me in his theatre and then and there handed me a season pass. . . . Belousov, the tailor, bought my book, is reading it aloud at home and prophesies a brilliant future for me. When medical colleagues meet me they heave a sigh, turn the conversation to literature and assure me that medicine disgusts them, etc.

As to the question you put to my sister about my having married: the reply is no, and I'm proud of it. I am above marriage! The widow Khludova[2] has arrived in Moscow. Save me, O Seraphim of Heaven! . . .

A few days ago I was at the Hermitage and ate oysters for the first time. Not very good. If you were to omit the Chablis and lemon, they'd be absolutely revolting. The end of this letter is in sight. . . . . Another six or seven months and—spring! Time to get the fishing tackle ready. Farewell, and believe the hypocritical A. Ch. when he says he is devoted heart and soul to your whole family.

I had barely finished this paragraph when the bell tinkled and I beheld the genius Levitan. Cocky hat, clothing of a dandy, thin as a rail. He went to see Aida twice, Rusalka once, ordered some picture frames, almost sold some sketches. . . . Says life is nothing but anguish and more anguish.

God knows what I would give to be in Babkino for a couple of days, says he, probably forgetting how bored he was the last few days there.

A. Chekhov

To MARIA KISELEVA

January 14, 1887, Moscow

Dear Maria Vladimirovna,

Your "Larka" is very nice; it has some roughness, but its conciseness and masculine style redeem it entirely. Since I don't want to set myself up as sole judge of your literary child, I am sending it to Suvorin, an extremely understanding person. I will send you his opinion in due course. And now permit me to dig into your criticism of me. Even your praise of my "On the Road" has not appeased the wrath I feel as an author, and I hasten to avenge myself for "Mire." Be careful and hold fast to your chair so as not to fall into a faint. Well, here goes.

Every critical article, even an unjustifiably abusive one, is customarily met with a silent nod—that is literary etiquette.

2 Khludova was a wealthy widow.

Answering is not admissible and those who do so are properly reproached for inordinate vanity. But since your criticism is, as you said, a sort of "conversation in the evening at Babkino, on the porch, or the terrace of the main house, with Ma-Pa,[1] your dog Counterfeiter and Levitan present." And because you pass over the story's literary aspects and because you carry the question onto general ground, I am therefore not sinning against etiquette if I allow myself to continue our conversation.

Let me say first of all that I, even as you, do not like literature of the kind we are discussing. As a reader and a man on the street, I am inclined to shy away from it, but if you ask my honest and sincere opinion, I will tell you that the question of its right to exist is still a moot one and not decided by anyone. Neither you, nor I, nor all the world's critics have any reliable data on which to base their right to reject such literature. I do not know who is right: Homer, Shakespeare, Lope de Vega, the ancient classical writers generally, who were not afraid of burrowing in the "manure pile," but who were morally better balanced than we; or our contemporary writers, who are strait-laced on paper but coldly cynical in their souls and lives. I don't know who it is that has bad taste: the Greeks maybe, who were not ashamed to sing of love as it really exists in all the beauty of nature, or the readers of Gaboriau, Marlitt and Pierre Bobo.[2] Like questions concerning non-resistance to evil, free will and so on, this one can only be decided in the future. We can only make mention of it, but we can't settle it because it is outside the limits of our sphere of competence. Quoting chapter and verse from Turgenev and Tolstoy, who avoided the "manure pile," does not clarify this question. Their fastidiousness does not demonstrate anything, for certainly even before their time there was a generation of writers who considered as beneath

1 Ma-Pa was a nickname of Maria Pavlovna, Chekhov's sister. He usually called her Masha.
2 Gaboriau, French writer of crime stores; Marlitt, pen-name of a German writer of popular novels; Bobo, nickname for Boborykin, Russian playwright and novelist.

their notice not only "male and female scoundrels" but even descriptions of peasants or officials lower in rank than the head of a small department. Yes indeed, a single period, no matter how fruitful, does not give us the right to draw a conclusion in favor of one or another trend. Talk about the degenerating influence of that trend does not resolve the question either. Everything in this world is relative and approximate. There are people who can be corrupted even by children's literature, who with particular pleasure skim through the Psalms and Proverbs on the lookout for piquant passages; there are also some who, the more they acquaint themselves with the sordidness of life, become all the cleaner. Publicists, jurists and physicians, absorbed in all the secrets of human frailty, are not regarded as immoral; and very often realistic writers are more moral than highly placed ecclesiastics. Yes, and in the last analysis no sort of literature can surpass real life in its cynicism; you cannot intoxicate with one glassful a person who has already drunk his way through a whole barrel.

2. It is true that the world teems with "scoundrels—male and female." Human nature is imperfect and it would therefore be strange to observe only the righteous in this world. Certainly, to believe that literature bears the responsibility for digging up the "pearls" from the heap of muck would mean rejecting literature itself. Literature is called artistic when it depicts life as it actually is. Its aim is absolute and honest truth. To constrict its function to such a specialty as digging for "pearls" is as fatal for it as if you were to require Levitan to draw a tree and omit the dirty bark and yellowing foliage. I agree that the "pearl" theory is a good thing, but surely a man of letters is not a pastry cook, nor an expert on cosmetics, nor an entertainer; he is a responsible person, under contract to his conscience and the consciousness of his duty; being in for a penny he has to be in for a pound, and no matter how distressing he finds it, he is in duty bound to battle with his fastidiousness and soil his imagination with the grime of life. He is like

any ordinary reporter. What would you say if a reporter, out of a feeling of squeamishness or from the desire to give pleasure to his readers, would describe only honest city administrators, high-minded matrons and virtuous railroad magnates?

To chemists there is nothing unclean in this world. A man of letters should be as objective as a chemist; he has to renounce ordinary subjectivity and realize that manure piles play a very respectable role in a landscape and that evil passions are as inherent in life as good ones.

3. Literary men are the children of their age, and so like all the rest of the lot must subordinate themselves to external conditions of living together. They must be absolutely decent. That is all we have the right to require from the realists. However, you have nothing to say against the presentation and form of "Mire." Accordingly, I must have been decent.

4. I confess that I rarely commune with my conscience when I write. This can be explained by habit and the triviality of my efforts. And that is why I don't take myself into consideration when I express this or that opinion on literature.

5. You write: "Were I the editor, I would have returned the article to you for your own good." Then why don't you go further? Why don't you hold responsible the editors who print such stories? Why not sternly take to task the Government Press Administration for not banning immoral papers?

Sad would be the fate of literature (whether serious or trivial) if it were delivered over to the mercy of personal views. That's first. Second, there is no police body which could consider itself competent on matters of literature. I agree that one cannot get along without restraint and the big stick, for sharpers will crawl even into literature, but no matter how you try, you can devise no better police for literature than criticism and the consciences of the authors themselves. People have been trying to invent some such thing since the creation of the world, but no one has yet discovered anything better

Here you would wish me to suffer a loss of 115 rubles and have the editor humiliate me. Others, among them your father, are ecstatic over the story Still others send Suvorin abusive letters, slandering the paper, me, etc., in every possible way. Who is right? Who is the real judge?

6. Further you write, "Leave the writing of such stuff to poor-spirited and unfortunate scribblers like . . ." May Allah forgive you if you wrote those lines in earnest! A condescendingly scornful tone toward little people merely because they are little does no honor to the human heart. In literature the low ranks are as indispensable as they are in the army—one's good sense says so, and the heart should repeat it even more emphatically.

Ooof! I have been wearying you with my fiddle-faddle. If I had known my criticism would have reached such length I would not have started the letter. Please forgive! . . .

Have you read my "On the Road?" Well, how do you like my courage? I am writing of "intellectual" things and am undaunted. In St. Pete it produced a resounding furore. Somewhat earlier I had treated of "non-resistance to evil" and had also astounded the reading public. Compliments have been heaped on me in the New Year's numbers of all the papers and in the December number of "Russian Wealth," which publishes Leo Tolstoy, there is an article by Obolenski (32 pages) entitled "Chekhov and Korolenko." The fellow is in raptures over me and argues that I am more of an artist than Korolenko. He is undoubtedly lying, but nevertheless I am beginning to feel that I possess one distinction: I am the sole person not being printed in the serious journals and writing journalistic trash who has gained the attention of the lop-eared critics. This is the only instance on record of such a case. The "Observer" scolded me —and did they get it! At the end of 1886 I felt like a bone that had been thrown to the dog. . . .

I have written a play on four sheets of paper.[3] It will run for

3 The play was *Swan Song.*

[21]

15 or 20 minutes. The smallest drama in existence. . . . It is being published in "The Season" and will therefore be available everywhere. On the whole, little things are much better to write than big ones: there is very little pretension and sure success . . . what more does one need? I wrote my drama in an hour and five minutes. I started another, but didn't finish, for I had no time. . . .

Best regards to all. You will of course forgive me for writing you such a long letter. My pen has run away with me. . . .

Devotedly and respectfully,
A. Chekhov

To ALEXANDER CHEKHOV

February 3 or 4, 1887, Moscow

My worthy friend,

Since you are a rentier and belong to the idle gilded youth of St. Pete, I find it desirable to give you a bit of work. See here, I need 20 (twenty) copies of Pushkin's works, Suvorin edition. They are absolutely unobtainable in Moscow—the edition was sold out in no time.

If you can intercede for me and buy the abovementioned copies from your benefactor and protector (whom you should respect, as you do me), and send them via the conductor of the express train (with a letter), let me know at once and I'll send the money. Do what you can, for the Pushkin is needed urgently.

You are not our oldest brother, but a rascal: why didn't you restrain your younger brothers from taking such a shameful step as subscribing to the "Sun"? I hope it gives you a good burn!

I haven't seen Nikolai. You're the one who corresponds with him, so please write and tell him to send or bring my new black trousers.

We are all well and send regards. Mother is dying to know whether your Kokosha has begun to talk.

With greetings to all,

Your talented brother,
A. Chekhov

To DMITRI GRIGOROVICH

February 12, 1887, Moscow

I have just read "Karelin's Dream" and am now seriously concerned with the question as to what extent the dream you portray is a dream. It seems to me, too, that the action of the brain and the general feeling of a person asleep are rendered with marvelous artistry and physiological fidelity. Of course, a dream is a subjective phenomenon and its inner aspect can be observed only in oneself, but since the process of dreaming is the same for all people, it seems to me that every reader must measure Karelin by his own yardstick, and every critic must of necessity be subjective. I am judging on the basis of my own dreams, which are frequent.

To begin with, the feeling of cold you convey is wonderfully subtle. When my blanket falls off at night, in my dreams I begin seeing enormous slippery boulders, cold autumnal water, bleak, barren shores—all this is vague, misty, without a patch of blue in the sky; I am dejected and melancholy, as if I had gone astray or been deserted, and I gaze upon the stones and feel a sort of compulsion to cross a deep river; at this time I see little rowboats pulling huge barges, floating logs, rafts and such. All of this is endlessly grim, raw and depressing. Then as I run from the shore, I encounter on my way the crumbling gates of a cemetery, funeral processions, my high school teacher. . . . And all this time I am utterly pervaded with that peculiar nightmarish cold which is impossible in reality and experienced only by sleepers. This all comes to mind very distinctly when one reads the first page of "Karelin," and particularly the top half of the fifth page, where you mention the cold and loneliness of the grave.

I believe that if I had been born and brought up in St. Petersburg I would certainly dream of the banks of the Neva, Senate Square and the massive masonry.

When I feel cold in my dream, I always see people. I happened to read the critic in the "St. Petersburg Reports," who scolds you for having portrayed a would-be cabinet officer, thus impairing the generally elevated tone of the story. I do not agree. It is not the people who spoil the tone, but the way you characterize them, which interrupts the picture of sleep in some places. The people one meets in dreams are bound to be unpleasant. During the sensation of cold, for example, I always dream of the good-looking and learned ecclesiastic who insulted my mother when I was a little boy; I dream of evil, persistently intriguing, maliciously smiling, vulgar people whom one never sees in one's waking hours. Laughter at the windows of a railway coach is a characteristic symptom of a Karelin nightmare. When you feel the pressure of an evil will during your dream and the inevitable ruin caused by some power over whom you have no control, there is always something like this kind of laughter. . . . I also dream of those I love, but usually they are suffering along with me.

When my body gets accustomed to the cold, or when someone in the family covers me up, the sensation of cold, loneliness and oppressive evil gradually vanishes. Along with the warmth I begin to feel as though I were treading on soft carpets or on green grass, I see the sun, women and children. The pictures change continually, more sharply than in real life, though, so that when I wake up it is hard to recollect the shifting from one picture to another. . . . This brusqueness comes through very well in your story and strengthens the impression of dreaming.

A natural phenomenon you have noted is also thrust forcefully before one's eyes: dreamers express their spiritual moods impulsively, in acute form, child-fashion. How true to life this is! People dreaming weep and cry out oftener than they do when they are awake.

I ask your pardon, Dmitri Vasilyevich, but I liked your story so much that I was prepared to run along for a dozen pages, although I am perfectly aware that I cannot tell you anything new, valuable or to the point. For fear of boring you and talking nonsense I am restraining myself and cutting my words short. Let me only say that I think your story is magnificent. The reading public finds it "misty," but for the writing man, who savors every line, such mists are more limpid than holy water. Despite all my efforts I could detect only two spotty places, both unimportant, and even these by dint of straining the interpretation: (1) the descriptions of the characters break up the picture of sleep and give the impression of explanatory notes of the sort which learned horticulturists tack on to trees in gardens, thus spoiling the landscape; (2) at the beginning of the story the feeling of cold is somewhat blunted for the reader and becomes monotonous through frequent repetition of the word "cold."

I can find nothing more, and acknowledge that when I feel an urgent need for refreshing little images in my literary work, "Karelin's Dream" provides a glittering example. That is why I could not restrain myself and had the temerity of imparting some of my impressions and thoughts to you.

Forgive the length of this letter and please accept the sincere good wishes of your devoted

A. Chekhov

To MARIA CHEKHOVA

April 7-19, 1887, Taganrog.

Gentle readers and devout listeners,

I am continuing with some trepidation, observing chronological order.

2nd of April. Traveling from Moscow to Serpukhov was

dull. . . . I arrived in Serpukhov at seven. The Oka is nice and clean. . . .

At eleven I arrived in Tula, that pearl of cities. . . . In Tula schnapps-trinken, a mild bun, and schlafen. I slept twisted into a pretzel . . . with my boot tops next to my nose. Nice weather. . . .

At twelve o'clock, Kursk. There was an hour's wait, a glass of vodka, a wash in the gent's room and some cabbage soup. Change of trains. The coach is full to bursting. Immediately after Kursk I strike up acquaintances: a Kharkov country gentleman, playful, like Yasha K[orneyev], a lady who was operated on in St. Petersburg, a Tomsk police officer, a Little Russian officer and a general wearing the insignia of a provost marshal. We settle social problems. The general thinks in a sane, terse and liberal manner; the police officer is a type of old, hard-drinking hussar sinner, homesick for his sweethearts—he puts on airs like a governor: before uttering a word, he keep his mouth open for a long time, and having pronounced the word he gives a long whine like a dog: e-e-e-e. The lady injects herself with morphine and sends the men out for ice at every station. . . .

Little burial mounds, water towers, buildings, all familiar and memorable. At the lunch counter a plate of unsually delicious and luscious sorrel soup. Then a stroll along the platform. Young ladies. At the last window of the second storey of the station building sits a young lady (or a young matron, for all I know) in a white blouse, languid and lovely. I look at her, she at me. I put on my glasses, she hers. . . . O wondrous vision! I contracted catarrh of the heart and travelled on. The weather is diabolically, shockingly fine. Little Russians, oxen, kites, white cottages, the southern rivulets, branch lines of the Donets railroad with one telegraph wire, daughters of country gentlemen and lease-holders, rust-colored dogs, greenery—all this flashes by like a vision. . . . Hot. The inspector becomes wearisome. The meat patties and pirojki are only half disposed of and are beginning to acquire a slight sour odor. I thrust them under somebody else's seat with the remainder of the vodka.

Five o'clock. The sea is in sight. There it is, the Rostov line, twisting beautifully; there is the jail, the poorhouse, the country boys, the freight cars. . . . Belov's hotel, St. Michael's Church with its clumsy architecture. . . . I am in Taganrog. I am "meeted" by Yegorushka,[1] a mighty young lad, dressed to kill: a hat, gloves costing one ruble fifty, a cane and all the rest. I don't recognize him, but he recognizes me. He hires a carriage and off we go. An impression as of Herculaneum and Pompeii: no people, but instead of mummies, sleepy local yokels and pumpkinheads. . . . We finally reach the house.

Why, it's—it's—Antoshichka!

Da-a-rr-rr-ll-ing!

Next to the house is a bench resembling the box that toilet soap comes in. The porch is in the last stages of decay. Of the front door only one quality has remained—an exemplary cleanliness. Uncle is just as he was, but has grayed considerably. As always he is kind, mild and sincere. Ludmila Pavlovna is so "awful glad" she plumb forgot to sprinkle the expensive tea into the pot and generally finds she has to make excuses and prattle when there is no need. She looks me over suspiciously: am I passing judgment? But still she is happy to make me welcome and at home. Yegorushka is a good lad and very proper according to Taganrog standards. He acts the dandy and likes to look at himself in the mirror. Bought himself a lady's gold watch for twenty-five rubles and goes out with nice young girls. . . . Vladimirchik[2] . . . is gentle and reserved, and is evidently a fine type of lad. He is preparing himself for the church, is entering a theological school and aspires to the career of metropolitan. . . . Sasha is unchanged. And Lelia is hardly distinguishable from Sasha. What is immediately apparent is the unusual gentleness of the children toward their parents and in their relations

1 Yegorushka was Chekhov's cousin.
2 Vladimirchik, Sasha, Lelia were young cousins.

with one another. . . . The rooms themselves are as they always have been: very bad prints and Coates and Clarke's posters tacked up everywhere. There is as little taste in their glaring pretensions to luxury and refinement as there is daintiness in a muddy boot. Crowding, heat, insufficient table space, and a lack of all conveniences. Irina, Volodya and Lelia sleep in one room; Uncle, Ludmila Pavlovna and Sasha in another. Yegor sleeps on a trunk in the vestibule; they probably don't have supper on purpose for fear that the extra heat might blow up the house. Hot air emanates both from the kitchen and from the stoves, which are still heated despite the warm weather. The toilet is miles off, beside a fence, and since occasionally rascally pranksters lurk thereabouts, going at night is more dangerous to life and limb than taking poison. There are no tables, if you do not count card tables and little round ones set up merely as ornaments. There aren't any cuspidors, nor a decent washbasin. The napkins are gray, Irinushka is flabby and slovenly . . . in a word, it's enough to drive a man wild! I don't like Taganrog manners, can't bear them, and, I think, would run to the ends of the earth to avoid them.

Selivanov's house is empty and deserted. Looking at it depresses me and I wouldn't have it at any price. How could we have lived in it, I wonder? . . .

At night I am home again. Uncle arrays himself in the uniform he wears as a church beadle. I help him put on his big medal, which he had never once worn previously. Laughter. We walk to St. Michael's. It is dark and there are no cabs. Walking along the streets you catch glimpses of the local yokels and dockworkers, roaming from church to church. Many people carry lanterns. Mitrofan's church is illuminated very effectively, with crosses from top to bottom. Loboda's home with its brightly lit windows stands out sharply in the shadows.

We reach the church. Gray, ordinary and drab. Little candles stuck in the windows are the extent of the display of illuminations. The avuncular countenance is lit with a most beatific smile—which takes the place of electric lighting. The church decorations are nothing to go wild about, and remind one of the Voskresensk church. We sell candles. Yegor, as a dandy and liberal, does not do so, but stands to one side and regards everyone with an indifferent eye. But Vladimirchik feels in his element.

The procession of the cross. Two foolish individuals walk ahead, waving fiery torches, which reek and sprinkle the celebrants with sparks. The congregation is pleased. In the vestibule of the temple stand the founders, benefactors and worshippers of the said edifice, with uncle at their head, and with icons in their hands await the return of the procession. Vladimirchik sits on top of the wardrobe where the vestments are kept, sprinkling incense into the brazier. There is so much smoke you can scarcely breathe. But now the priests and icon bearers enter. The moment of triumphant silence is at hand. All glances are turned toward Father Vasili.

"Pappy, shall I sprinkle in some more?" suddenly pipes Vladimirchik from aloft.

Matins begin. I pick up Yegor and we go to the cathedral together. There are no cabs and so we are obliged to go on foot. In the cathedral all is seemly, decorous and exultant. The choir is magnificent. The voices are glorious, though the discipline is good for nothing. . . .

We walk home from the cathedral. My legs ache and are numb. We break our fast in Irinusha's room: excellent Easter cake [kulich], abominable salami, gray napkins, closeness and the smell of children's clothing. Uncle is breaking his at Father Vassily's. After eating my fill and drinking some of our good local wine, I lie down and fall asleep to the sound of the "blah-blah-blah" of the women.

In the morning the invasion of priests and singers gets under way. I go to the Agalis'. Paulina Ivanovna is in a happy mood. Lipochka didn't come near me because her jealous husband won't let her. Nikolai Agali is a healthy idiot who is forever taking exams, doesn't pass them and hopes to attend Zurich University. Stupid. From the Agalis' I went to Mme. Savelyev's on Kontorskaya St., where she lives in the creaking wing of a decrepit house. In two tiny rooms are two virginal couches and a cradle. . . . Eugenia Jasonovna is living apart from her husband. She has two children and has become terribly ugly and like a bag of bones. From all appearances she is unhappy. Her Mitya is in the service in a Cossack village somewhere in the Caucasus and lives a bachelor's life. An unmitigated swine. . . .

Threading my way through the New Bazaar, I become aware of how dirty, drab, empty, lazy and illiterate is Taganrog. There isn't a single grammatical signboard and there is even a "Rushian Inn"; the streets are deserted; the dumb faces of the dock-workers are smugly satisfied; the dandies are arrayed in long overcoats and caps. Novostroyenka is decked out in olive-colored dresses; cavaliers, young leddies, peeling plaster, universal laziness, satisfaction with a futile present and an uncertain future —all this thrust before the eyes is so disheartening that even Moscow with its grime and typhus seems attractive. . . .

"I say, old man, how about coming over to my place?" asks one of the local clowns who pops in on me. "I always read your weekly articles. My old man is quite a type! Come on and look him over. I bet you forgot I'm married! I've got a little girl now. Ye gods, how you've changed!" and so on.

After dinner (soup with hard rice and chicken) I go over to Khodakovski's. Mr. K. doesn't live badly at all, although not on the luxurious scale he used to maintain when we knew him. His fair Manya is a fat, well-cooked Polish lump of flesh, agreeable in profile but unpleasant in full face. Bags under the eyes and intensified activity of the sebaceous glands. Obviously up to tricks. Later I learned that this past season she all but ran off with an actor and even sold her rings, earrings and so on. Of course, this is all being told you in confidence. I would say it's the fashion here in Taganrog to run off with actors. Many are they who find their wives and daughters missing. . . .

On my way home from Loboda's I meet Mme. Savelyeva and her daughter. The daughter takes right after her daddy; giggles a lot and is already a good talker. When I helped her put on an overshoe which had fallen off, as a token of gratitude she looked at me languidly and said, "Do come and spend the night with us."

At home I found Father John Yakimovski, an obese, over-stuffed priest who graciously deigned to interest himself in my medical career and, to Uncle's great satisfaction, condescendingly expressed himself, "It's very nice for parents to have such good children."

A reverend deacon who was present also deigned to interest himself in me and said that their choir at St. Michael's (a rabble of hungry jackals headed by a hard-drinking choir-master) was considered the best in town. I agreed with him, although I knew that Father John and the deacon don't under-stand a damned thing about singing. A little country deacon sat at a respectable distance and cast longing glances at the preserves and wine with which the priest and reverend deacon were regaling themselves. . . .

I sleep on a couch in the living room. The couch has not grown any bigger, is still as short as it used to be, and so, getting into bed, I had to poke my feet indecently into the air or put them down on the floor. It brings to mind Procrustes and his bed. I cover myself with a pink quilt, stiff and stuffy, which be-comes intolerably obnoxious at night when the stoves lit by Irina make their presence felt. A Yakov Andreyevich[3] is a fond but unattainable dream. Only two persons permit themselves this luxury in Taganrog: the mayor and Alferaki. All the rest must either pee in bed or take a trip to God's outdoors.

6th of April. I awaken at 5 A.M. The sky is clouded, and a cold, disagreeable wind, reminiscent of Moscow, is blowing. I am weary. I wait for the cathedral chimes and go to late mass. It is lovely, dignified and thrilling in the cathedral. The choir

[3] Chekhov's name for a chamber pot.

sings well, not like tradespeople and Philistines, while the
listeners consist wholly of young ladies in olive dresses and
chocolate jackets. There are many pretty ones, so many that I
am sorry I am not Mishka, who needs pretty faces so badly. The
majority of the local girls are well built, have splendid profiles
and are not averse to making a little amour. Of cavaliers there
are none, if you don't take into account the Greek brokers and
shady local sparks, and for that reason officers and male new-
comers here live in clover.

From the cathedral to Yeremeyev's. I find his wife at home, a
very nice little lady. Yeremeyev has set himself up not half bad,
in Moscow style, and looking at his huge apartment, I cannot
believe Alexander's statement that it is not possible to live
decently in Taganrog. A flock of visitors, including all the local
aristocrats—insignificant, cheap little people, amongst whom,
however, one can make a tolerable selection. . . . At 3 o'clock
Yeremeyev comes home, drunk as a lord. He is ecstatic over my
arrival, and swears eternal friendship; I was never on very good
terms with him but he swears he has only two true friends in
the world: Korobov and me. We sit down to eat and split a
bottle. A very decent dinner: good soup without hard rice, and
broilers. Despite the cold wind we visit Quarantine after dinner.
There are many summer cottages in this section, cheap and
comfortable; they can be rented for next year, but I am taken
aback by the abundance of places: wherever you have so many
of them, you are bound to have lots of people and noise. . . .
Many people advise me to drive out five miles from Taganrog to
Meeus, where there are more summer cottages. I'll write you
if I do. . . .

7th, 8th, 9th and 10th of April. The most boring days possible, cold and overcast. I "have to go" continually every day.
I run outside day and night. The nights are pure torture: pitch
darkness, wind, hard-to-open, creaking doors, groping through
dark yards, a suspicious quietness, no newspaper in the toilet.
. . . Every night I am constrained to swear at myself for volun-

tarily accepting torture, for having left Moscow for the land of
. . . pitch darkness, and toilets next to fences. The constant feeling of uncomfortable camping out, accompanied by the ceaseless
"blah-blah-blah," "you don't eat much, you should eat more,"
"but you forgot to use the good tea . . ." Only one consolation:
Yeremeyev and his wife and their comfortable apartment. Fate
has had mercy on me: I haven't run into Anisim Vasilich and
not once yet have I been forced to talk politics. If I meet him
I'll pop a bullet through my head.

I've "got to go" and so I rarely leave the house. It isn't possible to leave here right now, for it's coldish, and anyway I
would like to have a look at the procession through the cemetery. The 19th and 20th I shall be having a big time as best
man at a wedding in Novocherkassk, while before and after
those dates I'll be at Kravtsov's, where the daily discomforts are
a thousand times more comfortable than the Taganrog comforts.

11th of April. A drunken party at Yeremeyev's, then a trip
in gay company to the cemetery and Quarantine. . . .

I have been making the acquaintance of young girls every day,
i.e., the young girls visit Yeremeyev's to have a look at what kind
of bird this writer Chekhov is. Most of them are not bad-looking or stupid, but I am indifferent, for I have intestinal catarrh,
which stifles all tender emotions. . . .

Father Pavel is as always the somewhat soiled dandy and
never will say die; he informs on everyone, swears and finds
fault. . . .

Pokrovski is an archdeacon. He is cock of the roost on his
own dungheap. Comports himself like a bishop. His mamma
cheats at cards and doesn't pay up when she loses.

14th of April. Alas! the bitter cup has not passed me by:
yesterday that small potato, the asinine police officer Anisim
Vasilich stopped in. He spoke with a strong local accent, but as
loudly and shrilly as hundreds of local yokels together are not
in a condition to do.

"Wa-al, for the Lord's sake, I been telling your friend here where I live, so why ain't ya dropped in to see me? My little boy Firs, he's been sailin' all over the ocean. Has that brother Nikolai of yours finished that picture of his? He been showing them at these here exhibitions, ain't he?"

He told us that the police chief had made him give his word of honor that he wouldn't scribble for the newspapers, that the head of the entire police department had promised to send him beyond the Urals in twenty-four hours if he dared write even one line, etc. Further he discoursed on the weather, Socialists, Italy, immorality, marmots, spoke ceaselessly, with modulations and interjections and so loud that I almost had a fit, and I edged him out into the yard. He sat there until evening: to get rid of him I went to the park, and he after me; from the park I dashed to Yeremeyev's—he following. I didn't find Yeremeyev in, so I went home with the police scum in tow, etc. He promised to call for me today and accompany me to the cemetery. . . .

My intestinal catarrh continues to carry me from the room to the grassy spot and back again. My head cold is gone and in its place a new ailment has put in its appearance—phlebitis of the left shin. Three or four inches of the vein are as hard as a slate pencil, and it aches. My infirmities are endless! In me is being fulfilled what was written in Holy Scripture, that in sorrow thou shalt bring forth children. But my children are not Yegor, nor Vladimirchik, but tales and stories, which I cannot even think about now. Writing is repugnant to me.

Two of my stories are appearing in the "Petersburg Gazette," i.e., 65-70 rubles' worth. Sometime this April I'll be sending another, so you'll be receiving 100 rubles from the "Petersburg Gazette." As for "New Times," I can't tell you anything yet.

Father Vasili is dangerously ill. . . .

Loboda's business is very slow; Uncle's sales amount to a few kopeks apiece, and even those don't come easily. The choristers and church workers who get their wages from him are under some sort of obligation to buy merchandise in his shop. . . .

On Tuesday I was at the cemetery procession. This procession is so original that it merits a special description and for that reason I won't describe it now but put it off for another time. On Wednesday I should have been on my way but the phlebitis in my leg prevented my leaving. From Wednesday to Saturday I gadded about in the park, the club, and with the young ladies. Regardless of the tedium and boredom of life in Taganrog, it absorbs one remarkably and is not hard to get used to. During all the time I spent in Taganrog I could praise only the following: the wonderfully delicious ring rolls at the market, the local wine, fresh caviar, the excellent cabmen and Uncle's genuine hospitality. All the rest is inferior and unenviable. The local girls, true, are not bad-looking, but you have to get used to them. They are awkward in their movements, frivolous in their relations with men, run away from home with actors, giggle loudly, are oversexed, whistle like men, drink wine, and so on. Amongst them there are even cynics, like the fair-haired Manya Khodakovskaya. This individual makes fun not only of the living but of the dead as well. When I took her for a stroll in the cemetery she kept on laughing at the dead and their epitaphs, at the priests, deacons, etc.

What I detest about Taganrog is the way they keep their shutters closed. However, in the morning, when the shutters are opened and the sunlight bursts into the room, one's soul becomes joyful again.

On Saturday I traveled further. At Morskaya Station the air was wonderful and the very best caviar seventy kopeks a pound. In Rostov there was a two hours' wait; in Novocherkassk twenty hours to wait. I spent the night with an acquaintance. Come to think of it, I've spent nights in every damned place imaginable: on beds with bedbugs, on sofas, on couches, on trunks. . . . Last night I slept in a long and narrow room on a divan under a mirror. . . . I am now in Novocherkassk. I have just lunched: caviar, butter, divine "Chimpagne" and luscious meat croquettes with scallions.

To MARIA CHEKHOVA [*1887*]

The young lady for whom I am being best man has postponed her wedding until Friday. On Thursday I have to be in Novocherkassk again, and today at four I am on my way. . . . In the meantime, goodbye.

A. Ch.

I'm off tomorrow morning.

To MARIA CHEKHOVA

April 25, 1887, Cherkassk

. . . Yesterday and the day before that the wedding took place, a real Cossack affair, with music, old women bleating like goats and scandalous carousing. One gets such a mass of diverse impressions that it is impossible to give them to you in a letter, so I will put off any descriptions until I get back to Moscow. The bride is sixteen. The couple got married in the local cathedral. I was best man in somebody else's frock coat, with the very widest of trousers and without studs. Such a best man would be a laughing stock in Moscow, but out here I made more of an impression than anybody.

I saw lots of rich prospective brides. An enormous choice, but I was so drunk all the time that I took bottles for girls, and girls for bottles. Owing to my drunken condition, probably, the local girls found I was witty and "sarcastical." The girls here are absolute sheep: if one gets up to leave a room, the others follow after. The boldest and "smartest" of them, who wanted to show that she was not unaware of subtle niceties of behavior and the social graces, kept tapping me on the arm with her fan and saying, "You bad boy!" though she kept on darting timid glances at me all the time. I taught her to repeat to the local cavaliers, "How naive you are!" [with a Ukrainian accent].

The bridal pair, probably because of the force of local custom, kept exchanging resounding kisses every minute, their lips producing a minor explosion each time, as the air compressed; my own mouth acquired a taste as of oversweet raisins, and a spasm afflicted my left calf. My phlebitis in the left leg got worse what with all the kissing.

I cannot tell you how much fresh caviar I ate and how much liquor I drank. I don't know what kept me from bursting wide open. . . .

My intestinal catarrh left me the moment I left Uncle's. Evidently the odor of sanctity has a weakening effect on my insides.

Yesterday I sent the "Petersburg Gazette" a story. If you have no money by the fifteenth of May, you can get my fee from them without waiting until the end of the month by sending a bill for the two stories. It's dreadfully hard for me to write. . . . I have many themes in mind for "New Times" but the heat is such that even letter writing is a chore.

My money is coming to an end, and I have to live like a pimp. Wherever I go I live on other people's money and am beginning to resemble a Nizhni-Novgorod swindler who retains his sleekness even while sponging on others. . . .

Goodbye. I hope you're all well.

The cherry and apricot trees are in bloom.

A. Chekhov

To MARIA CHEKHOVA

May 11, 1887, Taganrog

. . . It is a superb morning. Because of the holiday (6th of May) the cathedral bells are pealing. I meet people on their way from mass, and see police officers, justices of the peace, military men and other ranks of the heavenly hierarchy issuing from the church. For two kopeks I buy some sunflower seeds and for six rubles hire a rubber-tired carriage to take me to Holy Mts. and back (2 days later). I leave town through some lanes literally submerged in the green of cherry, apricot and apple trees. The birds sing indefatigably. The passing Ukrainians, probably taking me for Turgenev, doff their caps; my coachman, Grigori

Polenichka, keeps jumping down from his seat to adjust the harness or flick the whip at the little boys running behind us. . . . A file of pilgrims stretches along the road. The mountains and hills are pale in color, and the horizon a bluish white; the rye stands high, oak forests flit past—and the only things lacking are crocodiles and rattlesnakes.

I reach Holy Mts. at twelve. The place is unique and remarkably beautiful; the monastery lies on the bank of the Donets River, at the foot of an enormous white rock on which, huddled together and suspended one above another are gardens, oaks and century-old pines. It is as if the trees cannot find enough room on the cliff and some power thrusts them higher and higher. The pines literally hang in the air and look as though they will topple over. The cuckoos and nightingales never hush night or day.

The monks, extremely agreeable people, gave me an extremely disagreeable room with a mattress as flat as a pancake. I spent two nights there and came away with a mass of impressions. During my sojourn, because of St. Nicholas Day, about fifteen thousand pilgrims thronged there, of whom nine-tenths were old women. If I had known there were so many old ladies in the world I would have shot myself a long time ago. Concerning the monks and my contact with them, the medical treatment I gave them and the old ladies, I will inform you in the pages of "New Times," and when we meet. The services are never-ending: at twelve midnight the bells ring for matins, at five A.M. for early mass, at nine for late mass, at three for the song of praise, at five for vespers, at six for canons. Before each service the pealing of bells may be heard in the corridors, and a scurrying monk exclaims in the voice of a creditor begging his debtor to pay him at least a measly five kopeks on the ruble: "Lord Jesus Christ, have mercy on us! Time for matins!"

Remaining in one's room is awkward, so you get up and go out. I found a favored haunt on the banks of the Donets and sat out all the services there.

To MARIA CHEKHOVA [*1887*]

I bought Aunty Feodosia Yakovlevna an icon.

The monastic food was offered free to all the 15,000: soup with dried fish and thin gruel. Both dishes, as well as the rye bread, were delicious.

The chimes are wonderful. The choir is bad. I took part in the procession of the cross on boats.

I am cutting short my description of Holy Mts. as it can't all be put down at one time, and only makes a hash.

On the return journey there was a six-hour wait at the station. I felt dejected. I saw Sozia Khodakovskaya in one of the coaches; she daubs and paints herself all the colors of the rainbow and looks like a mangy alley-cat.

Then followed a whole night in the third-class coach of an odious, broken-down, dragging freight and passenger train. I was all in.

Now I am in Taganrog. Once again "blah-blah-blah . . ." is with me, again the exiguous couch, Coates' pictures, the stinking water in the washbasin. . . .

A sign on the main street proclaims: "Artesial fruit sodas sold." In other words, the dunce had heard the word "artificial" but hadn't heard it right and so put it down as "artesial." . . .

I get a nauseous feeling when I write. I have no money and if I didn't have the faculty of living off other people I don't know what I'd do.

You can smell the acacias. Ludmila Pavlovna has gotten stout and resembles [...] very much No intelligence can fathom the profundities of her intellect. When I listen to her, I am lost in wonder before the inscrutable fates which sometimes create such rare pearls.

Incomprehensible creation! I haven't yet forgotten my anatomy, but contemplating her skull I begin to disbelieve in the existence of the substance termed brain.

Uncle is delightful and just about the best of anyone in town.

A Chekhov

To ALEXANDER CHEKHOV

November 20, 1887, Moscow

Well, the first night[1] is over. . . . I'll describe everything in order. To start with, Korsh promised ten rehearsals and gave me only four, and of those only two could properly be called rehearsals, since the other two were in the nature of tournaments where the lady and gentlemen actors practiced the art of controversy and abuse. Only Davidov and Glama knew their parts, while the rest followed the prompter and their inner convictions.

Act One. I sit behind the scenes in a little box resembling a police cell. The family is in an upper tier box and on edge. Contrary to expectations I myself am cool and feel no agitation. The actors are atremble, tense, and cross themselves. Curtain. Enter the benefit performer. Lack of assurance, the way he forgets his lines and the wreath brought in and presented to him combine to make the play unrecognizable to me from the very first words. Kiselevski, on whom I had placed great hopes, did not pronounce one phrase as he should have. Literally: *not one.* He just spoke his own lines. Despite this and the stage manager's blunders the first act went off successfully. Lots of curtain calls.

Act Two. A mass of people on the stage. Guests. They don't know their lines, mix everything up, and talk nonsense. Every word cuts like a knife thrust in the back. But—oh Muse!—This act was also a success. Everybody was called out, me too, twice. General congratulations all around.

Act Three. Not badly done. Enormous success. I am called before the curtain three times, with Davidov shaking my hand and Glama, in the style of Manilov, pressing my other hand to her heart. A triumph of talent and virtue.

Act Four. Scene One. Doesn't go badly. Curtain calls. Next a very, very long, wearisome intermission. The audience, which is unaccustomed to getting up and going to the refreshment bar

1 The first night of *Ivanov*.

between scenes, mutters. The curtain rises. Beautiful: in the archway, a supper table (the wedding). The orchestra plays flourishes. Out come the best men: they are drunk, and so, you see, they have to clown and kick up their heels. The side show and tavern atmosphere fills me with horror. At this point Kiselevski enters: this is a poetic interlude which grips the soul, but my Kiselevski does not know his part, is drunk as a sailor and something distressing and odious happens to the short, poetic dialogue. The audience is bewildered. At the end the hero dies because he cannot endure the insult hurled at him. The cooling and exhausted audience cannot make head or tail out of this death (which the actors had wrested out of me; I have another version). The actors and I are called before the curtain. During one of the curtain calls frank hissing can be heard, stifled in applause and the stamping of feet.

On the whole, I feel a sense of weariness and irritation. Disgusting, although the play had a solid success (denied by Kicheyev and Co.[2]).

The theatre people say they have never seen such turmoil, such general applause and hissing, and never had they ever had occasion to listen to such hot words as they heard that night. And there had never before been an occasion at Korsh's when the author had been called before the curtain after the second act.

The second performance is on the twenty-third, with the other version and with changes: I am taking out a couple of the actors in the wedding scene.

Details when we meet.

Your

A. Chekhov

Tell Burenin that after the play I snapped right back into my routine and sat myself down to my weekly piece.

---

2 Kicheyev was the critic on a Moscow newspaper who denounced the play as "coldly cynical," "profoundly immoral," etc.

To ALEXANDER CHEKHOV

November 24, 1887, Moscow

Well, dearest Gooseyev,

The dust has finally settled, and the clouds dispersed, and once again I sit at my desk composing stories with my mind at ease. You cannot imagine what went on! Heaven only knows what meaning they read into my poor little trashy play[1] (I sent one print to Maslov). I already wrote you that the first performance stirred up such excitement in the audience and behind the scenes as the prompter, who has worked in the theatre for thirty-two years, had never before witnessed. They shouted, raised Cain, clapped and hissed: in the refreshment bar they almost came to blows, while in the gallery the students wanted to chuck out somebody and the police escorted two people to the street. The place was in an uproar. Sister was on the verge of fainting. Dyukovski, who got palpitations of the heart, ran out of the theatre, while Kiselev for no good reason clutched his head in his hands and cried out in all sincerity, "Now what am I going to do?"

The actors were nervously tense. Everything I have written to you and Maslov about their playing and their attitude toward their parts should of course go no further than my letters. A great deal may be explained and excused. It seems that the little daughter of the actress who played the lead was close to death—what could acting mean to her?

The day after the performance Pyotr Kicheyev's review in the "Moscow News" called my play brashly cynical, immoral trash. It was praised in "Moscow Reports."

The second performance came off not too badly, although with surprises. Instead of the actress with the sick daughter, another one went on (without rehearsal). Again there were curtain calls after the third act (twice) and the fourth, but this time without the hissing.

There you have it. My "Ivanov" is on again on Wednesday.

1 *Ivanov.*

Now everything has calmed down and is back to normal. We have marked the nineteenth of November with a red letter and will celebrate it every year with a spree, for the said day will certainly be memorable to the family.

More I won't write about the play. If you want to have some understanding of it, ask Maslov to let you read his copy. A reading won't throw any light on the commotion I've described; you won't find anything in particular. Nikolai, Schechtel and Levitan, i.e., artists—assure me that on the stage the play is so original as to make it strange to look upon. In reading it, though, you won't notice anything of the sort.

See here, if anybody on "New Times" wants to scold the actors who took part in the play, do ask them to refrain from censure. At the second performance they were splendid.

Well, sir, I'll be off to St. Pete in a few days. I'll try to make it by the first of December. In any case we'll celebrate the birthday of your eldest together. Warn him there will be no cake.

Congratulations on your promotion. If you are indeed the secretary, insert a notice that " 'Ivanov' was given a second performance on November 23 at the Korsh Theatre. The actors, especially Davidov, Kiselevski, Gradov-Sokolov and Kosheva, had to take numerous curtain calls. The author was called out after the third and fourth acts." Something like that. If you put this note in they'll give my play an extra performance and I'll get an extra 50 or 100 rubles. If you find it inexpedient to insert a notice of that kind, don't do so.

What's wrong with Anna Ivanovna? Allah Kerim! The St. Petersburg climate is not for her.

I received the 40 rubles—thanks.

Have I wearied you? It seems to me I acted like a psychopath during all of November. . . .

Keep well and forgive my psychopathy. I won't do it again. Today I am normal. . . .

> Yours,
> Schiller Shakespearovich Goethe

To ALEXEI PLESHCHEYEV

February 9, 1888, Moscow

... In return for your promise to print "The Steppe" in its entirety and to send me your magazine, I am replying with an offer to treat you to some of the very finest Don wine when we take our trip on the Volga next summer. Unfortunately Korolenko is no drinker; and on such a journey, when the moon gleams and the crocodiles gaze forth at you from the water, not knowing how to drink is as uncomfortable as not being able to read. Wine and music have always served me as a most efficient corkscrew. When, during my travels, I have felt stopped up, in the head or in the heart, one little glass of wine would be enough to send me soaring aloft, a free soul.

So Korolenko will be with me tomorrow; he is a good soul. It's a pity the censor hacked at his "Along the Way." An artistic but obviously bald thing (not the censor, but "Along the Way"). But why did he send it to a censored magazine? Secondly, why did he entitle it a Christmas story?

I must get busy at once with some minor work, but am itching to undertake something big again. If you only knew what a subject for a novel I've got in my noodle! What marvelous women! What funerals, and what weddings! If I had the money I'd be off for the Crimea, sit myself under a cypress and write a novel in one or two months. I have 48 pages done already, imagine! However, I'm lying: if I had any money, I would embark upon such a mad whirl that all my novels would be shot to hell.

After writing the first part of this novel, if you allow me I will send it to you for reading, but not to the "Northern Herald," as it won't do for a publication which is subject to censorship. I am insatiable. I love crowds of people in my productions, and for that reason my novel will be a long one. Besides, I love the people I portray and find them attractive, and I like to fool around with attractive people for as long as I can. ...

To MIKHAIL CHEKHOV [*1888*]

You write that you liked Dymov.[1] . . . Life creates such natures as this arrogant Dymov—not to be heretics or hoboes, nor to lead settled lives, but as out-and-out revolutionists. . . . There will never be a revolution in Russia, and Dymov will wind up by drinking himself to death or landing in prison. He is a superfluous man. . . .

Tomorrow I am having a high time at the wedding of a tailor who writes verse not too badly and has mended a jacket of mine out of respect for my talent (honoris causa). I have wearied you with my nonsense, and so I shall stop. Keep well. I hope your creditors will vanish into Never-Never land. . . . An importunate breed, worse than mosquitoes.

Yours in spirit,
A. Chekhov

To MIKHAIL CHEKHOV

March 15, 1888, St. Petersburg

. . . I reached here safely but had a miserable trip, thanks to Leikin, the prattler. He kept me from reading, eating and sleeping. . . . The wretch kept boasting continually and pestering me with questions. I would just begin to drowse when he would nudge me and ask, "Did you know that my 'Bride of Christ' has been translated into Italian?"

I have been stopping at the Moscow Hotel, but am moving today to the "New Times" building, where Mme. Suvorina has offered me two rooms complete with grand piano and couch in an alcove. Taking up residence with the Suvorins will cramp my style a lot.

The biscuits have been given to Alexander. His family is in good health, well nourished and cleanly dressed. He does not touch liquor, which surprised me quite a bit.

It is cold and snowy. Wherever I go people talk about my

1 Dymov is a character in "The Steppe."

"The Steppe." I visited the Pleshcheyevs, Shcheglovs and some others and tonight I am going to Polonski's.

I have moved to my new diggings. Grand piano, harmonium, the couch in the alcove, a valet named Vasili, a bed, fireplace, an elegant desk—these are my conveniences. As for the inconveniences, you can't begin to count them. To begin with the least of them, there's not the remotest chance of my appearing home half drunk and with a lady guest. . . .

Before dinner—a lengthy conversation with Mme. S. on how she detests the human race, and that she bought herself a jacket today for 120 rubles.

After dinner, talk about migraine headaches, while the kiddies stare at me goggle-eyed, waiting for me to say something real clever. That's because they consider me a genius, as the author of "Kashtanka." . . .

From dinner to teatime I indulge in pacing back and forth in the Suvorin study, plus philosophy; the spouse injects herself into the conversation, but inappropriately, putting on a bass voice or yapping like a dog.

Tea. There is medical talk at the table. Finally I am free, and sit in my study in blessed silence. Tomorrow I am running away for the whole day: am going to Pleshcheyev's, Sabashnikov's "Messenger," Polonski's and Palkin's, and will return late at night worn to a frazzle. By the way: I have a special toilet and a separate exit—without it one might as well lie down and die. My Vasili is dressed more decently than I and has a well-bred physiognomy; it feels a bit strange to have him walking around me reverently on tiptoe and trying to anticipate my every wish.

On the whole, being a literary man has its inconveniences.

I am sleepy, but mine hosts retire at three. They don't have late supper and I'm too lazy to go to the Palkins.

I have the honor to send my compliments to all.

I'm too lazy to write, and there is too much going on anyway.

Votre à tous

A. Chekhov

To ALEXANDER CHEKHOV[1]

April 26, 1888, Moscow

Mr. Goosekov!

This is an answer to your last letter. Before all else I invite you to compose yourself and reflect upon the roots of things. Secondly, may I inform you of the following:

You can settle your children in Moscow, but only under the one condition that you guarantee before whomever or whatever you choose that neither cowardice, nor deluge, nor fire, nor sword, nor even pestilence, will prevent you from being punctual, i.e., from dispatching a definite number of rubles at a definite date each month. The substance of the matter lies in money. Neither Grandfather's piety nor Grandmother's goodness, neither Daddy's tender feelings nor the generosity of the uncles—*nothing can take its place*. Bear the above words in mind, as I do every moment. If you feel that the proposed condition is within your power to fulfill, read on.

Fifty rubles a month is enough. Less is impossible. The children will come under the sway of one of the grandmas, but which of them? . . . My place is *crowded* and there is positively no room for children. I pay 750 rubles for the apartment. If I were to add two rooms to accommodate the children, nurse, and juvenile paraphernalia, the apartment would cost 900. However, we would be crowded no matter how spacious the apartment might be. You know my place has a multitude of adults living under one roof only because we cannot separate, in view of certain incomprehensible circumstances. With me are Mother, Sister, Mishka[2] (who won't leave until he is graduated), Nikolai, drunk and half undressed, who does nothing whatever and has been abandoned by his *objet*, Auntie, and Alyosha[3] (the last two only use the apartment). Add to this that Ivan is around

---

1 Alexander Chekhov's wife was dying and he had written to ask if he could send his children to Moscow.

2 Mishka was the son of a family friend who was attending the University of Moscow.

3 Alyosha was Alexei Doljenko, a cousin.

from three in the afternoon until late at night and on all holidays, and that Papa comes evenings. They are all nice people, jolly but egoistic, pretentious, unusually talkative, prone to stamping their feet, impecunious. My head is in a whirl. . . . If you were to add two more beds for the children and a nurse, I would have to pour wax into my ears and put on dark glasses. . . . If I had a wife and children I would gladly take unto myself even a dozen youngsters, but with my present family, which is weighed down by abnormal communal life, which is noisy, financially irresponsible and held together unnaturally I cannot decide to take on any more people, let alone those who require educating and setting on their feet. Moreover, my little family group is southward bound at the beginning of May. To drag children there and back would be inconvenient and expensive.

The children can live with Auntie Feodosia Yakovlevna. I've already spoken to her on the subject, informed her of your motives and mine, and she has gladly consented. Alexei is a good man, and he too will probably have nothing against it.

Living with her will offer the children a number of comforts: (1) a quiet atmosphere, (2) the good will of their hosts, (3) the absence of annoyances, such as music, guests, and pious folks looking down their noses at the fruits of your irregular marriage and so on.

For fifty rubles Auntie will give the children lodging, food, servants and my medical care (apartment—eighteen to twenty-five rubles; Alex's fuel; nursemaid—five to six rubles, the rest to go for victuals and emergencies). Stipulations: the children must be brought from St. Pete by you or a servant; there is nobody here to call for them. An apartment must be found by the first of September. Until then the youngsters will stay with Auntie in my apartment (so twenty-five rubles a month will be enough for you to send until then).

My head is killing me; this letter is probably written incoherently. If such is the case, it's a pity. Generally speaking my head is in a bad state. I think you will understand me, i.e., you may not understand me and what goes on inside of me, but you will understand the reasons and considerations. Write to me, not to Auntie. When we have reached an understanding you may write to her, otherwise there will be many unnecessary conversations. Conversations have been driving me frantic. Keep well and as cheerful as you can.

Your A. Chekhov.

Tear up this letter. On the whole, get into the habit of tearing up letters, otherwise you will have them thrown around all over the apartment.

Come to see us in the south this summer. It doesn't cost much.

To IVAN LEONTIEV [SHCHEGLOV]

May 3, 1888, Moscow

Dear Alba,

. . . Pleshcheyev is arriving sometime after the tenth. How about your making the trip? Yes, you! In any event, I'll wait for you all summer. Perhaps you'll make up your mind to come. By the by, I won't expect you in June, when I'll be traveling. If you do come, bring along three pounds of good pork bologna, the very best (I'll pay you back).

. . . I sent a story to the "Northern Herald" and am slightly ashamed of it. Very dull and dripping with fancy philosophy. I hated to do it, but had to, for we run through money like water. Tomorrow I am finishing a story for "New Times." All summer I'll be writing only small things.

I had a letter from Lehman: he informs that "we" (i.e., all of you St. Petersburgers) "have agreed to carry announcements of one another's works in our books," invites me to concur in this proposal and warns that "only those persons more or less *in solidarity* with us" can be included in this elite. In reply I sent my consent and inquired as to how he knew who was or was not in solidarity with me. How smug all of you are in St. Pete! Don't tell me you aren't all oppressed by such words as solidarity, the unity of young writers, community of interest, and so on? Solidarity and such stuff I understand on the stock exchange, in politics, in religious affairs (of a sect), etc., but solidarity in young literary men is impossible and unnecessary. We cannot think and feel the same way, our aims are various or nonexistent, we know one another slightly or not at all, and so there isn't anything to which this solidarity might fasten itself securely. Is there any need for it? No. To lend a helping hand to one's colleague, to respect his personality and labors, not to gossip about him or envy him, not to lie or play the hypocrite before him—to act thus you've got to be not so much the young literary figure as just a plain human being. Let us be ordinary people, let us adopt the same attitude toward all and then an artificially wrought solidarity is not needed. This persistent striving to set up the private, professional, solid little group that you people want, would only mean unconscious spying on one another and suspicion and control; and without meaning to, we would turn ourselves into something like a Jesuit society. I am not in solidarity with you, dear Jan, but I promise you to the death full freedom as a writer; i.e., you can write where and how you like . . . change your convictions and tendencies a thousand times, and so forth and so on, but my human relations with you will not change one iota, and I'll always print announcements of your books in mine. I can promise the same to all my other colleagues, and would wish the same for myself. To my way of thinking these are the most normal relations. It is only thus that we can have mutual respect and even friendship, and compassion in life's bitter moments.

However, I have let my tongue run away with me. God keep you!

Your A. Chekhov

To ALEXEI SUVORIN

May 30, 1888, Sumy
Lintvareva's summer place

. . . I am living on the banks of the Psel in the wing of an old feudal country home. I hired the place sight unseen, hoping for the best, and thus far have not regretted it. The river is wide, deep, teeming with islands, fish and crayfish, the banks are beautiful and there is much greenery. But its chief virtue is its sense of spaciousness, which is such that it seems to me my hundred rubles have given me the right to live amidst a limitless expanse. Nature and life hereabouts are of a pattern that editors are rejecting as old-fashioned, let alone the nightingales, which sing day and night, the distant barking of dogs, the old neglected gardens, the tightly boarded, very sad and poetic country places, where dwell the souls of beautiful women, the venerable, doddering feudal retainers and the young girls athirst for the most conventional type of love; not far from here we even have such a worn-out device of romance as a watermill (sixteen wheels), along with a miller and his daughter who keeps sitting at her window, obviously waiting for something to happen. Everything I see and hear about me seems like the ancient tales and fairy stories I have known for so long. The only novelty is the presence of a mysterious bird—the water-bittern —that hides amongst the reeds in the distance and day and night utters a cry that is a cross between a blow on an empty barrel and the bellowing of a cow locked in a barn. Every Little Russian claims to have seen this bird during his lifetime, but each describes it differently, so actually no one has seen it. There is another novelty, too, but a superficial one, and maybe not so new, either.

Every day I row my boat to the mill, while evenings I make for the islands with fishermen fans from the Kharitonenko works to catch fish. The talk is interesting. Whitsunday Eve all the addicts are spending the night on the island to fish the night through: me too. There are some superb types.

My landlords have proved to be very fine, hospitable people. It is a family worth studying, and consists of six persons. The old mother is a very kind, rather faded and long-suffering woman; she reads Schopenhauer and goes to church to hear the Song of Praise, conscientiously cons every issue of the "Herald of Europe" and "Northern Herald," is acquainted with writers I never dreamed existed; considers it noteworthy that the artist Makovski once lived in the wing of her house and that now it houses a young man of letters; in conversing with Pleshcheyev feels a sacred tremor throughout her body and rejoices every instant that she has been "found worthy" to behold the great poet.

Her oldest daughter, a woman physician, is the pride of the whole household, and a saint, as the peasants call her, a truly unusual figure. She has a tumor on the brain which has rendered her completely blind; she suffers from epilepsy and constant headaches. She knows what awaits her, and speaks of her imminent death stoically in astounding cold blood. In my practice I have become accustomed to see people near death and have always had a sort of queer feeling when those about to die speak, smile, or cry in my presence, but here, when I see this blind figure on the terrace laughing, joking or listening to my "In the Twilight" being read to her, I always have a queer feeling not about this good lady doctor's dying, but about our own unawareness of approaching death, and writing "In the Twilight" as though we would never die.

The second daughter is also a woman doctor and an old maid, a quiet, shy, infinitely good, tender and homely being. Sick people are an absolute torment to her, and she is practically psychotic in her anxiety about them. At consultations we never agree: I am the messenger of cheer where she sees death, and I double the doses she gives. Where death is indeed obvious and inevitable my lady doctor's reaction is quite undoctorlike. One day I took over the sick from her at the medical clinic; a young Little Russian woman appeared with a malignant tumor of the glands on her cheek and at the nape of her neck. The affliction had spread to so many areas that any treatment would have been futile. And because this farm woman now felt no pain, but would die six months hence in frightful torment, the lady doctor looked at her with such a guilty expression that she seemed to be apologizing for her own health, ashamed of the helplessness of medical science. She attends to the housekeeping conscientiously and understands it in all its smallest details. She even knows horses. For example, when the side horse won't pull or starts getting restless, she will advise the coachman how to take care of the matter. She dearly loves family life, which it has not been her fate to enjoy, and dreams of it, I think; on nights when there are games and songs in the big house, she strides up and down along the dark avenue of trees quickly and nervously like a caged animal. I don't believe she would ever harm a fly, and to my mind never has been or will be happy for a single minute.

The third daughter, who was graduated from the college in Bestuzhevka, is a young girl of masculine frame, strong, bony as a shad, well muscled, tanned and vociferous. . . . She laughs so loud you can hear her half a mile off. A super-Ukrainimaniac. She has built a school on the estate at her own expense and teaches little Little Russians Krylov's fables translated into Little Russian. . . . She hasn't cut her hair, wears a corset and a bustle, busies herself with domestic duties, loves to sing and roar with laughter and doesn't deny herself the most conventional sort of love, despite her having read Marx; but it's scarcely likely she'll get married, she is so homely.

The oldest son is a quiet, modest, bright, unlucky and hard-working young person, unpretentious and apparently satisfied with what life has given him. He does not boast of his being expelled for political activity during his fourth year at the university.[1] He says little, loves domestic life and the earth and

---

[1] Undergraduate political activity, always radical, was considered, in those days, a mark of intellectual and moral distinction.

lives peaceably with his Little Russian neighbors.

The second son is a young man and a fanatic on the subject of Tchaikovski's genius. A pianist. He aspires to the Tolstoyan life. . . .

Pleshcheyev is my guest now. People regard him as a demigod, envy the great good fortune of some bumpkin who happens to attract his attention, bring him flowers, invite him everywhere and so on. Young Vata, a boarding school girl from Poltava who is visiting our landlady, is paying particular court to him. He "listens and eats" and smokes cigars which give his worshipers a headache. He is stiff in his movements and senilely indolent, but this does not deter the fair sex from taking boatrides with him, bearing him off to neighboring estates and singing him romantic ballads. He cuts the same figure here as he does in St. Petersburg, i.e., an icon which is worshipped because it happens to be old and once hung in the company of miracleworking icons. Personally I regard him as a receptacle full of traditions, interesting memoirs and platitudes, but at the same time a very kind, warm, sincere person. . . .

What you write about "The Lights" is perfectly true. Nikolai and Masha are overemphasized, but what can I do? Unaccustomed as I am to writing lengthily I become overanxious; when I do, the thought that my tale is disproportionately long always scares me and I attempt to write as tersely as I can. Kisochka's last scene with the engineer seemed to me an insignificant detail encumbering the story, and so I threw it out, substituting Nikolai and Masha for it.

You write that the talk about pessimism and Kisochka's story in no way develop or solve the problem of pessimism. It seems to me that it is not up to writers to solve such questions as God, pessimism and so on. The job of the writer is to depict only who, how and under what circumstances people have spoken or thought about God or pessimism. The artist should not be a judge of his characters or of what they say, but only an objective observer. I heard a confused, indecisive talk by two Russians on pessimism and so must convey this conversation in the same form in which I heard it, but it is up to the jury, i.e., the readers, to give it an evaluation. My job is only to be talented, i.e., to be able to throw light upon some figures and speak their language. Shcheglov-Leontiev finds fault with me for having ended my story with the sentence: "You can't appraise anything in this world!" In his opinion the artist-psychologist *must* analyze—that's why he's a psychologist. But I don't agree with him. It is high time for writing folk, especially artists, to admit you can't appraise anything in this world, as Socrates did in his day, and Voltaire. The crowd thinks it knows and understands everything: and the more stupid it is, the broader seems to be its scope. If the artist, in whom the crowd believes, dares to declare that he does not understand what he sees, that alone comprises deep knowledge in the domain of thought and a good step ahead. . . .

What a letter I've concocted! I must end. Give my regards to Anna Ivanovna, Nastya and Borya. . . . Goodbye, keep well, and may God be good to you.

Your sincerely devoted

A. Chekhov

To ALEXEI PLESHCHEYEV

October 4, 1888, Moscow

. . . I would be glad to read what Merejkowski[1] has to say. In the meantime, goodbye for now. Write me once you have read my story. You won't like it, but I am not afraid of you, nor of Anna Mikhailovna. Those I am afraid of are the ones who look for tendencies between the lines and want to put me down definitely as a liberal or conservative. I am not a liberal and not a conservative, not an evolutionist, nor a monk, nor indifferent

---

[1] Merejkowski, the author of *The Life of Leonardo Da Vinci*, in 1888 wrote an article, "An Old Question on New Talent," about Chekhov's short stories.

to the world. I would like to be a free artist—and that is all—and regret that God has not given me the strength to be one. I hate lies and coercion in all their aspects. . . . Pharisaism, stupidity and idle whim reign not only in the homes of the merchant class and within prison walls; I see them in science, in literature, amongst young people. I cannot therefore nurture any particularly warm feelings toward policemen, butchers, savants, writers, or youth. I consider trademarks or labels to be prejudices.

My holy of holies are the human body, health, intelligence, talent, inspiration, love, and the most absolute freedom—freedom from force and falsity, in whatever form these last may be expressed. This is the program I would maintain, were I a great artist.

However, I've run on too much as it is. Keep well,

Yours,

A. Chekhov

To ALEXEI SUVORIN

October 27, 1888, Moscow

. . . I sometimes preach heresies, but have never once gone as far as the absolute negation of problems in art. In talks with the writing fraternity I always insist it is not the business of the artist to solve narrowly specialized questions. It is bad for an artist to tackle what he does not understand. For special problems we have specialists: it is their business to judge the community, the fate of capitalism, the evil of drunkenness, boots, female maladies. . . . The artist, though, must pass judgment only on what he understands; his circle is as limited as that of any other specialist—this I repeat and on this I always insist. Only one who has never written and has had no business with images can say there are no problems in his sphere, only answers. The artist observes, chooses, guesses, combines—these acts in themselves presuppose a problem; if he has not put this problem to himself from the very beginning, then there will be nothing to guess and no choice to make. To be more concise, let me finish with psychiatry; if one denies problem and purpose in creative work, then one must concede that the artist is creating undesignedly, without intention, temporarily deranged; and therefore, if some author were to boast to me that he had written a story without a previously considered intention, guided by inspiration, I would call him insane.

You are right to require a conscious attitude from the artist toward his work, but you mix up two ideas: *the solution of the problem and a correct presentation of the problem*. Only the latter is obligatory for the artist. In "Anna Karenina" and "Onegin" not a single problem is solved, but they satisfy you completely just because all their problems are correctly presented. The court is obliged to submit the case fairly, but let the jury do the deciding, each according to its own judgment. . . .

Tomorrow my "Bear" is on at Korsh's theatre. I have written another one-act play; two male parts, one female.

You write that the hero of my "The Party" is a figure which it would be well for me to develop further. Good Lord, surely I am not an unfeeling brute, I understand that. I know that I deface and even murder my characters, and that good material perishes needlessly. . . . I would gladly have sat half a year over "The Party." And that is speaking the truth. I love to relax at my ease, and see no delight in hasty bursting into print. Gladly, with pleasure, with feeling and with deliberation would I describe *all* of my hero. I would depict his spirit while his wife was giving birth, his trial, his miserable state of mind after he was exonerated, I would portray the midwife and doctor drinking tea at night, I would describe the rain. This would afford me only pleasure, because I love to fool around and fuss. But what am I to do? I begin the story on the tenth of September with the thought that it must be completed by the fifth of October, which is the deadline; if I put it off, I'll be

tricking the publisher and will remain without money. I write
the beginning serenely, let myself go, but in the middle I have
already begun cowering and fearing lest my story turn out to
be long; I have to remember that the "Northern Herald" hasn't
much money and that I am one of its expensive contributors.
My start, therefore, is full of promise, as though I were beginning a novel; the middle section is difficult and broken up,
while the end, as in a short short story, is like fireworks. In
writing, therefore, one is bound to concentrate first of all upon
the story's framework; from the mass of greater and lesser figures you pick one particular person—the husband or wife—
place him in the foreground, draw him in and underscore him
alone, then you throw the others about the background like
loose change, and the result is not unlike the vault of heaven:
one big moon and around it a mass of very small stars. The
moon, however, cannot come through successfully, because it
can only be interpreted properly when the other stars are understood; and the stars in the meantime have not been clearly
explained. So what emerges is not literature, but something on
the order of the sewing of Trishkin's coat. What shall I do?
I simply don't know. I put my trust in all-healing time.

If I may again speak of my conscience, well then, I haven't
yet begun my literary career, despite the receipt of a prize.
Subjects for five big stories and two novels swarm in my head.
One of the novels was conceived a long time ago, so that several
in the cast of characters have grown old without ever having
been put down on paper. There is a regular army of people in
my brain begging to be summoned forth and only waiting for
the word to be given. All I have written hitherto is trash in
comparison with what I would like to write and what I would
write exultantly. It's all the same to me whether I write "The
Party" or "The Lights" or a one-act comedy, or a letter to a
friend—it is all tedious, mechanical, faded; I feel aggrieved
against the critic who, let us say, attributes some significance
to "The Lights," for it seems to me that I am misleading him,

as I have misled many people with my immoderately serious or merry face. I am not pleased that I am successful; the subjects that sit in my head are vexatiously jealous of those already on paper; it is insulting that the trash is already on view while the good stuff lies about in the storehouse, like discarded books. Of course, there is much in this lamentation of mine that is exaggerated, much that only *seems* so to me, but there is some portion of truth, and a big one. What do I call good? Those images which seem best to me, which I love and jealously guard so as not to waste and trample them down on account of some "The Party," written to meet a deadline. . . . If my love is mistaken, then I am not right, but surely it is possible that it may not be mistaken! I am either a fool and a presumptuous person or I am actually an organism capable of being a good writer; all that now issues from my pen does not please me and causes me weariness, but all that sits in my head interests me, touches and stirs me. Wherefore I conclude that nobody knows the secret of doing the right thing but me. It is very likely that everyone who writes reasons thus. However, the devil himself would break his neck on questions such as these.

In determining what kind of person I should be and what I should do *money will not help.* An extra thousand rubles does not solve the problem, while a hundred thousand is a pipe dream. Moreover, when I have money (perhaps this is from want of habit, I don't know) I become extremely heedless and lazy; the world is my oyster then. I need solitude and time.

Forgive me for forcing my personality on you. My pen has run away with me. Somehow I cannot work now.

Thanks for placing my little articles. For the love of God, don't stand on ceremony with them; abridge, lengthen, alter, throw out or do with them what you will. I give you, as Korsh says, carte blanche. I will be happy if my articles do not usurp somebody else's place. . . .

Tell me what Anna Ivanovna's eye disease is called in Latin. I will let you know how serious it is. If she was prescribed atropin it is serious, though not categorically so. And what is wrong with Nastya? If you are thinking of curing your boredom in Moscow, a journey will prove fruitless: there is frightful tedium here. Many literary men have been arrested, among them, too, old busybody Goltsev, author of the "Ninth Symphony." V. S. Mamyshev, who visited me today, is interceding for one of them.

Greetings to all your family.

Your A. Chekhov

A mosquito is flying about in my room. How did he ever get here? Thank you for the striking ads of my books.

To ALEXEI SUVORIN

November 3, 1888, Moscow

Greetings, Alexei Sergeyevich,

I am now arraying myself in a frock coat to attend the opening evening of the "Society of Arts and Literature" to which I have been specially invited. There's going to be a formal ball. What the aims and resources of this society are, who constitutes the membership and so on, I don't know. . . . I have not been elected to membership, and am very glad of it since contributing twenty-five rubles for the right to be bored is far from my desire. . . .

In the "Northern Herald" for November there is an article devoted to yours truly by Merejkowski, the poet. A long one. I recommend its conclusion to your attention. It is characteristic. Merejkowski is still very young and a student—I believe he is a naturalist. People who have mastered the wisdom of the scientific method and who therefore know how to reason scientifically are subject to a number of irresistible temptations. Archimedes wanted to turn the earth upside down, and nowadays the hotheads want to embrace the scientifically unembraceable, to discover physical laws for the creative impulse, to bring to light a general law and formulae which the artist feels and

[60]

follows instinctively in composing music, painting landscapes, writing novels and so on. These formulae probably exist in nature. We know that there is A, B, C, do, re, mi, fa and sol in nature, there is the curve, the straight line, the circle, the square, green, red and blue . . . we know that these factors in some particular combination produce a melody or verse or a picture, just as simple chemical bodies in some particular combination produce wood, or stone, or the sea, but the only thing we know is that there is a combination, and that the working of this combination is unknown to us. Those who have assimilated the scientific method are deeply aware that there is something in common between the piece of music and the tree, that both are created as a result of equally true and simple laws. So the question arises: what are these laws? . . . Reasoning scientifically is always a good idea, but the trouble is that this scientific reasoning on the subject of creative power is in the end certain to degenerate into looking for "cells" or "centres" which control the creative impulse; then some ponderous German will discover these cellules somewhere in the occipital lobes, another countryman of his will dissent, a third will concur, and the Russian will skim through an article on cells and dash off an essay for the "Northern Herald"; the "Herald of Europe" will set to work picking this essay to pieces, and for about three years after that an epidemic of nonsense will hover in the Russian air which will provide earnings and popularity for the dunces, and inspire nothing but annoyance in intelligent people.

For those whom the scientific method has wearied, to whom God has given the rare gift of reasoning scientifically, there is, in my opinion, a single way out, and that is the philosophy of creative power. You can heap together all the best that has been created by artists throughout the centuries, and, utilizing the scientific method, extract from them the qualities they have in common with one another and which condition their value. That common quality will be the criterion. The works called immortal have a great deal in common; if you omit from each of them this *common quality,* the work loses its value and delight. In other words, this *common quality* is indispensable, and constitutes the condition sine qua non of every work with pretensions to immortality.

For the younger generation, writing criticism is more useful than composing poems. Merejkowski writes smoothly and youthfully, but on every page he quavers, makes reservations and advances concessions—this is a sign that he himself has not clarified the question in his own mind. . . . He calls me a poet, my stories are novellas, my heroes—ill-starred, that is to say, he has nothing new to offer. It is about time he discarded these victims of fate, superfluous people and so on, and thought up something of his own. Merejkowski calls my monk, the composer of the "Song of Praise," an unfortunate. But in what respect was he a failure? God grant that all may live as he: he believed in God, was well fed and could write creatively. . . . Dividing people into successes and failures means looking upon human nature from the narrow, preconceived point of view. . . . Are you a failure or not? Am I? Napoleon? Your servant Vasili? Where is the criterion? One must be God to be able to distinguish successes from failures and not make mistakes. . . . I'm going to the ball.

I have returned. The aim of the society is "unity." A learned German taught a cat, a mouse, a hawk and a sparrow to eat out of one plate. . . . Deathly boredom reigned. People sauntered through the rooms and made believe they weren't bored. A young lady sang. Lenski read my story (one of the listeners remarked: "A rather weak story!" and Levinski had the stupidity and cruelty to interrupt him with, "And here is the author himself! Allow me to introduce him," while the listener almost sank into the floor in embarrassment), people danced, ate a bad supper, were held up for tips by the flunkies. If actors, artists and men of letters really constitute the best part of society, what a pity it is! A fine type of society it must be with an elite so poor in desires, intentions, taste, beautiful women, and initiative. A Japanese stuffed animal had been placed in the foyer, a Chinese parasol thrust into a corner, a rug hung over the banisters, and this they consider artistic. They have a Chinese parasol, but no newspapers. If an artist decorates his apartment with nothing more than a stuffed mummy, a halberd, escutcheons, and fans on the wall, if all of this is not unplanned, but carefully thought out and emphasized, he is not an artist, but a pompous monkey.

I had a letter from Leikin today. He writes that he paid you a visit. He is a genial and harmless person, but a bourgeois to the marrow of his bones. If he goes anywhere or says anything it is always with an ulterior motive. Every one of his words is seriously pondered and every one of your words, no matter how casually pronounced, he puts into his pipe for a smoking in the full assurance that he, Leikin, must do things this way; if he doesn't his books won't sell, his enemies will triumph, his friends will desert him and his credit union won't re-elect him to its board of directors. The fox constantly fears for his skin, and so does he. A subtle diplomat! . . .

There is confusion at Korsh's. A steam coffeepot burst and scalded Rybchinskaya's face. . . . There is nobody here to perform, no one follows orders, everybody shouts and quarrels. Evidently the spectacular costume play will be a horrible flop . . . though I would like to have them present "The Seducer of Seville."[1] . . . We must strive with all our power to see to it that the stage passes out of the hands of the grocers and into literary hands, otherwise the theatre is lost.

The coffeepot killed my "Bear." Rybchinskaya is ill and there's no one to play her part.

All our folks ask to be remembered. My hearty regards to Anna Ivanovna, Nastya and Borya.

Yours,
A. Chekhov

[1] By Maslov-Bejetski.

One-act comedies can be published in the summer; winter is not suitable, though. I'm going to compose a one-acter every month during the summer season, but must deny myself this pleasure in the winter.

Please enter me as a member of the Literary Society. . . . I'll attend the meetings when I arrive.

To ALEXEI SUVORIN

November 20-25, 1888, Moscow

. . . You write that authors are God's elect. I won't bother disputing. Shcheglov calls me the Potemkin of literature, and so it is not for me to speak of the thorny path, disappointments and so on. I don't know whether I have ever suffered more than shoemakers, mathematicians or train conductors; I don't know who it is that prophesies through my lips, God or somebody worse. I allow myself to mention only one little unpleasantness I have experienced with which you, too, are undoubtedly familiar. This is it. Both of us like ordinary people; we, on the other hand, are liked because people regard us as extraordinary. I am invited everywhere, for example am wined and dined like a general at a wedding; my sister is aggrieved because she is invited everywhere as the writer's sister.

Nobody wants to like what is ordinary in us. The consequence is that were we tomorrow to appear like ordinary mortals in the eyes of our good acquantances, people would stop liking us and only pity us. This is very bad. And it's bad because what people like in us is often what we ourselves do not like or respect in ourselves. It is too bad that I was right when I wrote "The First-Class Passenger," wherein my engineer and professor discourse on glory.

I am going to the farm. The devil with them! You have Feodosia.

Incidentally, as to Feodosia and the Tatars. Although the Tatars' land was stolen from them, nobody is concerned with their welfare. Schools for the Tatars are badly needed. Write an article saying that the ministry should assign the money wasted on sausage-like Derpt University, which is full of useless Germans, to schools for Tatars, who are of use to Russia. I myself would write on the subject but don't know how.

Leikin sent me a very amusing one-act comedy that he has written. This man is the only one of his kind.

Be well and happy.

Your A. Chekhov

To ALEXEI SUVORIN

December 23, 1888, Moscow

Dear Alexei Sergeyevich,

. . . I have read your play again. In it there is a great deal that is good and original which has not previously appeared in dramatic literature, and much that is not good (for example, the language). Its merits and defects constitute a capital from which we could derive much profit, if we had any criticism. But this capital will lie about unproductively to no purpose until it becomes obsolete and goes out of print. There is no criticism. Tatischev, who follows the beaten path, the donkey Mikhnevich and the indifferent Burenin—comprise the entire Russian critical battery. And it is not worth the trouble to write for this battery, just as it is no use thrusting flowers at the nose of somebody who has a head cold. There are moments when I positively lose heart. For whom and what do I write? For the public? But I don't see it and don't believe in it any more than I do in spirits: it is uncultured and badly educated, while its best elements are not conscientious or sincere toward us. I cannot figure out whether or not I am needed by this public. Burenin says that I am not and that I occupy myself with trifles, but the Academy has awarded me a prize—the devil himself wouldn't be able to make head or tail of the rights of the matter. Do I write for money? But I never have any, and from chronic lack of it I am almost indifferent in my attitude toward it. I work for money sluggishly. Do I write for praise? But praise only irritates me. The literary society, the students, Yevreinova, Pleshcheyev, the young girls and so on extolled my "Nervous Breakdown" to the skies, but it was only Grigorovich who remarked upon my description of the first snowfall. Etc., etc. Had we any criticism, I would know that I provide material to work with—good or bad, it doesn't matter—and that to people devoting themselves to the study of life I am as necessary as a star to an astronomer. Then I would work painstakingly, and would know wherefore I was working. As it is now, you, I, Muravlin and the rest resemble maniacs writing books and plays for their own satisfaction. One's own personal satisfaction is, of course, a fine thing: one senses it during the writing process, but what of it? But . . . I must call a halt. . . .

Many races, religions, languages and cultures have vanished without a trace—vanished because there were no historians and biologists. Just so a mass of lives and works of art is vanishing before our eyes, owing to the complete absence of criticism. People may say there is nothing for our critics to do, that all our contemporary works are meaningless and inferior. But that is a narrow view. Life must be observed not only on the plus side, but also on the minus. The conviction in itself that the eighties have not produced a single worthwhile writer may serve as material for five volumes. . . .

My "Bear" is going into a second edition. And you say I am not a superb dramatist. I have cooked up a one-act comedy entitled "Thunder and Lightning" for Savina, Davidov and the other ministers of culture. One night during a thunderstorm I have the district doctor Davidov pay a call upon the maiden Savina. Davidov has a toothache, and Savina has an odious disposition. Interesting conversations, interrupted by the thunder. At the end I marry them off. When I write myself out I'm going to turn to composing one-acters and making my living off them. I believe I could write about a hundred a year. Subjects for one-act plays sprout out of me like oil from Baku soil. Why can't I give my oil-bearing plot of ground to Shcheglov?

I sent Khudekov a story for a hundred rubles which I ask you not to read. I'm ashamed of it. Last night I sat down to write a tale for "New Times," but some dame appeared and bore me off to Pluschikha to see Palmin the poet, who in a state of drunkenness fell and fractured his forehead. I fooled around with this drunken character for a good one-and-a-half to two hours, wore myself out, stank of iodoform, got into a bad temper and returned home tired to death. Today it would be too late to do the story. On the whole I lead a tedious life and am beginning to feel hatred from time to time, something that has never happened to me before. Long, silly conversations, guests, people asking for help, to the tune of one-, two- and three-ruble contributions, money spent on cabs to visit patients who don't pay me a kopek—in short, everything is in such a muddle that one feels like running out of the house. People get loans and don't repay them, take away my books, have no regard for my time. . . . All I lack is an unhappy love affair. . . .

You will get this letter on the first day of Christmas, and may I wish you a merry one. Have a good rest. My sister sends her compliments to you, Anna Ivanovna and the children. I also salute you most humbly and remain your bored

A. Chekhov

To ALEXEI SUVORIN

December 26, 1888, Moscow

. . . You write that one should work not for criticism but for the public, and that it's too soon for me to complain. It is pleasant to think that one works for the public, of course, but how do I know that I am actually doing so? What with its scantiness and some other qualities, I myself do not feel any satisfaction in my work; the public, though (I did not call it ignoble), is unscrupulous and insincere in its attitude toward us; you will never hear the truth from it and so you can't figure out whether or not it needs me. It may be early for me to complain, but never too early to ask myself whether I am engaged in serious business or nonsense. Criticism is silent, the public lies and my own instinct tells me I am busying myself with trash. Do I complain? I don't recall the tone of my letter, but if I did so, I complained not on my own behalf but for all our writing fraternity, whom I pity infinitely.

All week I have been as mean as a son of a bitch. Hemorrhoids accompanied by itching and bleeding, visitors, Palmin and his fractured skull, tedium. On the first evening of the holiday I hovered over a sick man who died before my eyes. On the whole, there have been plenty of morbid motifs. Spitefulness is a type of pusillanimity. I confess it and curse myself. Above all I am vexed with myself for letting you into the secrets of my melancholy, very uninteresting and shameful for one of my years, which the poets have exalted as a time of bloom.

I will try to do a story for you by the New Year, and soon after the first will send "The Princess."

You should print one-act plays in the summertime only, not in winter.

You wish me to turn Sasha loose at all costs. But surely "Ivanov" can hardly be put on in that form. If it can be done, then by all means I will do as you wish, but please excuse me if I give it to her properly, the nasty creature! (You say that women love out of compassion and marry out of compassion. And how about men? I don't care to have realistic novelists slander women, but I don't like it either when people like Yuzhin lift womankind onto their shoulders and attempt to show that even when she is worse than a man, the man is nevertheless a scoundrel and the woman an angel. Both men and women are a dime a dozen, except that man is more intelligent and just.)

. . . My painter continues in the same condition.

In the autumn I am moving to Petersburg and am taking

my mother and sister along. I have to do some serious work. . . .

Don't be angry with me and forgive my melancholy, which I don't find attractive either. It has been evoked in me by circumstances over which I had no control.

Read me a moral lecture and don't apologize. If you knew how often I read moral lectures to young people in my letters! I have even made a habit of it. I have long, redundant, overfancy phrases, while you have short ones. Yours come out better.

. . . Goodbye. My greetings to Anna Ivanovna and all your family.

Heartily yours,
A. Chekhov

To ALEXEI SUVORIN

December 30, 1888, Moscow

. . . The producer considers Ivanov[1] a superfluous man in the Turgenev tradition; and Savina asks why Ivanov is a scoundrel. You write: "You have to endow Ivanov with some sort of quality which will make it apparent why he has two women hanging onto him and why he is a scoundrel, and why the doctor is a great man." If you three people have understood me in this fashion, it means that my play is no good. My wit and reason have probably deserted me and I have not put down on paper what I have wished to write. If Ivanov emerges as a rogue or superfluous man, and the doctor as a great person, Sara's and Sasha's love for Ivanov is incomprehensible, obviously my play hasn't been properly realized and there can be no question of producing it.

1 *Ivanov.* The main character of this play is a well-educated, liberal, humane man who, in spite of his excellent intentions, brings ruin on himself and those who love him. His wife, a Jewess, has given up her family and her fortune to marry him and, as the play opens, she is dying. Ivanov is in love with Sasha, a young girl who lives in the neighborhood. As Chekhov says, Sasha "is a woman who loves men in the period of their decline," and she loves the romantic chance to redeem a lost man. But he is a lost man, and in the end of the play he commits suicide.

This is how I understand my characters. Ivanov, an upper-class gentleman and a university man, was not remarkable in any way; he had an easily excitable nature, was fervent, with a strong bent for distractions, and honest and straightforward, like the majority of the educated upper class. He has been living in his country home and serving in the district council. What he has been doing and how he has been behaving, what has engrossed and fascinated him, is evident from these following words of his, addressed to the doctor (Act I, scene 5), "Don't marry a Jewess, or a psychopath, or a bluestocking . . . don't battle alone against thousands, don't tilt against windmills, don't knock your head against a wall . . . and may God save you from all kinds of scientific farming, progressive schools, impassioned talk. . . ." That's his past. Sara, who was witness to his scientific farming and other such ventures, speaks of him to the doctor: "He is a remarkable man, Doctor, and I am sorry you did not know him as he was two or three years ago. Now he is depressed and silent, he doesn't do anything, but . . . what a charmer he was then!" (Act I, scene 7). His past was admirable, as is the case with the majority of Russian intellectuals. There is scarcely a Russian gentleman or university graduate who could not boast of his past. The present is always worse than the past; and why? Because our excitability has one specific quality: it quickly gives way to exhaustion. A man who has hardly clambered off the school bench, rashly takes on a burden beyond his powers, simultaneously takes up schools, peasants, scientific farming and the "Herald of Europe," makes speeches, writes to the minister, struggles with evil, applauds the good, does not fall in love simply and any old way, but inevitably with either bluestockings or psychopaths . . . or even prostitutes whom he tries to save from their fate, and so on and so forth. But hardly has he reached the age of thirty or thirty-five when he begins to feel weariness and ennui. He hasn't even cultivated decent moustaches but he says in a tone of authority, "Don't get married, old man. You'd better trust my experience." Or, "After all, in essence what is liberalism?" . . . Such is the tone of these prematurely exhausted people. Further, sighing very positively, he advises, "Don't marry thus and so (see one of the passages above), but choose something run-of-the-mill, grayish, without bright colors, without extra flourishes. . . . On the whole, try to plan a quiet life for yourself. The grayer, the more monotonous the background, the better. . . . But the life I have been leading, how wearing it has been!—how wearing!"

Though he feels physical weariness and boredom, he does not understand what the trouble is and what has happened. In terror he says to the doctor (Act I, scene 3), "You tell me she is dying, but I don't feel any love, or pity, but a sort of loneliness and weariness. If you just judge me as a stranger, you would probably think this horrible. I myself do not understand what is happening to me."

When narrow and unconscientious people find themselves in such a situation, they usually place the blame on their environment, or enter the ranks of the unwanted and unneeded Hamlets, and then their minds are at rest. . . . But Ivanov, who is straightforward, openly declares to the doctor and audience that he does not understand himself. "I don't understand, don't understand . . ." That he really does not understand himself is apparent from the long monologue in Act III, where, speaking directly to the audience, he confesses to it, and even weeps!

The change taking place within him outrages his integrity. He seeks reasons from within and doesn't find them; he begins to seek outside of himself and finds only an undefined feeling of guilt. This feeling is Russian. If someone dies in a Russian's house, or falls sick, or if somebody owes him money, or if he wants to make a loan—the Russian always feels a sense of guilt. Ivanov is continually discoursing on some fault or other that he has, and every jolt increases the sense of guilt. In Act I he says, "Probably I am terribly guilty, but my thoughts have become confused, my soul is shackled with a kind of indolence, and I am not in a strong enough state to understand myself. . . ." In Act II he says to Sasha, "Day and night my conscience aches, I feel I am profoundly to blame, but I do not understand where I have done anything wrong."

To exhaustion, boredom and the sense of guilt add still another enemy. That is solitude. Were Ivanov a government official, an actor, a priest or professor, he would get used to his situation. But he lives on an estate in the country, in a rural district. The people there are either drunkards or card players, or such as the doctor. They are not concerned with his feelings and with the changes occurring within him. He is lonely. The long winters, the long evenings, the empty garden, the empty rooms, the morose count, the ailing wife . . . There is nowhere to go. Hence he is continually tormented by the question of what to do with himself.

Now for the fifth enemy. Ivanov is tired, doesn't understand himself, but life is not concerned with these things. It sets its legitimate demands before him and he—like it or not—must solve the problems. The sick wife is a problem. It should be plain from the monologue in Act III and from the contents of the last two acts how he resolves these problems. Such people as Ivanov do not settle questions, they are crushed by them. They are at their wit's end, throw up their hands, their nerves are on edge, they complain, commit stupidities and in the last analysis, in giving way to their loose, flabby nerves, the ground slips from under their feet and they join the ranks of the "broken" and "misunderstood."

Disillusion, apathy, nervousness and exhaustion are the inevitable consequences of inordinate excitability, and this characteristic is inherent in our young people to an extreme degree. Take literature. Take the present day. . . . Socialism is one aspect of excitability. . . Where is liberalism? Even Mikhailovski says there is nothing worth fighting for. And what do all these

Russian enthusiasms come to? The war has wearied, Bulgaria has degenerated into a joke. . . .

This weariness (and Dr. Bertenson will corroborate it) doesn't only express itself in grumbling or in the sensation of boredom. You cannot chart the life of a tired man this way [here Chekhov drew a gently undulating line], for it is very uneven. All these tired people don't lose their capacity for emotional stimulation, but they aren't able to remain at that pitch for any length of time; rather an ever greater apathy follows every state of excitement: Graphically you can represent it this way [here Chekhov drew an undulating line interrupted by peaks and valleys]:

As you can see, the depressed condition doesn't show up as a gradual drop, but follows a rather different course. When Sasha declares her love, Ivanov cries in ecstasy, "A new life!" but by next morning his belief in this life is as sincere as his belief in fairies (monologue in Act III); when his wife's words outrage him, he is beside himself and in a fit of nerves he flings a cruel insult at her. People call him a scoundrel. Either this will prove fatal to his crumbling brain or else will arouse him to fresh heights and he is done for.

So as not to weary you to a state of exhaustion, I'll transfer my attention to Dr. Lvov. He is a type of honest, straight-forward, ardent but narrow and strait-laced person. Clever people refer to his kind like this: "He may be stupid, but he's got a good heart." Anything that resembles breadth of view or spontaneity of feeling is foreign to Lvov. He is a stereotype incarnate, a walking tendency. He looks out of his narrow frame on every phenomenon and face, and judges everything preconceivedly. He idolizes the man who exclaims, "Make way for honest toil!" and anyone who does not echo these sentiments is a rascal and a kulak. There is no middle way. He was educated on the novels of Mikhailov;[2] he has seen "new people" on the stage, i.e., kulaks and children of the age depicted by the new

[2] Mikhailov was the author of social-political novels.

playwrights, "moneygrubbers". . . . He has turned all of this over in his mind and done it so forcibly that when he reads "Rudin" he is bound to ask himself, "Is Rudin a scoundrel or isn't he?" Literature and the stage have so educated him that he applies this question to every person he meets in life or literature. . . .

He arrived in the country district already convinced. He could immediately discern that all the well-to-do peasants were kulaks, and that Ivanov, whom he couldn't figure out, was a knave. The man's wife is ill and he visits a rich woman neighbor—isn't he a villain? He is obviously killing his wife in order to marry the rich woman.

Lvov is honest, direct, and hits straight from the shoulder, whatever the consequences. If necessary he would throw a bomb under a carriage, punch an official in the puss, call a man a scoundrel to his face. He stops at nothing. He never feels pangs of conscience—he is an "honest toiler" with a mission, and is out to battle with "the powers of darkness."

We need people like him and for the most part they are likable. It is dishonest as well as pointless to portray them in caricature, merely to heighten the dramatic interest. True, a caricature is sharper and therefore easier to understand, but it is better to blur the portrait than to overdo it.

. . . Now as to the women. Why do they love him? Sara loves Ivanov because he is a good man, ardent, brilliant and quite as fervent a talker as Lvov (Act I, scene 7). She loves him as long as he is high-spirited and attractive; but when his personality becomes shrouded in gloom and loses its distinctive quality, she can no longer understand him and at the end of the third act she unburdens herself directly and sharply.

Sasha is a maiden poured from the newest mold. She is cultivated, intelligent, honest and so on. Among the blind the one-eyed is king, and that is why she makes much of the thirty-five-year-old Ivanov. He is the best person she knows. She knew him when she was small and observed his activities at close range at a period when he was not yet exhausted. He is a friend of her father's.

She is the type of female whom males do not conquer with the brilliance of their plumage, nor with their suppleness, nor with their courage, but with their laments, whimpers and recitals of failure. This is a woman who loves men in the period of their decline. Ivanov hardly had time to become disheartened before the young lady was Johnny-on-the-spot. She was only waiting for this moment. Goodness, she has such a noble, sacred problem! She will raise the fallen, get him up onto his feet, give him happiness. . . . It is not Ivanov she loves, but this problem. . . . Sasha struggles with Ivanov a whole year but he just will not rise from the dead and keeps sinking lower.

My fingers ache, and so I'll conclude. . . . If all the above-mentioned points are not in the play, then there's no sense even talking about producing it. It would mean I had not written what I had intended. Take the play back. I do not wish to preach heresy on the stage. If the audience leaves the theatre with the consciousness that Ivanovs are villains, while the Doctor Lvovs are great people, I will be forced to resign from the theatre and send my pen to hell. And you can't accomplish anything with revisions and interpolations. No revisions can make a great man step down from his pedestal and no interpolations can turn a scoundrel into an ordinary mortal. Sasha can be brought on at the final curtain, but I simply cannot add any more to Ivanov and Lvov. I don't know why. If I add anything, I merely feel that I will spoil it even more. Please believe my instincts, which after all are those of an author.

. . . Don't for any reason whatever allow Kiselevski to play the count! My play caused him a good deal of grief in Moscow! Wherever he went he complained he had been forced to act this son-of-a-bitch role. Why should I distress him again?

. . . God, how I must have wearied you with this letter! Enough, basta!

Happy New Year! Hurrah!

You lucky ones, you will be drinking, or have already drunk, champagne, while I indulge in slops!

. . . My compliments to you all, and I kiss Anna Ivanovna's hand. Keep well.

Your

A. Chekhov

If the audience does not understand "blood and iron," then the hell with it, i.e., with the blood in which there is no iron.

I have read over this letter. In characterizing Ivanov the word "Russian" occurs frequently. Don't be angry on its account. When I wrote the play I had in view only what really mattered, that is, only typical Russian traits. In that light, excessive excitability, the sense of guilt, and the inclination to weariness are purely Russian. Germans never get worked up and therefore Germany knows neither disillusioned people nor superfluous and overweary ones. . . . The excitation of the French always remains at the same level, without acute rises or falls, and therefore the Frenchman, until advanced senility sets in, is normally excited. In other words, the Frenchman doesn't have to waste his energy on inordinate excitement; he dispenses his strength with common sense, and that is why he never goes bankrupt.

In my play, naturally I did not employ such terms as Russian, excitability, exhaustion and so on—in full confidence that the reader and spectator would be attentive and would not require a sign reading: Dis ain't no melon, dis is a plum." I tried to express myself simply, did not resort to deceptions and had no suspicion that my readers and spectators would trip up my characters in every phrase they uttered, stress the talks about the dowry, etc.

I was not able to write the play I wished to write. Of course it's a pity. In my imagination Ivanov and Lvov appear as living people. I am telling you in all sincerity and in accordance with the dictates of my conscience that these people were born in my head and not out of ocean spray, or preconceived ideas, not out of "intellectuality," and not by sheer accident. They are the result of observation and the study of life. They are still in my brain and I feel I have not lied, not by a single centimetre, nor have I been too smart-alecky by a single iota. If these figures have emerged on paper lifeless and indistinct, it is not they who are to blame, but my lack of ability to convey my ideas. Seems as though it's too soon for me to take up play writing.

To ALEXEI SUVORIN

January 7, 1889, Moscow

. . . Davidov is playing Ivanov. Which is to say I must write as tersely and colorlessly as possible, remembering that all subtleties and "nuances" will merge into a gray mass and produce nothing but tedium. Can Davidov actually be first tender and then raging? When he plays serious rôles, a little grinding machine sits in his throat, monotonous and weak voiced, and performs in his stead. . . .

Ivanov has two long monologues which are decisive for the play: one in Act III and the other at the end of Act IV. The first should be sung, the second read savagely. Both are impossible for Davidov. He will deliver both monologues "intelligently," i.e., with overwhelming languor.

. . . I would with great pleasure read an essay before the Literary Society whence came the idea of writing "Ivanov." I would make a public confession. I have long cherished the audacious notion of summing up all that has hitherto been written about complaining and melancholy people, and would have my Ivanov proclaim the ultimate in such writing. It seems to me that all Russian novelists and playwrights have felt a need to depict the mournful man and that they have all written instinctively, without having definite images or a point of view. I tried consciously to get on the right track, and practically did so, but my manner of presentation is not worth a hoot in hell. It would have ben much better to wait! I rejoice that I did not heed Grigorovich's advice two or three years ago and write a novel! I can imagine how much good stuff I would have spoiled if I had listened to him. He says "talent and freshness will overcome everything." Talent and freshness can spoil a great deal—that would be more true. Besides an abundance of material and talent, other qualities of no less importance are also required. What you must have is maturity—that's one; second, you must have a *feeling of personal freedom,* and this feeling began kindling within me only a short time ago. I hadn't had it previously; frivolity, carelessness and lack of respect for my work had successfully served instead.

Self-made intellectuals buy at the price of their youth what gently born and bred writers have been endowed with by nature. Go ahead and write a story about a young man, the son of a serf, an ex-small shopkeeper, a choir boy, high school and university student, brought up on respect for rank, kissing priests' hands, and the worship of others' ideas, offering thanks for every mouthful of bread, often whipped, going to school without shoes, fighting, torturing animals, fond of dining with rich relatives, playing the hypocrite before God and people without any cause, except out of a consciousness of his own insignificance—then tell how this young man presses the slave out of himself one drop at a time and how he wakes up one fine morning to feel that in his veins flows not the blood of a slave, but real human blood. . . .

Keep well then, and forgive the long letter.

Yours,

A. Chekhov

To ALEXEI SUVORIN

March 11, 1889, Moscow

... What do you know? I am writing a novel!! I am keeping at it, but can't see the end in sight. I have begun doing it, i.e., the novel, all over again, revising and abridging considerably what had already been written. I have already clearly sketched in nine individuals. What a plot! I have called it "Tales from the Life of my Friends" and am writing it in the form of separate, complete stories, tightly held together by the common basis of plot, idea and characters. There is a special chapter for each story. Don't think that the novel will consist of odds and ends. No indeed. It will be a real novel, a complete whole, in which each person will be organically indispensable. . . .

I am having a hard time coping with technical problems. I am still weak in this quarter and have the feeling I am making loads of mistakes. There are going to be overlong passages, and inanities. Faithless wives, suicides, kulaks, virtuous peasants, devoted slaves, moralizing old ladies, kind old nurses, rustic wits, red-nosed captains and "new" people I shall endeavor to avoid, although in spots I do stray into conventional types. . . .

By the way, amongst your papers and magazines there was a quotation from some newspaper praising German housemaids for working *all day long,* like convict labor, and getting only two or three rubles a month pay for it. "New Times" endorses this praise and adds as its own commentary that one of our misfortunes is that we keep many unnecessary servants. In my opinion the Germans are scoundrels and bad political economists. In the first place one should not talk about servants in a tone implying they are criminals; in the second place, servants are worthy people and composed of the same flesh and blood as Bismarck; they are not slaves, but free workers; in the third place, the better labor is paid, the happier the country is, and each of us should strive to see that labor is paid better. Not to speak of the Christian point of view! As to unnecessary servants, well, they are kept only where there is plenty of money and are paid more than the heads of departments. They should not be taken into account, for they constitute an accidental phenomenon and not an organic one.

Why don't you come to Moscow? How well we would get along together!

Your

A. Chekhov

To ALEXEI SUVORIN

May 4, 1889, Sumy

Dear Alexei Sergeyevich,

I am writing you upon my return from a crabbing expedition. The weather is superb. Everything sings, blooms and gleams with beauty. The garden is already completely green, and even the oaks have blossomed forth. The busy worms have given a white coat to the trunks of the apple, pear, cherry and plum trees. All these trees bloom white, which makes them startlingly like brides in their wedding dresses: white frocks, white flowers and a look of innocence, as though they were ashamed to have people stare at them. Every day billions of beings are born. Nightingales, bitterns, cuckoos and other winged creatures lift their voices night and day, with frogs to accompany them. Every hour of the day and night has some particular quality. Thus, at nine in the evening the garden literally roars with May beetles. The nights are moonlit, the days bright. What with all the foregoing I am in a good mood, and were it not for the coughing artist and the mosquitoes, against which even Elpe's prescription is no help, I would be a perfect Potemkin. Nature is an excellent sedative. It pacifies, i.e., makes a man carefree. And being carefree is of the essence in this world. Only such people are able to look upon things clearly, to be just and to work properly—of course, this pertains only to clever and

[80]

generous people; egoists and empty heads are indifferent enough as it is.

You write that I have grown lazy. This doesn't mean I have become any lazier than I used to be. I do as much work now as I did three or five years ago. Working and looking like a working person at intervals from nine in the morning to dinner and from evening tea until retiring have become habits with me, and in this respect I am like a regular official. If two stories a month don't emerge out of my efforts, or 10,000 yearly income, it is not laziness that is to blame, but my basic psychological makeup; for medicine I am not fond enough of money, and for literature I don't have sufficient passion, and, consequently, talent. My creative fire burns at a slow, even pace, without flash and crackle, although sometimes I may write fifty or sixty pages at one swoop in one night or, absorbed by my work, I will keep myself from going to bed when I feel sleepy; for the same reason I am not remarkable either for stupidity or brilliance. I am afraid that in this respect I am very like Goncharov,[1] whom I don't like although he stands miles above me in talent. I don't have much passion; add to this fact the following symptom of a psychopathic condition: for the past two years and for no earthly reason I have become sick of seeing my works in print, have grown indifferent to reviews, talks on literature, slanders, successes, failures, and big fees—in short, I have become an utter fool. There is a sort of stagnation in my soul. I explain this by the stagnation in my personal life. I am not disillusioned, not weary, not dispirited, but everything has just become less interesting somehow. I must add some gunpowder to my makeup.

Imagine, the first act of my "Wood Demon" is ready. It's a fair piece of work, though long. I feel a much greater sense of power than I did while I was writing "Ivanov." The play will be ready by the beginning of June. Look out, you directors, the 5,000 are mine! The play is awfully queer, and I am amazed

1 Goncharov was best known as the author of the famous novel *Oblomov.*

that such peculiar things can issue from my pen. My one fear is that the censor won't allow it. I am also writing a novel that is more to my liking and closer to my heart than the "Wood Demon," which obliges me to resort to slyness and act like an idiot. Last night I recalled that I had promised Varlamov I'd write him a one-act comedy. I did so today and sent it off. You see what a ferment goes on within me! And you write that I've grown lazy!

... My brother writes that he has tortured himself with his play. I am glad. Let him. He viewed "Tatiana Repina" and "Ivanov" at the theatre with frightful condescension and during the intermissions drank cognac and deigned to criticize graciously. All these people judge plays in a manner which supposes they are very easy to write. They aren't aware, either, that writing a good play is difficult, and writing a bad one is twice as hard and a horrible job. I would like the entire public merged into a single person and have it write a play, whereupon you and I would sit in a box and hiss it. ...

Please bring me some forbidden books and newspapers from abroad. Were it not for our artist, I would go with you. ...

If you should play roulette, put twenty-five francs on for me just for luck.

Well, God grant you health and all the best.

Yours,

A. Chekhov

To ALEXEI SUVORIN

May 15, 1889, Sumy

If you haven't left yet for abroad, I will reply to your letter on Bourget,[1] and will be brief. Among other things you write: "Let us pursue the science of matter as usual, but let us also

---

[1] Paul Bourget, the French novelist.

keep for ourselves a place of refuge from this everlasting concern with matter." The science of matter is being pursued as usual, and the places of refuge are also on hand, and I don't think anybody is intruding there. If there is any intrusion, it will certainly be that of the natural sciences and not of the sacred places where one can take refuge from them. In my letter the problem was put more correctly and inoffensively than in yours, and I am closer to the "life of the spirit" than you. You speak of the right of one or another field of learning to exist, while I, on the other hand, speak not of any right, but of peace. I don't want people to see war where there isn't any. Branches of knowledge have always got along peaceably. Anatomy and elegant letters have an equally illustrious ancestry, the same aims, the same enemy—the devil—and there is no reason for them to battle with each other. They don't struggle against each other for existence. If a man understands the circulatory system, he is rich; if in addition he also studies the history of religion and knows the ballad "I Recall the Wond'rous Moment," he is the gainer thereby; accordingly we are treating only of plus quantities. That is why geniuses have never struggled and in Goethe the naturalist lived in harmony along with the poet.

It is not that branches of knowledge fight with one another, not poetry with anatomy, but fallacies, i.e., people. When a man does not understand a thing, he feels discord within himself: he seeks causes for this dissonance not in himself, as he should, but outside himself, and the result is war with something he does not understand. During the Middle Ages alchemy developed gradually, naturally and peacefully into chemistry; astrology into astronomy; the monks did not understand what was taking place, saw the process as war, and so gave battle. . . .

Bourget is fascinating to the Russian reader, like thunder after a drought, and it is easy to understand why. The reader of his novel saw that the characters and author were wiser than he, and observed a life richer than his own; whereas Russian fiction writers are stupider than the readers, their characters are pale and unimportant, the life of which they treat is barren and uninteresting. The Russian writer lives in a miserable hole, eats mold, is fond of low creatures and laundresses, doesn't know history, or geography, or the natural sciences, or the religion of his own country, or administration, or navigation . . . in short, doesn't know beans. In comparison with Bourget he is a web-footed goose and that's all. One can understand why people should be fond of Bourget. . . .

. . . I am bored. . . .

I'll soon be sending you a letter in French and German. My compliments to Anna Ivanovna, Nastya and Borya.

Have a fine trip.

Yours,

A. Chekhov

To MIKHAIL GALKIN-VRASKI[1]

January 20, 1890, St. Petersburg

Dear Sir,

As I propose in the spring of the present year to take a trip to Eastern Siberia with scientific and literary aims in view, and as I desire among other things to visit the island of Sakhalin, both in its central and southern portions, I have made so bold as to request most humbly that Your Excellency lend any support in my behalf you may find possible toward the attainment of the aims I have mentioned above.

[1] Chekhov took this letter to the office of the Main Prison Administration, of which Galkin-Vraski was the head. He explained to Galkin-Vraski, in great detail, the aims of his journey and asked permission to inspect prisons and industries. Galkin-Vraski was so agreeable and polite that Chekhov felt sure he would get the aid he needed. But Galkin-Vraski did not help him and, after the Bolshevik government opened the Prison Administration's archives, it was found that he had given orders that Chekhov was not to be allowed to see certain categories of political prisoners and exiles.

With sincere respect and devotion, I have the honor to be the most humble servant of Your Excellency,

Anton Chekhov

To ALEXEI PLESHCHEYEV

February 15, 1890, Moscow

. . . You really didn't like the "Kreutzer Sonata"? I won't say it is a work of genius, or a work for all eternity, for I am no judge of these matters, but in my opinion, amongst the mass of things being written here and abroad, you will hardly find anything its equal in seriousness of conception and beauty of execution, not to mention its artistic merits, which in spots are astounding. You must thank the story for just the one point that it is extremely thought-provoking. As I read it I could hardly keep myself from exclaiming, "That's true!" or "That's ridiculous!" Of course it does have some very annoying defects. Besides those you enumerated, there is still another point that one won't readily forgive its author, to wit, Tolstoy's stubborn brashness in treating of things he doesn't know and doesn't understand. Thus, his pronouncements on syphilis, foundling homes, women's repugnance to cohabitation and so on are not only debatable but also show him to be an ignoramus who has never taken the trouble during the course of his long life to read two or three books written by specialists. Still, these defects fly like feathers before the wind; considering the story's great qualities you just do not notice them, or if you do, it is only to be peeved that the story did not avoid the fate of all works created by man, none of which are perfect or free from error.

So my Petersburg friends and acquaintances are all angry with me? Why? Because I didn't bore them much with my presence, which has been a bore to myself for so long! Calm their minds, tell them that I ate a lot of dinners and suppers there, but did not captivate a *single* lady, that every day I felt sure I would be leaving on that evening's express, but that I was detained by my friends and "The Marine Miscellany" which I had to leaf through in its entirety, going back to 1852. I did as much in one month in St. Pete as my young friends would not be able to do in a year. However, let them rave! . . .

Goodbye, dear fellow, please pay us a visit. Regards to your family. My sister and mother send their compliments.

A. Chekhov

II

1890-1897

Sakhalin was a half forgotten island off the Pacific coast of Siberia, used by the Czarist government as a colony for criminals and political prisoners. Chekhov decided in 1890 to make a trip to Sakhalin. Up to that time he had shown no interest in penology, had not belonged to any organizations doing rehabilitation work or prison reform, had little interest in Siberia. The climate of the flat lands of Siberia in early spring was obviously too harsh for a man with tuberculosis, the trip was expensive and Chekhov didn't have much money, and the three months' journey from Moscow to Sakhalin had to be made under incredibly primitive and uncomfortable condition.[1]

Why did he go? He gave many answers to his bewildered and protesting friends. Sometimes he said he was worried about his work: "Sketches, stupidities, vaudevilles, 'A Tiresome Tale' . . . paper filled with writing, the Pushkin Prize[2] . . . and all the time not a single line which has any serious literary importance in my own eyes." Sometimes he said he was worried about the staleness of his life in Moscow: "Even if I get nothing out of it all there are bound to be two or three days which I will remember all my life with joy or grief." Sometimes he said he was going to Sakhalin to pay his debt to medicine, but some of his

---

[1] Fifty years later, I made almost the same trip across Siberia. Even though I went in a good airplane and took only fourteen days, it was still rough going.

[2] Chekhov had won the Pushkin Prize but the judges had made the whole thing mingy by cutting the money award in half.

friends thought he was running away from a love affair that he was afraid of.

There is nothing in the Chekhov letters or notes or in the memoirs of his friends that truly explains the reasons for this daring journey. Perhaps it was undertaken simply out of pity for the people on Sakhalin and a humane desire to help them, but, on the other hand, the trip was made at a time when many intellectuals were accusing him of being a man without convictions, without social ideals. Perhaps he felt—certainly he said it often enough in other places—that ideals are proved in action and not in fireplace chit-chat. Whatever the reasons, or mixture of reasons, he took off for Sakhalin in the spring of 1890.

The letters about the journey speak for themselves. The trip proved to be a kind of catharsis for Chekhov. The misery of the people on Sakhalin put his own physical-social-literary problems in their proper place. He said, for example, that before he went to Sakhalin the publication of *The Kreutzer Sonata* was a tremendous event, but that after the trip the book made him laugh.

Chekhov's book, *Sakhalin Island,* is said to be an excellent example of a creative writer making use of research material. The book did have influence: it caused so much comment that a special government investigating committe was sent to Sakhalin. There is no record that the committee accomplished anything, and Chekhov's book was soon forgotten. But what he had seen on the island of Sakhalin was important to Chekhov for the rest of his life.

In 1892 Chekhov bought a country house for his family in the village of Melikhovo, about fifty miles from Moscow. The Melikhovo letters are happy letters. Even his father, Pavel Chekhov, finally found a niche for himself: he became the village choirmaster and the peasants understood and accepted this old man who was so like themselves. Chekhov, as the years went on, took an active part in village life. He doctored the peasants, he was a man of importance in local government, he built three schools with his own money, and he worked hard on projects for new roads and new housing. These were good and fruitful years in Melikhovo. Much of his very best work was done in this period.

In 1894, with Suvorin, he took his second trip to Europe. Western Europe was an impressive place for a Russian. The beauty of the cities, the comfort of hotels and railroads and houses, the easy freedom of intellectual life lived without the fears and pressures of censorship—Chekhov was enchanted with all of it. But it is amusing to watch the enchantment wear off. He soon begins to tire of the beauties of Vienna and Venice and to remember the rough virtues of home. It has been said that Russians are the greatest complainers in history, but whatever it is that holds them to their land holds them forever. Homesick, Chekhov went back to Melikhovo.

Melikhovo, like all the houses of the Chekhov family, was always full of guests. One of the frequent visitors was Lydia Mizinova, a beautiful and charming young girl, a friend of Maria Chekhova's. Letters from Lydia Mizinova, found in recently opened archives, are said to prove that she was very much in love with Chekhov. But he was not in love with her. His letters to her are affectionate and flirtatious but they make clear that whatever she wanted, he wanted nothing. Lydia consoled herself with the painter Levitan. But Levitan, a famous beau, never consoled any woman for very long and so, in time, Lydia moved from Levitan to the novelist Potapenko. Chekhov watched this affair carefully and when he sat down to write *The Seagull*,[3] he very possibly made use of the Lydia-Potapenko relationship. Trigorin, in *The Seagull,* was so like Potapenko

---

[3] *The Seagull* was, of course, a famous failure in its first production in St. Petersburg. Two years later the newly formed Moscow Art Theatre produced it with great success.

that Suvorin spotted the resemblance immediately. Chekhov altered Trigorin in the next version of the play.

The Seagull was Chekhov's third full length play. (The earlier *Wood Demon* would later become *Uncle Vanya*.) The play does not reach the artistic purity and depth of *The Three Sisters*, but it is full of good things, and a daring departure in stage technique.

The serious theatre can be uncomfortable. How often we go to a play with high expectations which, as the evening wears on, turn into a kind of impatient discomfort. We grow conscious of strains and stresses, and something irritates us although we do not know its name. But sometimes we go to a play and after the curtain has been up five minutes we have a sense of being able to settle back in the arms of the playwright. Instinctively we know that the playwright knows his business. Neatness in design and execution is, after all, only the proper use of material, but it has a beauty of its own. It is exhilarating to watch a good workman at work, to see each detail fall into useful place, to know that the shortest line, the smallest stage movement, has an end in view and is not being used to trick us or deceive or pull fashionable wool over our eyes. It is then that we say to ourselves, this writer knows what he is doing, he has paid us the compliment of learning his trade. To such writers, in whatever field they be, we give our full attention and they deserve it.

It is that way with Chekhov. The smallest detail has meaning. In *The Seagull*, for example, Arkadina, many years before the play begins, married a man whose social standing she considered too low. This seems of no importance—the line about it is thrown away—until the third act when the whole Hamlet-Gertrude theme of the play is given new meaning: Arkadina, turning on her son, calls him a "Kiev artisan," which is what she had once called his father. And suddenly we understand that the son never had a chance: his father was not a gentleman to Arkadina and the child was made to pay for it from the day he was born. Chekhov knew all there was to know about his characters and every line he wrote advanced the play and moved it to its end. It is strange that neither his interpreters nor his imitators have been impressed with the fine, hard core of the design.

To ALEXEI SUVORIN

March 9, 1890, Moscow

March 9th, 40 Martyrs
and 10,000 skylarks

We are both mistaken about Sakhalin, but you probably more than I. I am leaving in the firm conviction that my expedition will not yield anything valuable in the way of either literature or science, as I haven't enough knowledge, time or pretensions. I haven't the plans of a Humboldt[1] or even of a Kennan.[2] I want to write a couple of hundred pages and thereby atone in some degree for my medicine, which, as you know, I have piggishly neglected.

Perhaps I shall not be able to write anything worthwhile, but the trip still has not lost its allure for me: in reading, looking about and listening, my researches will teach me a great deal. Although I have not yet left, thanks to the books I have gone through, I have been forced to learn much that people should be beaten for not knowing and which in my ignorance I had not known before this. Moreover, I am of the opinion that the trip will turn out to be six months at hard labor, physical and mental, and for me this is also essential, as I am a Little Russian and have already begun to get lazy. I have to discipline myself. Though the trip may be nonsense, stubbornness, a whim, still, think it over and tell me what I have to lose by going. Time?

1 Alexander Humboldt, the German scientist, made a journey to Asiatic Russia in 1829 to get geological and geophysical data.

2 George Kennan (1845-1924), an American engineer and explorer who, in 1886, made a famous tour of Siberian prisons. He was a great-uncle of George Kennan, former U. S. Ambassador to the Soviet Union.

Money? Will I have to undergo hardships? My time isn't worth anything, I'll never have any money anyway; as to hardships, I'll be traveling by horse for twenty-five or thirty days, not longer, and all the rest of the time I'll be sitting on the deck of a steamer or in a room and will be bombarding you with letters. Let's say I find the trip absolutely unrewarding. I still feel there are bound to be two or three days which I'll remember all my life with the greatest pleasure or the greatest pain, etc. That's how I figure it, my dear sir. All I say may be unconvincing, but certainly you too write just as unconvincingly. For example, you write that Sakhalin is of no use or interest to anybody. Do you really think that's so? Sakhalin is useless and uninteresting only to a society that does not exile thousands of people to it and spends millions maintaining it. Except for Australia in the old days and Cayenne today, Sakhalin is the only place where one can study convict colonization: all Europe is interested in it, but it's no use to us? No more than twenty-five or thirty years back our Russian researchers in Sakhalin did a tremendous job, a job that should make us proud of being men, but we have no use for this sort of thing, have we, nor do we know what kind of people we've got there; so we just sit shut within our four walls and complain of the bad job that God has made of man. Sakhalin is a place of intolerable sufferings, the kind that only free and unfree people together can inflict. Men there and elsewhere have solved terribly serious problems and are doing so now. I regret I am not sentimental, or I would say that we ought to journey to places like Sakhalin to worship as Turks go to Mecca; while sailors and penologists in particular ought to look upon Sakhalin as military men regard Sevastopol. From the books I have read and am now reading it is evident that we have let *millions* of people rot in prison, let them rot to no good purpose, barbarously, without giving the matter a thought; we have driven people in chains through the cold thousands of miles, infected them with syphilis, depraved them, multiplied criminals and shifted the blame onto the red-nosed prison overseers. Now, all educated Europe knows it is not the overseers who are the guilty parties, but all of us; but this does not interest us in the slightest. The celebrated sixties did *nothing* for the sick and imprisoned, thereby transgressing against the most important commandment of Christian civilization. In our times something is being done for the sick, but nothing at all for the imprisoned; penology just doesn't interest our jurists. No, I assure you, Sakhalin is of use and of interest and my sole regret is that it is I who goes there and not someone else who knows more about the business and is more capable of arousing public interest. My going won't mean very much. . . .

We have been having tremendous student riots. They began at Petrovski Academy, where the authorities banned the admission of young ladies into student quarters, suspecting these latter not only of prostitution but also of political activity. From the academy it spread to the university where, surrounded by Hectors and Achilleses heavily armed and mounted, and equipped with lances, the students are making the following demands:

1. Complete autonomy of the universities.
2. Complete freedom of teaching.
3. Free access to the university without distinction of creed, nationality, sex and social background.
4. Admission of Jews to the university without restrictions and equal rights for them with the other students.
5. Freedom of assemblage and recognition of student associations.
6. Establishment of a university and student tribunal.
7. Abolition of the police function of the inspectors.
8. Lowering of fees for courses.

This I have copied from a manifesto, with some abridgements. I think most of the fuss has been kicked up by the bunch of [. . .] and the sex that craves admission to the university, although it is five times worse prepared than the male. The latter is miserably enough prepared as it is, and its university career is, with rare exceptions, inglorious.

. . . I sympathize with Hay[3] with all my heart, but he is grieving needlessly. Syphilis is now treated very easily and we will cure him—no doubt of that.

Along with the books please send my one-acter "The Wedding." That's all. . . .

Keep well and happy. I put as much credence in old age creeping up on you as I do in the fourth dimension. First, you are not yet an old man; you think and work enough for ten and your ability to reason is certainly far from senile; second, and this I am prepared to state under oath, you have no illnesses except migraine headaches; third, old age is bad only for bad old people, and wearisome only to the weary, while you are good and anything but weary. Fourth, the difference between youth and age is extremely relative and conditional. Saying which, allow me to express my admiration for you by throwing myself into a deep pit and knocking out my brains.

Your

A. Chekhov

The other day I wrote you of Ostrovski. He has been to see me again. What shall I tell him? . . .

To MODEST TCHAIKOVSKI

March 16, 1890, Moscow

. . . I have been staying home without budging and reading about the price of Sakhalin coal per ton in 1863 and the price of coal in Shanghai, reading of latitudes and NO, NW, SO and other winds that will be whistling about my head when I observe my own seasickness along the Sakhalin shores. I am reading about the soil, subsoil, sandy clay and clayey sand. However, I haven't yet gone out of my mind and even sent a story yester-

[3] Hay, a contributor to *New Times*.

day to "New Times" and will soon be dispatching the "Wood Demon" to the "Northern Herald"—and doing so most unwillingly, as I don't like seeing my plays in print.

In a week and a half or two weeks my little book[1] dedicated to Pyotr Ilich will be coming out. I would feel it an honor to stand on guard, night and day, in front of any house where he happened to be living, so profoundly do I esteem him. If one were to speak of ranks in Russian art, he now occupies the place next to Leo Tolstoy, who has long stood at its head. (Third place I bestow on Repin[2] and take No. 98 for myself.) I have long held within me the daring dream of dedicating something to him. Such a step, I thought, would be the least I could do, inadequate as it might be, to express the tremendous critical approval in which I, a writing man, hold his magnificent talent; an approval I canot commit to paper because of my lack of a musical gift. To my regret I had to realize this dream through the medium of a book that I do not consider my best. It is composed of especially gloomy psychopathological sketches and bears a gloomy title that makes my dedication alien to Peter Ilich's taste and that of his admirers.

You are a Chekhist? I thank you humbly. No, you are not a Chekhist, but simply indulgent. Keep well. My best wishes.

Yours,

A. Chekhov

To IVAN LEONTIEV (SHCHEGLOV)

March 22, 1890, Moscow

How are you, dear Johnchik,

Thanks for your long letter and for its true kindness. I shall be glad to read your war story. Is it appearing in the Easter

---

1 *Gloomy People,* a collection of Chekhov stories.

2 Repin, the most famous of Russian painters, the man whose traditional and conservative work is still overrated in the Soviet Union.

issue? I haven't read anything of yours, or of mine, for a long
time.

You write that you wish to pick a violent quarrel with me
"especially on matters of morality and artistry," you speak
vaguely of certain crimes I have committed which merit a
friendly reproach and threaten me even "with influential newspaper criticism." If you cross out the word "artistry," the entire
phrase between quotation marks becomes clearer, but acquires
a significance which, to speak frankly, perplexes me considerably. John, what is it all about? How is this matter to be understood? Do you mean to say my understanding of morality puts
me in a different camp from people like you and even to such
an extent as to merit a reproach and the special attention of
influential criticism? I cannot suppose you have in view some
sort of abstruse lofty morality, since there are no low, high or
medium moralities, but only one, namely, that given us in his
day by Jesus Christ and which now deters you, and me . . .
from stealing, offending, lying and so on. In all my life, if I
can rely upon the repose of my own conscience, neither by word,
deed or intention, nor in my stories or plays have I coveted my
neighbor's wife, or his manservant, or his ox or his ass, or anything that is my neighbor's; I have not stolen, dissembled,
flattered the powerful or sought their favor, have not blackmailed or lived on other people. It is true that in idleness I
have wasted by substance, laughing madly, overeating, drinking
to excess, have played the prodigal, but surely all of this is personal to me and does not deprive me of the right to think that
in the morality section I do not deviate much either up or down
from the normal. No notable feats, no mean acts—that is how
I am, like the majority; my sins are many, but in morality we
are quits, since I am atoning lavishly for those sins through the
discomforts they bring in their wake. If you really wish to quarrel with me violently because I am not a hero, then throw your
savagery out of the window and substitute for the harsh words
your amiable tragic laugh—that would be better.

To IVAN LEONTIEV [1890]

But that word "artistry" I fear as merchants' wives are supposed to fear bogey men. When people talk to me of what is artistic or inartistic, of what is stageable or not stageable, of tendency, realism and so forth I am at my wit's end, assent irresolutely and reply with banal half-truths that aren't worth a hoot. I divide all productions into two categories: those I like and those I don't like. I have no other criterion, and if you ask me why I like Shakespeare and don't like Zlatovratski[1], I cannot tell you. Perhaps in time, when I get smarter, I will acquire a criterion, but in the meantime all talks about "artistry" only weary me and seem a continuation of those scholastic polemics with which people wore themselves out during the Middle Ages.

If criticism, whose authority you refer to, knows what you and I do not know, why has it been silent until now, why doesn't it reveal the truth and the immutable laws to us? If it knew, then believe me, it would long since have shown us the way and we would know what to do, Fofanov[2] would not be in an insane asylum, Garshin[3] would still be alive . . . and we wouldn't find existence as boring and tedious as it is now. You wouldn't be lured into the theatre and I to Sakhalin. But criticism is solidly silent or actually disposes of us with idle, rubbishy prattle. If it seems influential to you, it is only because it is stupid, immodest, arrogant and noisy, because it rumbles like an empty barrel which you can't avoid hearing.

However, let's spit on all this and sing a tune from another opera. Please do not have any literary hopes for my Sakhalin expedition. I am not going to observe or get impressions, but simply to be able to live for a half year as I have not lived hitherto. Don't expect anything from me, old man; if I have the time and ability to achieve anything, then glory be to

1 Zlatovratski, a popular author of the period.
2 Fofanov, the poet, was a contributor to *New Times*.
3 Garshin, a well-known writer who had committed suicide.

God—if not, don't find fault. I'll be leaving after Easter Week. . . .

Be a nice little staff captain with moustachios and keep well and happy.

Your
A. Chekhov

To ALEXEI SUVORIN

April 1, 1890, Moscow

Christ has risen! Happy Easter, dear fellow, to all of you, and every good wish for your happiness.

I am leaving during St. Thomas week or somewhat later, depending on when the Kama opens for traffic. I am soon going to make the round of farewell visits. Before my departure I shall be asking you for a correspondent's blank and some money. Please send the first, but as for the second I must wait a little since I don't know how much I'll require. I am now gathering all the capital I have any claim to from the far ends of the earth, have not got it together yet, but when I do I'll be able to tell how much more I need.

My family is taken care of until October—in this regard my mind is already at ease. . . .

You scold me for objectivity, calling it indifference to good and evil, lack of ideals and ideas and so on. When I portray horse thieves, you would want me to say that stealing horses is an evil. But certainly this has always been obvious without my saying so. Let the jury pass judgment on them; it is my business solely to show them as they are. Here is the way I write: you are considering the subject of horse thieves, so bear in mind they are not beggars but well-fed people, that they are members of a cult and that with them stealing horses is not just theft but a passion. Of course it would be nice to combine art with sermonizing, but that kind of thing I find extraordinarily difficult and well-nigh impossible because of technical considerations. Certainly if I am to depict horse thieves in seven hundred lines, I must speak and think as they would and feel with their feelings; I add a subjective point of view if I don't and then my characters will grow dim and the story won't be as compact as all little short stories should be. When I write I count upon my reader fully, assuming that he himself will add the subjective elements that are lacking in the telling.

All good wishes.

Your
A. Chekhov

To VUKOL LAVROV

April 10, 1890, Moscow

Vukol Mikhailovich,

In the March issue of "Russian Thought," on page 147 of the biographical section, I happened to come upon the following sentence: "Only yesterday even the pontiffs of unprincipled writing, such as Messrs. Yasinski and Chekhov, whose names . . ." etc. Generally one does not reply to criticism, but in the present instance the question is perhaps not one of criticism but simply of calumny. As a matter of fact I would not even reply to slander, except that in a few days I shall be leaving Russia for a long period, perhaps never to return, and I do not have the will power to refrain from a reply.

I have never been an unprincipled writer, or what amounts to the same thing, an unscrupulous person.

True, my literary career has consisted of an uninterrupted series of mistakes, sometimes crude ones, but this can be explained by the dimensions of my talent, and certainly not by whether I am good or bad. I have never blackmailed, written lampoons, informed on others; I have not toadied, or lied, or insulted anyone, in short, I am the author of a great number of stories and editorial articles that I would gladly throw out because of their worthlessness, but there is not a single line of which I need be ashamed. Let us say you subscribe to the theory of considering as lack of principle the grievous circumstance that I, a well-educated, popular writer, have not exerted myself at all in behalf of those I admire, that my literary endeavors have left no trace, for example in promoting local self-government, the new court procedure, freedom of the press, freedom in general and so on; in this respect "Russian Thought" should in all fairness look upon me as its comrade and not point a finger at me, since up until the present it has not done any more than I have in this field—and neither you nor I am to blame for the omission.

Let us say you are judging me as a writer from the external point of view; even then I do not merit a public dressing-down for lack of principle. I have always led a reserved life, within the four walls of my home. . . . I have always persistently avoided participation in literary evenings, evening parties, meetings, etc., have never shown myself without an invitation in any editorial office, have always striven to have my acquaintances consider me a physician rather than a writer; in brief, I have been a modest writing man and the letter I am now writing is the first immodesty committed during ten years of activity. With my comrades I maintain excellent relations; I have never taken upon myself the rôle of judging them or the newspapers and magazines on which they work, as I do not consider myself competent, and find the present dependent position of the press is such that every word uttered against a paper or a writer is not only merciless and tactless, but in point of fact criminal. I have always clung to my decision to turn down offers from newspapers and magazines whose bad quality has been apparent and proved; and when it came to choosing among them, I have given the preference to those which have been in greater need of my services because of material or other circumstances, and that is why I have worked not for you and not for the "European Herald," but for the "Northern Herald" and consequently have received half as much as I might have, had I another point of view toward my obligations.

Your accusation is a slander. I cannot request you to take it back, since the damage has already been done and can't be cut out with an axe. I cannot explain it as carelessness, frivolity or anything of that sort either, as I know your editorial office to be staffed by undoubtedly decent, cultured people who read and write articles, I trust, not casually but with a consciousness of responsibility for every word. It only remains for me to point out your error and ask you to believe in the sincerity of the unhappy feeling that caused me to write you this letter. It is of course obvious that in view of your accusation, not only business dealings between us, but even formal social relations are out of the question.

A. Chekhov

To MARIA CHEKHOVA

April 23, 1890, on the Volga aboard the S.S. Alexander Nevsky early in the morning.

Dear clan of Tunguses,

. . . My first impression of the Volga was spoiled by the rain, the tear-stained cabin windows and the wet nose of Gurland who came to meet me at the station. . . .

Once on the boat I paid first honors to my special talent, i.e., I went to sleep. When I awoke it was to behold the sun. The Volga is not bad, with water-drenched meadows, monasteries flooded with sunlight, white churches; a wonderful sense of expansive ease, and wherever you look you see nice places to sit and fish. . . .

The steamer itself is not so wonderful. The best thing about it is the toilet. This stands on high, four steps leading to it, so that an inexperienced person, say Ivanenko, might easily mistake it for a royal throne. The boat's worst feature is the dinner it serves. Here is the menu, with original spelling retained: veg. soupe, frankfurts and cab, sturgon frit, baked kat pudding; kat, it develops, means kasha. Since my money has been earned by blood and sweat, I should have wished the reverse order of things, i.e., to have the dinner better than the toilet facilities, all the more so since after the wine I drank at Korneyev's my insides have become completely clogged and I'll be doing without the toilet all the way through to Tomsk.

Madame Kundasova[1] is traveling on this boat. I haven't any idea where she is going, or why. When I start asking questions, she launches into extremely hazy conjectures on the subject of somebody who was supposed to meet her in a ravine near Kineshma, then bursts into furious laughter and stamps her foot or pokes her elbow into whatever is handy, not sparing [. . .] ribs. We have sailed past Kineshma, and the ravines as well, but she has continued on the boat, which has been very nice as far as I am concerned. By the way: yesterday, for the first time in my life, I saw her eat. She doesn't eat less than other folks, but she eats mechanically, as though she were champing oats. . . .

It's coldish and somewhat tiresome—but on the whole interesting.

The boat whistles every few minutes, sounding halfway between a donkey's bray and an Aeolian harp. In five or six hours I'll be in Nizhni-Novgorod. The sun is rising. I slept artistically all night. My money is intact—because I'm always clutching at my stomach. . . .

The sun has hidden behind a cloud, the sky is overcast and the broad Volga wears a dismal look. Levitan should not be living on the Volga. The river sheds gloom on the soul. Although a nice little estate along its banks would not be too bad.

Best regards to all. Hearty greetings and a thousand salutations. . . .

If the steward were awake, I should have some coffee, but as

1 Kundasova was a friend of the Chekhov family, a mathematician and astronomer.

it is I must drink water disconsolately. Greetings to Maryusha and Olga.[2]

Keep well and happy. I'll write regularly.

Your bored Volgaman,

Homo Sakhaliensis,

A. Chekhov

Greetings to Grandma.

To MARIA CHEKHOVA

April 24, 1890, Kama

S.S. Perm

My dear Tungus friends,

I am sailing on the Kama, but cannot tell you exactly where we are; around Chistopol, I think. Nor can I extol the beauty of the banks since it is devilishly cold; the birches haven't yet put forth their leaves, here and there lie patches of snow, ice floats in the river, in brief, all aesthetic considerations are shot to hell. I am sitting in the deck cabin where people of all classes are at table and am listening to conversations and asking myself whether it isn't time for some tea. If it were up to me I would do nothing but eat from morning to night; but as I haven't the money for continuous eating I sleep or wait for sleep. I haven't been going out on deck—it's too cold. It rains at night and daytime an unpleasant wind blows.

Ah, caviar! I keep on eating it, but can never get my fill. Like olives. It's a lucky thing it's not salty.

It's a shame I didn't think of sewing myself a little bag for tea and sugar. I have to order it one glass at a time, which is a bore and expensive to boot. This morning I wanted to buy some tea and sugar in Kazan but slept too late.

Rejoice, Mother! It seems I'll be spending twenty-four hours in Ekaterinburg and am going to see our relatives. Perhaps their

2 Maryusha and Olga were servants in the Chekhov household.

hearts have grown tender and they will give me three rubles and a little packet of tea.

From the conversations now under way, I take it that a circuit court is making the trip with us. These people are not overburdened with intellect and so the merchants who only rarely put in a word seem very clever. You run across frightfully rich people everywhere.

Small sturgeon are cheaper than dirt, but you get tired of them very fast. What more is there to write? Nothing. Oh yes, we have a general on board and an emaciated man with fair hair. The former rushes back and forth from his cabin to the deck and keeps sending photos to people; the latter . . . seeks to give the impression that he is a writer; today at dinner he lied to some lady that Suvorin had published a little book of his; I, of course, expressed the proper awe on my face.

My money is intact with the exception of what I've eaten up. The scoundrels won't feed me free!

I am neither gay nor sad but seem to have a soul of gelatin. I am content to sit motionless and silent. Today, for example, I hardly spoke five words. Hold on, I'm not telling the truth: I had a talk with a priest on deck.

We are starting to meet up with natives. There are great numbers of Tatars, who appear to be a respectable and decorous people. . . .

I send my humblest greetings to all of you. I plead with Mama and Papa not to worry about me and not to imagine dangers that do not exist. . . .

Keep well and happy.

Yours,

A. Chekhov

Forgive me for writing only of food. If I didn't write of it I would have to write of the cold; there are no other themes.

The circuit court has decreed that we are to have tea. It has picked up somewhere along the line two candidates for court duties who are now serving as the office staff. One looks like our sartorial poet Byelousov and the other like Yezhov. Both respectfully listen to Messrs. the bosses. They don't dare have an opinion of their own and try to look as though they themselves were acquiring wisdom in listening to these sage speeches. I like model young people.

To MARIA CHEKHOVA

April 29, 1890, Ekaterinburg

Dear Tungus friends,

The Kama is the very dullest of rivers; to grasp its beauty one should be a Pecheneg, sit motionless on a barge near a barrel filled with oil or a sack with fish from the Caspian and continually take swigs of liquor. The banks are bare, the trees bare, the earth a mat-brown, patches of snow stretch ahead and the wind is such that even the devil himself couldn't blow as sharply or unpleasantly. When the cold wind blows and ripples the water, which after the spring's flooding has taken on the color of coffee slops, everything turns cold and lonely and wretched; the accordion sounds on the shore seem mournful and the figures in torn sheepskin coats standing motionless on the barges we encounter appear permanently stiff with sorrow. The cities of the Kama are gray; it looks as though their inhabitants occupied themselves exclusively in the manufacture of lowering clouds, boredom, wet fences and street filth. The quays swarm with intelligentsia, for whom the arrival of a boat is an event. . . .

I have already written that a circuit court is aboard: presiding officer, judge and public prosecutor. The presiding officer is a healthy, sturdy old German fellow converted to Orthodoxy, pious, a homeopath, and obviously an assiduous ladies' man; the judge is an old fellow of the type our departed Nikolai used to draw; he walks badly bent, coughs and likes comic themes; the prosecutor is a man of forty-three, dissatisfied with life, a liberal, skeptic and really big-hearted fellow. During the entire trip this judicial group has employed its time eating, deciding important questions, eating, reading and eating. There is a library on board, and I saw the prosecutor reading my "In the Twilight." The talk was about me. Around this part of the world their favorite is Sibiryak-Mamin and his descriptions of the Urals. They have more to say about him than they do about Tolstoy. . . .

[Later]

After awakening yesterday morning and looking out of the coach window I felt an aversion to nature; the ground was white-covered, trees were cloaked in hoar frost and a genuine blizzard was catching up with the train. Wasn't it revolting! What sons of bitches these natural phenomena are! I had no overshoes, so I drew on my big boots and on my trip to the re-freshment bar for coffee I perfumed the whole Ural region with tar. Upon arriving in Ekaterinburg I found rain, snow and hail and put on my leather coat. The cabs are inconceivable as far as their squalor is concerned—filthy, dripping, no springs; the horses' front feet are arranged this way [drawing], their hoofs are enormous and their spines spindly. . . . The local droshkis are a clumsy parody of our surreys. . . .

All cities look alike in Russia. Ekaterinburg is just exactly like Perm or Tula. The bells chime magnificently, in velvet tones. I put up at the American Hotel (not half bad) and im-mediately let Alexander Simonov know of my arrival, inform-ing him that I intended sitting tight in my rooms for about two days and drinking Hunyadi water, which I am taking, and—I mention this not without pride—with great success.

The people here inspire the newcomer with something like horror; they are high-cheekboned, with jutting foreheads, broad-shouldered, have little eyes and enormously big fists. They are born at the local iron foundries and it is a mechanic, and not a midwife, who officiates. One of them will walk into your room with a samovar or water carafe and you may well fear he will murder you. I steer clear of them. This morning one such creature entered—high cheekbones, bulging brow, morose, almost as tall as the ceiling, shoulders five feet across and, to top it all, wearing a sheepskin coat.

Well, I think to myself, this one will certainly murder me. He turned out to be Alexander Simonov! We had a long talk. He serves as a member of the local government council, is manager of his cousin's mill, which is lit by electricity, is the editor of the "Ekaterinburg Weekly," which is censored by Police Chief Baron Taube, is married, has two children, is getting rich and fat, is aging, and lives "substantially." Says he has no time to be bored. He advised me to visit the museum, factories and mines; I thanked him for the advice. Then he invited me to take tea with him tomorrow; I invited him to have dinner with me. He did not ask me for dinner and generally did not insist on my visiting him. From this Mama may conclude that the heart of her relative has not softened and that both of us— Simonov and I—have no use for each other. . . .

There is snow on the streets and I have purposely pulled the curtains over the window so as not to have to look out upon all Asiatica. . . .

All night long sheets of iron are struck at every corner. People have to have iron heads not to go out of their minds with the incessant hammering. Today I attempted to boil myself some coffee; the result was like our cheap Taganrog wine. I drank it and shrugged it off. . . .

Keep well and happy, all of you, and may God look after you. . . . My money is intact. If Mama has a screen made in Nikolai's memory, I shall have nothing against it. I would like it.

Will I find a letter from you in Irkutsk?

Your Homo Sakhaliensis,

A. Chekhov

To MARIA CHEKHOVA

May 14-17, 1890, Krasni Yar to Tomsk
May 14, 1890, Village of Krasni Yar,
30 miles from Tomsk

My wonderful Mama, excellent Masha,
sweet Misha and everybody at home,

. . . I left Tyumen on May the third after a stop of two or three days in Ekaterinburg, which I applied to the repair of my coughing and hemorrhoidal personage. Both post and private drivers make the trans-Siberian trip. I elected to use the latter, as it was all the same to me. They put your humble servant into a vehicle resembling a little wicker basket and off we drove with a pair of horses. You sit in the basket, and look out upon God's earth like a bird in a cage, without a thought on your mind.

It looks to me as if the Siberian plain commences right at Ekaterinburg and ends the devil knows where; I would say it is very like our South Russian steppe, were it not for the small birch groves encountered here and there and the cold wind stinging one's cheeks. Spring hasn't yet arrived here. There is absolutely no greenery, the forests are bare, the snow has not all melted and lusterless ice sheathes the lakes. On the ninth of May, St. Nicholas Day, there was a frost, and today, the fourteenth, we had a snowfall of about three inches. Only the ducks hint of spring. How many of them there are! I have never in my life seen such a superabundance of ducks. They fly over your head, take wing over the carriage, swim the lakes and pools, in short, I could have shot a thousand of them in one day with a poor gun. You can hear the wild geese honking; they are also numerous here. Often files of cranes and swans head our way. . . . In the birch groves flutter grouse and woodcock. Rabbits, which are not eaten or shot here, sit up on their hind paws in a relaxed way and prick up their ears as they stare inquisitively at all comers. They run across the road so often that here it is not considered bad luck.

Traveling is a cold business. I am wearing my sheepskin jacket. I don't mind my body, that's all right, but my feet are always freezing. I wrap them in my leather coat but it doesn't help. I am wearing two pairs of trousers. Well, you go on and on. Road signs flash by, ponds, little birch groves. . . . Now we drive past a group of new settlers, then a file of prisoners. . . . We've met tramps with pots on their backs; these gentlemen promenade all over the Siberian plain without hindrance. On occasion they will murder a poor old woman to obtain her skirt for leg puttees; or they will tear off the tin numbers from the road signs, on the chance they may find them useful; another time they will bash in the head of a passing beggar or knock out the eyes of one of their own banished brotherhood, but they won't touch people in vehicles. On the whole, as far as robbery is concerned, traveling hereabouts is absolutely safe. From Tyumen to Tomsk neither the drivers of the post coaches nor the independent drivers can recall anything ever having been stolen from a traveler; when you get to a station, you leave your things outside; when you ask whether they won't be stolen you get a smile in reply. It is not good form to mention burglaries and murders on the road. I really believe that were I to lose my money at a station or in a vehicle the driver would return it to me without fail if he found it and wouldn't boast of his honesty. On the whole, the people here are good, kind, and have splendid traditions. Their rooms are furnished simply, but cleanly, with some pretension to luxury; the beds are soft, with feather mattresses and big pillows, the floors are painted or covered with handmade linen rugs. All this is due, of course, to their prosperity, to the fact that a family gets an allotment of about 50 acres of good black earth, and that good wheat grows on it (wheat flour here is 30 kopeks for 36 pounds). But not everything can be explained by comfortable circumstances and plenty to eat, some reference must be made to their way of life as well. When you enter a room full of sleeping people at night your nose isn't assailed, especially not by that notorious Russian smell. I must say, one old lady wiped a teaspoon on her hind-side before handing it to me, but still you do not sit down to tea without a tablecloth, people do not belch in your presence and don't search for things in their heads; when they hand you water or milk, they don't put their fingers inside the glass, the dishes are clean, the kvas is as transparent as beer—in fact, they practice cleanliness of a sort our Little Russians can only dream about, and certainly Little Russians are far and away cleaner than Great Russians! They bake the most delicious bread; the first few days I made a pig of myself. Delicious also are the pies and pancakes, the fritters and dinner rolls which remind one of Little Russian spongy ring rolls. The pancakes are thin. . . . On the other hand, the rest of their cuisine is not for the European stomach. For instance, I have been treated everywhere to "duck soup." This is absolutely awful, consisting of a muddy liquid in which float bits of wild duck and un-cooked onion; the duck stomachs haven't been entirely cleaned of their contents and so, when you bite into them, cause you to think your mouth and rectum have changed places. One time I asked for soup cooked with meat and some fried perch. The soup was served oversalted, dirty, with weatherbeaten bits of skin instead of meat, and the perch arrived complete with scales. They cook cabbage soup here with corned beef; they also roast corned beef. I've just been served some of the latter; it's vile stuff and after chewing a little of it I pushed it aside. Brick tea is their beverage. This is an infusion of sage and cockroaches—both in taste and color—not tea but something like our horrible Taganrog wine. I might mention that I brought a quarter of a pound of tea with me from Ekaterin-burg, five pounds of sugar and three lemons. I've run out of tea and now there's no place to buy any. In the dumpy little towns even the officials drink brick tea and the very best shops don't sell any more expensive than 1 ruble 50 a pound. So I've just had to drink sage.

The distance between stations is determined by the distance

between the villages, usually 14 to 28 miles. The villages here are large, and there are no hamlets or farms. Churches and schools are everywhere. You see wooden cabins, some of them of two storeys.

Toward evening the pools and roads begin freezing, and at night there is a regular frost; an extra fur coat would not be amiss. Br-r-r-! The vehicle jolts because the mud has turned into hillocks. It is heartbreaking. By dawn you are terribly tired with the cold, the jolting and the jingle of the bells on your horses; you passionately crave warmth and a bed. While the horses are being changed, you curl up in some corner and immediately fall asleep, but a moment later your driver is already tugging at your sleeve and saying, "Get up, friend, time to leave!" On the second night I began feeling a sharp toothache in my heels. It was intolerably painful and I wondered whether they hadn't got frost-bitten. . . .

Tomsk, May 16

The guilty party turned out to be my jack boots, too narrow in the back. Sweet Misha, if you ever have children, which I don't doubt will happen, advise them not to look for cheapness. A cheap price on Russian merchandise is a guarantee of its worthlessness. In my opinion going barefoot is preferable to wearing cheap boots. . . . I had to buy felt boots in Ishim. . . . So I have been traveling in felt boots until they decompose on me from dampness and mud.

Tea drinking in the cabins goes on at five or six in the morning. Tea on the road is a true boon. . . . It warms you up, dispels sleep and with it you eat a lot of bread; in the absence of other food, bread should be eaten in large amounts and that is why the peasant eats such a quantity of bread and starchy things. You drink tea and talk with the peasant women, who here are sensible, home-loving, tenderhearted, hard-working and more free than they are in Europe; their husbands do not curse or beat them because they are just as tall, and strong, and clever as their lords; when their husbands are not at home it is they who do the driving. They are great punsters. They do not raise their children strictly but are inclined to indulge them. The children sleep in comfortable beds for as long as they like, drink tea, ride with the peasants and use swear words when the latter tease them playfully. There is no diphtheria. Smallpox is widespread but curiously enough it is not as contagious here as it is elsewhere; two or three will come down with it and die—and that's the end of the epidemic. There are no hospitals or doctors. The doctoring is done by medical assistants. They go in for bloodletting and cupping on a grandiose, brutal scale. On the road I examined a Jew with cancer of the liver. The Jew was emaciated and hardly breathing, but this did not deter the medical assistant from putting twelve cupping glasses on him. By the way, on the subject of Jews. Here they work the land, drive, run ferryboats, trade and call themselves peasants,[1] because they actually are de jure and de facto peasants. They enjoy universal respect and according to the police officer are not infrequently elected village elders. I saw a tall, thin Jew scowling in revulsion and spitting when the police officer told obscene stories; he had a clean mind and his wife cooked excellent fish soup. The wife of the Jew with the cancer treated me to some pike roe and the most delicious white bread. Exploitation by Jews is unheard of.

By the way, about the Poles. You run across exiles sent here from Poland in 1864. They are kind, hospitable and most considerate. Some enjoy real wealth, others are poverty-stricken and work as clerks at the stations. After the amnesty the former returned to their homeland, but soon came back to Siberia, where life is more opulent; the latter dream of their native land, although they are already old and ailing. In Ishim a certain Pan Zalesski, who is rich and whose daughter resembles Sasha Kiseleva, served me an excellent dinner for a ruble and

[1] The Russian word for peasant derives from the word "Christian" because it was taken for granted that all peasants were Christians.

gave me a room where I slept very well; he keeps a tavern, has become a kulak to the marrow of his bones, swindles everybody, but nevertheless the gentleman makes itself felt in his manners, in the table he sets, in everything. He won't go back home out of greed, out of greed he puts up with snow on St. Nicholas Day; when he dies his daughter, born in Ishim, will remain here forever, and so black eyes and delicate features will keep on multiplying in Siberia! These random mixtures of blood are all to the good, since Siberians are not handsome. There are absolutely no brunettes. Perhaps you'd like to hear about the Tatars as well? Here goes. They are not numerous here. Good people. In Kazan Province even the priests speak well of them, and in Siberia they are "better than the Russians" —so stated the police officer in the presence of Russians, whose silence gave assent. My God, how rich Russia is in good people! If it were not for the cold which deprives Siberia of summer, and were it not for the officials who corrupt the peasants and exiles, Siberia would be the very richest and happiest of territories.

Dinners are nothing in particular. . . . During the entire trip I have only had a real dinner twice, if you don't count the Yiddish fish soup which I ate after having filled up on tea. I haven't been drinking any vodka; the Siberian brand is vile, and besides I had got out of the habit of drinking before reaching Ekaterinburg. One should drink vodka, though. It acts as a stimulant on the brain, which, flabby and inert with the continual movement, makes one stupid and weak. . . .

The first three days of the voyage, what with the shaking and jolting, my collarbones, shoulders and vertebrae started aching. I couldn't sit, walk or lie down. On the other hand, though, all my chest and head aches disappeared, my appetite took an unbelievable spurt and the hemorrhoids—keep your fingers crossed—have given up the ghost. The strain, the continual worry over trunks and such, and perhaps the farewell drinking bouts in Moscow, gave rise to some blood-spitting in the mornings, and this infected me with a kind of despondency and stirred up gloomy thoughts; but it ceased toward the end of the trip and now I don't even have a cough; it is a long time since I have coughed as little as now, after two weeks spent in the fresh air. After the first three days of the trip my body accustomed itself to the jolts and the time arrived when I began not to notice the way midday arrived after morning, followed by evening and night. The days flitted by quickly, as in a lingering illness. . . .

Now let me tell you of an adventure for which I am indebted to Siberian driving. Except that I ask Mama not to groan or lament, for everything came out all right. On the sixth of May, before dawn, I was being driven by a very nice old man with a team of horses. I was in a little buggy. I was drowsing and to make time pass was observing the tongues of flame darting about the fields and birch groves; people here burn the previous year's grass this way. Suddenly I heard the broken thud of wheels. Coming toward us at full tilt, like a bird, dashed a three-horse carriage. My old man quickly turned to the right, the post carriage sailed past and then I discerned in the shadows an enormous, heavy three-horse post wagon with a driver making the return trip. Behind this wagon I could see another tearing along, also at full speed. We hurried to turn right. . . . To my great bewilderment and alarm the cart turned to the left, not the right. I scarcely had time to think to myself, "My God, we'll collide!" when there was a desperate crash, the horses mingled into one dark mass, the yokes fell, my buggy stood on end, I lay on the ground and my baggage on top of me. But that wasn't all. . . . A third cart dashed upon us. . . . Verily, this should have crushed me and my suitcases, but thank God, I was not sleeping, didn't fracture any bones and managed to jump up quickly enough to run to one side. "Stop!" I yelled at the third cart, "Stop!" It hurled itself upon the second one and came to a halt. Of course, if I had been able to sleep in my buggy, or if the third wagon had flung itself immediately upon the second, I would have returned home a cripple or a headless horseman. Results of the collision: broken shafts, torn harness, yokes and baggage on the ground, scared, exhausted horses and terror at the thought of having experienced a moment of peril. It seemed that the first driver had urged on his horses, while the drivers of the other two wagons were asleep; nobody was steering. After recovering from the tumult my old fellow and the drivers of all three vehicles began swearing furiously at one another. How they cursed! I thought it would wind up in a free-for-all. You cannot conceive how alone you feel in the midst of this wild, cursing horde, in the open country, at dawn, in sight of flames lapping up the grass in the distance and close at hand, but not throwing off a bit of heat into the frigid night air! How grief-stricken was my soul! You listen to the swearing, look down at the broken shafts and your own torn baggage and you seem to be thrust into another world, about to be trampled down. After an hour long of cursing, my old man began tying up the shafts and harness with cord; my straps were pressed into service too. We dragged ourselves to the station somehow, with plenty of stops in between, and barely made it.

After the fifth or sixth day the rains began, accompanied by a stiff wind. It poured day and night. Out came the leather coat to save me from the rain and wind. It is a marvelous coat. The mud became practically impassable and the drivers were unwilling to drive by night. But the most terrible business of all, which I won't ever forget, were the river crossings. You reach a river at night. You and the driver both start shouting. . . . Rain, wind, sheets of ice creep along the river, you hear a splash. To enliven things appropriately, we hear a bittern screeching. These birds live on Siberian rivers. That means they don't recognize climate, but geographical position. Well, sir, in an hour a massive ferryboat in the form of a barge looms in the shadows; it has immense oars resembling the pincers of a crab. The ferrymen are a mischievous lot, for the most part exiles, deported here by society to atone for their sins. They use foul language to an intolerable degree, shout, demand money for vodka. . . . It is a long, long trip across the river . . . one long agony! . . .

The seventh of May, when I asked the driver for horses, he told me the Irtish had overflown its banks and flooded the meadows, that yesterday Kuzma had gone that way and had scarcely managed to return, and that it was impossible to go on, that we would have to wait. I asked until when. Reply: "The Lord only knows!" Here was an indefinite answer for me, and besides, I had promised myself to get rid of two vices en route which had caused me considerable expense, trouble and inconvenience: a readiness to comply and let myself be talked into things. I would quickly come to terms with a driver and find myself riding on the devil knows what, sometimes paying twice the usual price, and waiting for hours on end. I decided not to give in and not to believe what was told me and I've had less aches and pains. For instance, they would get out a plain, jolting wagon instead of a carriage. I'd refuse to ride in it, lay down the law, and a carriage would inevitably appear, although previously I had been assured there wasn't a single one in the whole village, etc.

Well, sir, suspecting that the flood on the Irtish had been dreamed up expressly to avoid driving through the mud at night, I protested and gave orders to go on. . . . Off we went. Mud, rain, a furious wind, cold . . . and felt boots on. Do you know what wet felt boots are like? They are footwear made of gelatin. We kept on and suddenly before my vision spread an immense lake, with mounds of earth and bushes jutting out in clumps—these were the inundated meadows. In the distance ranged the Irtish's steep bank and on it the patches of snow lay white. We started negotiating the lake. We should have turned back, but my obstinacy stood in the way, I was in a sort of defiant fervor, that same fervor that compelled me to bathe in the midst of the Black Sea from the yacht, and which has led me to perform all sorts of foolish acts. It's probably a psychotic condition. On we went, picking out little islets and strips of land. Big and little bridges are supposed to show the way, but they had been washed out. To get past them the horses had to be unharnessed and led one at a time. The driver did so, and I jumped into the water—in my felt boots—to hold the horses. . . . What sport! And with it the rain, the wind. Save us, Heavenly Mother! Finally we made our way to an islet with a roofless cabin. Wet horses were wandering about in wet manure. A mujik with a long stick came out of the cabin and volunteered to show us the way. He measured the depth of the water with his stick and tested the ground. God bless him, he steered us to a long strip of ground which he called a "ridge." He showed us how to get our bearings from this ridge and take the road to the right, or maybe the left, I don't remember exactly, and land on another ridge. This we did.

On we went. . . . Finally—O Joy—we reached the Irtish. The other bank was steep, on our side it sloped. . . The Irtish does not murmur, or roar, but resigns itself to its fate, which, as it were, is to hammer as though coffins were reposing on its bottom. Cursed impression! The other bank was high, mat-brown, desolate.

We came to the cabin where the ferrymen lived. One of them came out to announce it was impossible to allow a ferry across, as a storm was brewing. The river, they told us, was wide and the wind strong. What to do? We had to spend the night in the cabin. I recall that night, the snoring of the ferrymen, and of my driver, the howl of the wind, the patter of the rain, the growling of the Irtish. . . .

In the morning they were reluctant to ferry us across because of the wind. So we had to row our way over. There I was sailing across the river, with the rain beating down, the wind blowing, the baggage getting drenched, the felt boots, which had been dried overnight in the stove, again turning into jelly. . . .

. . . Seated on my suitcase I spent a full hour waiting for horses to be sent from the village. As I recall, climbing the bank was very slippery business. In the village I warmed up and had some tea. Some exiles approached me for alms. Every family makes about forty pounds of wheat flour into bread for them every day, as a sort of compulsory service.

The exiles sell the bread for liquor in the taverns. One such, a ragged, shaven old fellow, whose eyes his fellow prisoners had *knocked out* in the tavern, upon hearing there was a traveler in the room, and taking me for a merchant, began chanting and saying prayers. Prayers for health, requiescats, the Easter "God Has Risen," and "Peace With the Saints"—what didn't he sing! Then he began lying that he came of a Moscow merchant family. I noticed that this sot held in contempt the mujiks on whose necks he hung!

On the 11th I travelled on post horses. To pass the time I read the complaint book at the stations. I made a discovery that astounded me and which in the rain and dampness constitutes a pearl beyond price: and that is that there are toilets in the entrance halls of the post stations. You cannot put too high a value on them!

. . . In Tomsk the mud is impassable. Of the city and way of life here I will write in a few days, but so long for now. I have worn myself out writing. . . .

. . . I embrace you all, kiss and bless you.

Your

A. Chekhov

Misha's letter has arrived. Thanks.

Excuse the letter's resembling a hotchpotch. It rambles, but what can I do? One can't do better sitting in a hotel room. Excuse its length, but I am not to blame. My pen has run away with me, and besides, I wanted to be talking to you for as long as I could. It's three in the morning, and my hand has wearied. The wick has burned down on the candle and I can scarcely make things out. Write me at Sakhalin every four or five days.

It seems the mails reach there not only by the sea route, but also across Siberia, which means I will be receiving them in good time and often. . . .

To ALEXEI SUVORIN

May 20, 1890, Tomsk

Greetings at last! Greetings from your Siberian, dear Alexei Sergeyevich. I have missed you and our correspondence terribly. . . .

When I left I promised to send you my travel notes, beginning with Tomsk, as the road between Tyumen and Tomsk has long since been described and exploited a thousand times over. But in your telegram you expressed the desire of having some Siberian impressions as soon as possible and even, sir, had the cruelty to reproach me with a lapse of memory, i.e., of having forgotten you. It was absolutely out of the question writing on the road: I kept up a short diary in pencil and can only now offer you what has been set down in it. So as not to write at great length and make a muddle, I divided all my written impressions into chapters. I am sending you six of them. They are written *for you personally;* I wrote only for you and so haven't been afraid of being too subjective in my remarks and of putting in more of Chekhov's feelings and thoughts than of Siberia. If you find some parts interesting and deserving of print, give them beneficent publicity, sign my name and publish them, also in separate chapterlets, one tablespoon an hour. They could be given a general title: "From Siberia," later, "From the Trans-Baikal," then "From the Amur" and so on. . . .

I starved like a dog all along the way. I crammed my belly with bread in order not to think of turbot, asparagus and the like. I even dreamt of kasha. Reveries for hours on end.

In Tyumen I bought some sausage to eat along the way, but what an abomination! When you put a piece in your mouth, the odor was as if you had entered a stable at the moment the coachman was unwinding his leg puttees; when you started chewing the stuff you experienced a sensation like sinking your teeth in to a tar-smeared dog's tail. Phew! I tried some twice and then threw it away.

I got a telegram and letter from you in which you say you would like to publish an encyclopedic dictionary. I don't know why, but the news of this dictionary gave me great pleasure. Go on with it, dear man! If I would do for the job, I would give you November and December; I'd spend those months in St. Pete and sit at my work from morning to night.

I made a fair copy of my notes in Tomsk, in the utterly vile surroundings of a hotel room, but with application and not without the desire of pleasing you. I thought to myself, he must find it somewhat hot and tiresome in Feodosia, so let him read about the cold. These notes are going to you in lieu of the letter which was storing itself up in my head all through the trip. In return you must send to Sakhalin all your critical articles except the first two, which I have read; arrange also that I be sent Peshel's "Ethnology," except for the first two installments, which I already have.

God, what expenses! On account of the floods I had to keep paying my drivers almost double and sometimes triple, for their work is hellish, as bad as penal servitude. My suitcase, my adorable little trunk, turned out to be unsuitable for the road; takes up a lot of room, pushes into your side, clatters, and most important—threatens to fall apart. Kind people counseled me not to take a trunk on a long journey, but this advice was only recalled when I had gone half the way. Now what? I am deporting it to Tomsk and instead have bought a piece of leather trash which has the convenience of flattening itself into any shape you please on the floor of the carriage. I paid 16 rubles for it. Further . . . galloping to the Amur on post horses is torture. You shatter both yourself and your baggage. I had been advised to purchase a small carriage and bought one today for 130 rubles. If I do not manage to sell it in Sretensk where my trip by horse comes to an end, I will be flat broke and will set up a howl. I dined today with the editor of the "Siberian Herald," Kartamyshev. The local Nozdrev, and an expansive soul . . . he drank up 6 rubles' worth.

Stop! I have been informed that the Assistant Chief of Police wishes to see me. What now?

False alarm. The arm of the law turned out to be a devotee of literature and even a writing man; came to pay his respects. He went back home for his drama and I think he wants to treat me to a reading of it. He'll be returning presently and interfering with my writing to you.

Write me of Feodosia, Tolstoy, the sea, the bulls, of mutual acquaintances. . . .

Stop! Our policeman has returned. He did not read his drama, although he did bring it along, but regaled me with a story. Not bad, only too localized. He showed me a gold nugget and asked for some vodka. I cannot recall one Siberian intellectual who has called on me and not asked for vodka. Told me he was in the midst of a "little affair" with a married woman; let me read a petition to the All Highest regarding a divorce. Then he offered to drive me downtown to look over the Tomsk houses of prostitution.

I have returned from these houses. Revolting. Two o'clock in the morning.

. . . From now on I shall be writing you punctually, from every city and every station where I am not given horses, i.e., where I am forced to spend the night. And how delighted I am when I am compelled to remain somewhere overnight! I hardly have time to plop into bed before I am already asleep. Living as I am at the moment, where one keeps on going and doesn't sleep nights, one values sleep above all else; there is no higher felicity on earth than sleep, when sleep is desired. In Moscow and in Russia generally I never really desired sleep, as I now understand the word. I went to bed only because it was the thing to do. But now! Here's another observation: traveling like this you don't crave liquor. I haven't been able to drink, but have smoked a great deal. Thinking coherently is difficult; somehow your thoughts don't knit together. Time runs on rapidly, so that you don't notice the interval between 10 A.M. and 7 P.M. Evening follows morning in a twinkling. This sort of thing occurs during a lingering illness. The wind and rain have made my face scaly, and looking at myself in the mirror I cannot recognize my former noble lineaments. . . .

I embrace you warmly. I kiss Anna Ivanovna's both hands and bow to the ground before her. It is raining. So long, and be well and happy. If my letters are short, negligent or dry, don't grumble, for one cannot always be oneself on one's travels and write as one would wish. The ink is miserable, and little hairs and lumps are eternally sitting on my pen.

Your

A. Chekhov

To EVGENIA CHEKHOVA

June 7, 1890, Irkutsk

. . . I have changed my route drastically. From Khabarovsk (see map) I am journeying not to Nikolayevsk but to Vladivostok along the Ussuri and from there to Sakhalin. I must have a look at the Ussuri region. In Vladivostok I'm going to do some sea bathing and eat oysters.

It was cold until Kansk; starting from there we began heading south. The greenery is just as dense as at your place, and even the oaks have put forth their leaves. The birches are darker here than in Russia and in their foliage not as sentimental. There are masses of sweet cherries, which here take the place of lilacs and sour cherries. They say they make excellent preserves. I ate some, pickled; nothing special.

I have two lieutenants and a medical corps doctor as company on the trip. They got a travel allowance three times the usual amount but have gone through it, although the three of them are making the trip in only one carriage. They are without a sou and waiting for fresh funds. Nice people. Each of them has had an allowance of around 1500-2000 rubles, with the expenses of the road amounting to practically nothing (not counting stopovers, of course). They pass their time calling down people in hotels and at stations, so that everybody is terribly afraid to ask them for payments. I spend less than usual when in their company.

It would be best to request an accounting from the bookstore in August, around the tenth or twentieth; then send the letter to Kondratiev. . . .

For the first time in my life I saw a Siberian cat today. It has long, soft fur and a gentle disposition.

I felt lonesome for you and sent off a wire today, asking you to pool your funds and answer me at greater length. It wouldn't be a tragedy for all you Luka residents to ruin yourself to the extent of five rubles.

How do matters stand with regard to civilian admirers and psychic influence? With whom has Misha fallen in love and what lucky girl is Ivanenko telling about his uncle? And what about Vata? I must be in love with Jamais, for I saw her in my dreams last night. In comparison . . . with all these oafs who don't know how to dress, sing, or laugh, our Jamais, Drishkas and Gundasikhas are virtual queens. Siberian women and misses are frozen fish. You'd have to be a walrus or seal to have an affair with them. . . .

Mama, how are your legs? Are you following the advice of Kuzmin, who charged you five rubles for it? How are Auntie and Alyosha? Send my regards when you write. . . .

The Siberian highways have their scurvy little stations, like the Ukraine. They pop up every 20 or 25 miles. You drive at night, on and on, until you feel giddy and ill, but you keep on going, and if you venture to ask the driver how many miles it is to the next station, he invariably says not less than twelve.

This is particularly agonizing when you have to drive at a walk along a muddy, rutted road, and when you are thirsty. I have taught myself how to get along without sleep and don't care a bit if I am awakened. Ordinarily you won't sleep for a day and a night, then at dinnertime of the following day you begin feeling tension in the eyelids; that evening and late at night, particularly at daybreak and the morning of the following day, you drowse in the carriage and you may happen to fall asleep in a sitting position for a moment; at dinner and after dinner, while the horses are being harnessed at the stations, you loll about on the sofa and it is only that night that the ordeal begins. In the evening, after having drunk five glasses of tea, your face starts flaming and your entire body suddenly droops with fatigue and wants to bend backward; your eyelids stick together, your feet itch in your big boots, your brain is in confusion. If you allow yourself to spend the night somewhere you immediately fall into a dead stupor; if you have sufficient will power to continue, you fall asleep in the carriage, no matter how strong the jolting is; at the stations the drivers wake you up, as you have to crawl out of the carriage and pay the charges; they wake you not so much with their voices and tugging at your sleeve as with the stench of garlic emanating from their mouths; they stink of onion and garlic to a point of nausea. I taught myself to sleep in a vehicle only after Krasnoyarsk. On the way to Irkutsk I once slept through 40 miles, during which I was awakened only once. But slumber in a vehicle does not refresh. It is not sleep, but a sort of unconscious situation which results in a muddy head and vile-tasting mouth. . . .

By the way, you ought to be looking for a farm. Upon my return to Russia I am going to have a rest for five years or so, i.e., am going to stay put and take it easy. A farm would be most appropriate. I believe money can be found, for my affairs are not going badly. If I work off the advance I have had (I'm halfway there), next spring I shall certainly take two or three thousands' advance to be paid off in installments over a five-year period. This won't trouble my conscience, as my books have already earned the "New Times" bookstore more than two or three thousands, and will earn even more. I plan not to take up anything serious until I am thirty-five; I'd like to have a try at personal life, which I once had but didn't have any regard for owing to various circumstances. . . .

Anyway, keep well. There's nothing more to write about. My regards to all.

Your
A. Chekhov

To NIKOLAI LEIKIN
> *June 20, 1890, The Amur near Gorbitza*
Greetings, my dear Nikolai Alexeyevich,

I write the above lines as I approach Gorbitza, one of the Cossack settlements on the banks of the Shilka, a tributary of the Amur. So this is where I have got to! I am sailing the Amur

I sent you a letter from Irkutsk. Did you get it? More than a week has elapsed since then, during which I made the crossing of the Baikal and traversed the Baikal region. The Baikal is astonishing, and it is with good cause that the Siberians entitle it not a lake, but a sea. The water is unusually limpid, so that you can see through it as you do through air; its color is tenderly turquoise, pleasant to the eye. The shores are mountainous and wooded; all about are impenetrable, sunless thickets. There is an abundance of bears, sables, wild goats and all kinds of wild game, which occupies itself in existing in the taiga and making meals out of one another. I spent two days on the banks of the Baikal.

It was quiet and hot during the sailing.

The Baikal area is magnificent; it is a mixture of Switzerland, the Don and Finland.

I covered over 2600 miles on horses. The trip was entirely

satisfactory. I was well throughout and of all my baggage lost only a penknife. God grant that everyone make as good a journey. Traveling is absolutely safe, and all those stories about runaways, night assaults and such are nothing but fairy tales, legends of days gone by. A revolver is a completely superfluous article. I am now sitting in a first-class cabin and feel I am in Europe. My spirits are as high as if I had just passed an examination.

A whistle. That's Gorbitza. So long, then, keep healthy and happy. If I am lucky I will post this letter, if not, I will wait until we reach the Cossack village of Pokrovsk, where I expect to be tomorrow. The mails go but seldom from the Amur, scarcely more than three times a month.

Regards to Praskovya Nikiforovna and Fedya.

Your

A. Chekhov

The banks of the Shilka are exquisite, like a stage setting, but alas! the utter absence of human beings depresses me. The place is like a cage without a bird.

To ALEXEI SUVORIN

June 27, 1890, Blagoveshchensk

Greetings, my dear friend,

The Amur is a very fine river; I derived more pleasure from it than I had a right to expect, and have for a long time been wishing to share my delight with you, but the villainous boat quivered for all seven days of the trip and hindered me from writing. In addition, I am absolutely unable to convey such beauty as one finds on the banks of the Amur; I confess I am bankrupt before beauty which is beyond my powers to describe. How can I, though? Imagine the Suram Pass transformed into the bank of a river—that is the Amur for you. Cliffs, crags, forests, thousands of ducks, herons and assorted long-nosed rascals, and utter wilderness. To the left the Russian bank, to the right the Chinese. I can look at Russia or China, whichever suits me. China is just as wild and desolate as Russia; villages and sentry boxes are few. My head is in a whirl, and small wonder, Your Excellency! I sailed the Amur for more than 650 miles, in the process of which I gazed upon millions of landscapes; and as you are aware, the Amur was preceded by the Baikal and Trans-Baikal. Verily, I saw such wealth and derived such enjoyment that I can now look upon death with equanimity. The Amur people are singular, the life they lead interesting and unlike ours. All the talk is about gold. Gold, gold and more gold. . . .

I am in love with the Amur and would be delighted to remain here a couple of years. It is beautiful, and expansive, and free and warm. Switzerland and France have never known such freedom. The lowliest exile breathes more freely on the Amur than the top general in Russia. If you had spent some time here you would have set down a lot of good material of interest to readers, but I am not up to it.

You begin running across Chinese from Irkutsk on, and here they are thicker than flies. They are a most good-natured race. . . .

From Blagoveshchensk on you meet Japanese, or, more precisely, Japanese women. They are petite brunettes with big, complicated hair-dos, handsome torsos and, the way it looks to me, short thighs. They dress beautifully. The sound "ts" predominates in their language. . . .

When I asked a Chinese to join me at the refreshment counter in a glass of vodka, he extended his glass to me, the bartender and the flunkies before drinking and said, "Taste!" This is a Chinese ritual. He did not drain the glass at one gulp as we do, but in small sips, nibbling a bite of food after each one and then, to thank me, gave me a few Chinese coins. They are terribly polite people. They dress poorly but beautifully, eat delicious food in ceremonious fashion.

To ALEXEI SUVORIN [1890]

The Chinese are going to take the Amur from us—no doubt of it. They themselves may not do so, but it will be given them by others, the English, for example, who are the ruling group there and are even building forts. The people living along the Amur are a scoffing lot; they remark jeeringly that Russia is making a fuss over Bulgaria, which isn't worth a damn, and is forgetting the Amur entirely. This is neither prudent nor intelligent. However, more about politics later, when we meet.

You have wired me to return via America. I myself was thinking of doing so. But people frighten me with the expenses involved. A transfer of money can be arranged not only in New York but also in Vladivostok, via the Siberian Bank in Irkutsk, which treated me with overwhelming courtesy. My money has not all disappeared yet, although I spend it godlessly. I took a loss of more than 160 rubles on the carriage and my fellow-traveling lieutenants did me out of more than 150 rubles. But still I will hardly require a transfer of funds. If the need arises I will apply to you in due course. I am completely well. You can judge for yourself; here it is more than two months that I have been living day and night under the open skies. What exercise! . . .

I am treating patients along the way. In the village of Reinov on the Amur, inhabited exclusively by gold miners, a husband asked me to have a look at his pregnant wife. As I left he thrust a wad of bills into my hand; I was ashamed and started protesting, assuring him I was a very rich man who didn't need the money. The patient's spouse began assuring me he was also a very rich man. We wound up by giving him back the wad, but still fifteen rubles remained with me.

Yesterday I treated a little boy and refused six rubles which his Mama shoved into my hand. I regret I did so.

Be well and happy. Forgive me for writing so badly and without giving details. Have you sent letters to Sakhalin for me?

To ALEXEI SUVORIN [*1890*]

I am bathing in the Amur. Bathing in the river, conversing and dining with gold smugglers—don't you find it interesting? I must hurry now to the "Yermak." So long! Thanks for the news of your family.

Yours,

A. Chekhov

To ALEXEI SUVORIN

September 11, 1890, S.S. Baikal, *Tatar Straits*

Greetings!

I am sailing along Tatar Sound from North Sakhalin to South. I write this letter though I am not sure it will reach you. I am well, although green-eyed cholera, which is all set to trap me, gazes at me everywhere. In Vladivostok, Japan, Shanghai, Chifu, Suez and even on the moon, I suppose, there is cholera; everywhere there is quarantine and fear. They are waiting for it in Sakhalin and holding all boats in quarantine. To put it briefly, it's a bad business. Europeans are dying in Vladivostok, among others a general's wife.

I spent exactly two months in North Sakhalin. I was welcomed with extreme cordiality by the local administration, although Galkin had not sent ahead a word about me. Neither Galkin nor Baroness Muskrat[1] nor the other genii to whom I had the stupidity to turn for help gave me any assistance; I had to proceed on my own hook.

The General of Sakhalin, Kononovich, is an intelligent and honorable man. We quickly hit it off and everything went along smoothly. I am bringing some papers with me which will show you that the conditions under which I worked from the very beginning were most favorable. I saw *everything;* now the question is not *what* I saw, but *how* I saw it.

I do not know what will come of it, but I have done quite a bit. The material gathered would be sufficient for three

[1] Chekhov's nickname for the Baroness Barbara Ichschul von Hildeband.

dissertations. I rose every morning at five, went to bed late and every day felt under intense strain in the realization that a great deal had not yet been done, and now that I have already finished my study of the penal system my feeling is that I have seen the trees but missed the forest.

By the way, let me tell you that I was patient enough to take a census of the entire population of Sakhalin. I made the rounds of every settlement, entered every cabin and spoke with every individual; I used a card system and have already accounted for approximately ten thousand convicts and penal settlers. In other words, there is not a single convict or penal settler on Sakhalin with whom I have not had a word. My inventory of the children was particularly successful, and I lay a great deal of hope in it.

I had dinner at Landsberg's and sat in the kitchen of ex-Baroness Hembruck. . . . I paid calls on all the celebrities. I witnessed a flogging, after which I had nightmares for three or four nights about the flogger and his horrible accessories. I spoke with people chained to their wheelbarrows. One day when I was having tea in a mine, the former Petersburg merchant Borodavkin,[2] sent up for arson, pulled a teaspoon out of his pocket and presented it to me, with the result that my nerves were upset and I vowed I would never more visit Sakhalin.

I would write you more, but in the cabin sits a lady roaring away with laughter and prattling without mercy. I haven't the strength to continue. She hasn't stopped laughing boisterously and chattering since last night.

This letter is traveling across America, but I probably won't. Everybody says the American trip is more expensive and more tiresome.

Tomorrow I shall see Japan from afar—Matsmai Island. It is now twelve midnight. The sea is dark and a wind is blowing.

[2] Landsberg was an ex-army officer, Hembruck an aristocrat, Borodavkin a prominent businessman. They were all exiled to Sakhalin for criminal offenses.

I cannot understand how this boat can keep on going and orient itself when it is pitch-dark, and moreover in such wild, little-known waters as Tatar Sound.

When I remind myself that six thousand miles separate me from my world, apathy overcomes me. I feel as though I won't get home for a hundred years.

Respectful salutations and hearty greetings to Anna Ivanovna and all of you. God grant you happiness and all the best.

Yours,

A. Chekhov

I'm lonesome.

To ALEXEI SUVORIN

December 9, 1890, Moscow

Greetings, my very dear friend,

Hurrah! Well, here I am, back at my own desk at last, with a prayer to my fading penates and a letter to you. I feel very well, as if I had never left home, healthy and happy to the very marrow of my bones. Now for a very brief report. I stayed in Sakhalin not two months, as was reported in your paper, but three months plus two days. It was high-pressure work; I made a full, detailed census of the entire Sakhalin population and saw *everything* except capital punishment. When we get together I will show you a whole trunkful of penal colony paraphernalia which should be unusually valuable as raw material. I know a lot now, but brought back a nasty feeling. While I was on the island I felt a kind of bitter taste, as of rancid butter, in the pit of my stomach, but now in retrospect Sakhalin seems a regular hell. I worked intensively for two months without sparing myself, but the third month, began giving way to the bitter taste I mention above, to the tedium and to thinking about the cholera due by way of Vladivostok, so that I stood the risk of wintering in the convict colony. But thank heaven the cholera came to an end and on the thirteenth of October the steamer bore me off from Sakhalin. I stopped in Vladivostok. Of the Maritime Province and our eastern shore generally, with its fleets, problems and Pacific Ocean aspirations, I have but one thing to say: crying poverty! Poverty, ignorance and nothingness, enough to drive one to despair. There is one honest man for ninety-nine thieves befouling the name of Russia. . . . We sailed past Japan, as it has some cholera cases, and so I didn't buy you anything Japanese, and the five hundred rubles you gave me for the purpose I spent on myself, for which reason you have a legal right to have me transported to Siberia. The first foreign port on my journey was Hong Kong. It has a glorious bay, the movement of ships on the ocean is beyond anything I have seen even in pictures, excellent roads, trolleys, a railway to the mountains, museums, botanical gardens; wherever you turn you will note evidences of the most tender solicitude on the part of the English for men in their service; there is even a sailors' club. I drove around in a rickshaw, i.e., was borne by humans, bought all sorts of rubbish from the Chinese and got indignant listening to my Russian traveling companions abusing the English for exploiting the natives. Thought I to myself, yes, the English exploit the Chinese, the Sepoys and the Hindus, but they do give them roads, plumbing and Christianity; you exploit them too, but what do you give them?

As we left Hong Kong the sea got really rough. The steamer wasn't carrying a load and dipped at a 38° angle, so that we were afraid it might turn over. The discovery that I am not susceptible to seasickness surprised me pleasantly. On our way to Singapore two dead bodies were flung into the sea. When you look at a corpse sewed into canvas flying head over heels into the water and when you realize it is a couple of miles to the bottom, your sensation is one of horror, as if, somehow, you yourself were about to die and be thrown into the ocean. Our cattle got sick and upon the sentence of Dr. Shcherbak and your humble servant were killed and thrown into the sea.

I recall Singapore only vaguely as I was sad somehow, close to tears, as I traveled past it. But then Ceylon followed, a heavenly place. In this paradise I made more than seventy miles by train and steeped myself in palm forests and bronze-hued women up to the neck [. . .] From Ceylon we sailed thirteen days and nights without a halt and were stupefied with boredom. I stand the heat very well. The Red Sea is dismal; looking upon Mt. Sinai I was moved.

God's earth is good. It is only we on it who are bad. How little justice and humility we have, how poor our understanding of patriotism! A drunken, worn-out, good-for-nothing husband loves his wife and children, but what good is this love? The newspapers tell us we love our mighty land, but how does this love express itself? Instead of knowledge, there is insolence and boundless conceit, instead of labor, idleness and caddishness; there is no justice, the understanding of honor does not go beyound "the honor of the uniform," a uniform usually adorning our prisoners' dock. We must work, the hell with everything else. The important thing is that we must be just, and all the rest will be added unto us.

I want terribly to speak with you. My soul is in upheaval. I don't want to see anyone but you, because you are the only one I can talk to. The hell with Pleshcheyev. And the hell with the actors, too.

I got your telegrams in deplorable condition, all of them torn. . . .

God keep you.

Yours,

A. Chekhov

To ALEXEI SUVORIN

December 24, 1890, Moscow

We felicitate you and all your respected family on the occasion of the holidays and wish you many more of them to be enjoyed in good health and happiness.

[133]

I believe both in Koch and in sperm and praise God I do. The public regards all this, i.e., Kochini, spermini, etc., as some miracle leaping without warning from the brain of a Pallas Athene, but people in the know see it only as a logical result of everything that has been done during the past twenty years. And much has been done, my dear man! Surgery alone has accomplished so much that the very thought of it is frightening. The period of twenty years ago appears just pitiful to anybody studying medicine nowadays. My dear man, if I were presented the choice of one of the two: the "ideals" of the celebrated sixties, or the worst community hospital of the present time, I wouldn't hesitate a moment in choosing the latter.

Do Kochini cure syphilis? Possibly. As to cancer, permit me to have my doubts. Cancer is not a microbe; it is tissue growing in the wrong place which, like a weed, chokes all the tissues in its vicinity. If Hay's uncle shows improvement, it would be merely because the erysipelas germ, i.e., the elements producing the disease of erysipelas—are also elements of the Kochini. It has long been noted that the growth of malignant tumors halts for a time when this disease is present. . . .

I brought some utterly fascinating animals with me from India. They are called mongooses and are the natural enemies of cobras; they are very inquisitive, are fond of humans and break dishes. . . . During the day the mongoose wanders through the rooms and sticks close to people, at night he sleeps on any bed handy and purrs like a kitten. He might bite through Trésor's throat, or vice versa. . . . He cannot stand animals.

Following your custom of previous years, would you send me some stories for polishing. I like this occupation.

Funny—journeying to Sakhalin and back I felt absolutely well, but now that I am home the devil only knows what goes on within me. I have a continual slight headache, a general feeling of lassitude, I tire easily, am apathetic, and the thing that bothers me most—have palpitations of the heart. Every minute my heart stops for several seconds and does *not* beat.

Misha got himself the uniform of a Grade VI official and is wearing it tomorrow on his round of holiday calls. Mother and Father look at him with tender pride, with expressions on their faces like those in paintings of the Blessed St. Simeon when he says, "Now absolve the sins of thy slave, O Lord . . ."

Baroness Ichschul (Madam Muskrat) is printing little books for popular consumption. Every booklet is adorned with the slogan "Truth"; and the price for truth runs from three to five kopeks a copy. Here you will find Uspenski, and Korolenko, and Potapenko, and other eminent personages. She asked my advice on what to publish. I couldn't reply to her question but in passing recommended that she poke around in old papers, almanacs, etc. . . . When she complained that it was hard for her to obtain books, I promised to get your help. If she comes with a request, don't refuse it. The Baroness is an honest lady and won't muss or soil the books. She'll return them and will reward you with an enchanting smile at the same time.

Alexei Alexeyevich sent me some elegant wine. According to the testimony of all who have drunk it, it is good enough to warrant your being boldly proud of your son. He also sent me a letter in Latin. Splendid.

I mailed you a story yesterday. I'm afraid I was late. It's a choppy affair, but the hell with it.

Our medical circles in Moscow have adopted a cautious attitude toward Koch, and nine tenths of the doctors don't believe in him.

God grant you the best of everything, and, principally, good health.

Yours,

A. Chekhov

To MARIA CHEKHOVA

January 14, 1891, St. Petersburg

I am as weary as a ballerina after five acts and eight tableaux. Dinners, letters I am too lazy to answer, conversations and assorted nonsense. Right now I must drive to Vassili Island for dinner, but I am bored and ought to be at work. . . .

I am enveloped in a heavy aura of bad feeling, extremely vague and to me incomprehensible. People feed me dinners and sing me vulgar hymns of praise, but at the same time are ready to devour me, the devil only knows why. If I were to shoot myself I would afford great pleasure to nine-tenths of my friends and admirers. And how pettily they express their petty feelings! Burenin's[1] article abuses me, although abusing one's colleagues in print just isn't done; Maslov [Bejetski] won't have dinner with the Suvorins; Shcheglov gossips about me to everyone he meets, etc. All this is terribly stupid and dreary. They are not people, but a sort of fungus growth. . . .

My "Children" has come out in a second edition. I got one hundred rubles on the occasion.

I am well but go to bed late. . . .

I spoke to Suvorin about you: you are not to work with him— I have decreed it. He is terribly well disposed toward you, and enamored of Kundasova. . . .

My respects to Lydia. . . . Tell her not to eat starchy things and to avoid Levitan. She won't find a more devoted admirer than me in the Duma or in high society.

Shcheglov has arrived.

Yesterday Grigorovich came to see me; he kissed me fondly, lied, and kept begging me to tell him about Japanese women. . . .

My greetings to all.

Your

A. Chekhov.

---

[1] Burenin was a critic on *New Times* who seldom had a good word for anybody. In one article he said that it would be a good idea for Chekhov to return to Sakhalin and stay there.

To ANATOL KONI

January 26, 1891, St. Petersburg

Dear Sir,

I have not answered your letter in a hurry, as I am not leaving St. Petersburg before Saturday.

I shall attempt to describe in detail the situation of Sakhalin children and adolescents. It is extraordinary. I saw hungry children, thirteen-year-old mistresses, girls of fifteen pregnant. Little girls enter upon prostitution at the age of twelve, sometimes before the coming of menstruation. The church and the school exist only on paper, the children are educated instead by their environment and convict atmosphere. By the way, I wrote down a conversation I had with a ten-year old boy. I was taking the census of the village of Upper Armudan; its inhabitants are to a man beggars, and notorious as reckless stoss players. I entered a hut: the parents were not at home, and on a bench sat a towheaded little fellow, round-shouldered, barefooted, in a brown study. We started talking:

I. What is your father's middle name?

He. I don't know.

I. How's that? You live with your father and don't know his name? You ought to be ashamed of yourself.

He. He isn't my real father.

I. What do you mean—not real?

He. He's living with Mom.

I. Does your mother have a husband or is she a widow?

He. A widow. She came here on account of her husband.

I. What do you mean by that?

He. She killed him.

I. Do you remember your father?

He. No. I'm illegitimate. She gave birth to me on Kara.

A prisoner, in foot shackles, who had murdered his wife, was with us on the Amur boat to Sakhalin. His poor half-orphaned daughter, a little girl of about six, was with him. I noticed that

[137]

when the father went down from the upper to the lower deck, where the toilet was, his guard and daughter followed; while the former sat in the toilet the armed soldier and the little girl stood at the door. When the prisoner climbed the staircase on his way back, the little girl clambered up and held on to his fetters. At night the little girl slept in a heap with the convicts and soldiers. Then I remember attending a funeral in Sakhalin. The wife of a transported criminal, who had left for Nikolay-evsk, was being buried. Around the open grave stood four convicts as pallbearers—ex officio; the island treasurer and I in the capacity of Hamlet and Horatio, roamed about the cemetery; the dead woman's lodger, a Circassian, who had nothing else to do; and a peasant woman prisoner, who was here out of pity; she had brought along two children of the deceased—one an infant and the other little Alyosha, a boy of four dressed in a woman's jacket and blue pants with brightly colored patches on the knees. It was cold, raw, there was water in the grave, and the convicts stood around laughing. The sea was visible. Alyosha looked at the grave with curiosity; he wanted to wipe his chilly nose, but the long sleeves of the jacket got in the way. While the grave was being filled I asked him, "Where is your mother, Alyosha?"

He waved his arm like a gentleman who had lost at cards, laughed and said, "Buried!"

The prisoners laughed; the Circassian turned to us and asked what he was to do with the children, as he was not obliged to take care of them.

I did not come upon infectious diseases in Sakhalin, there was very little congenital syphilis, but I did see children blind, filthy, covered with rashes—all maladies symptomatic of neglect.

Of course I shall not solve the children's problem, and I don't know what should be done. But it seems to me you will not get anywhere with charity and leftovers from prison appropriations and other sums. To my way of thinking, it is harmful to approach this important problem by depending upon charity, which in Russia is a casual affair, or upon nonexistent funds. I should prefer to have the government be financially responsible.

My Moscow address is c/o Firgang, M. Dmitrovka Street.

Permit me to thank you for your cordiality and for your promise to visit me and to remain,

Your sincerely respectful and devoted,

A. Chekhov

To MARIA CHEKHOVA

March 17, 1891, St. Petersburg

I have just seen Duse, the Italian actress, in Shakespeare's "Cleopatra." I don't understand Italian, but she performed so brilliantly I seemed to understand every word. What an actress! I have never seen anything like her. [I looked at Duse and worked myself into a state of anguish at the thought that we have to educate our temperaments and tastes through the medium of such wooden actresses as X and her like, whom we consider great because we haven't any better. After Duse I could understand why the Russian theatre is so dreary.][1]

I sent you a draft today for three hundred rubles. Did you get it? . . .

Tomorrow at half past one we leave for Warsaw. All of you keep alive and well. My regards to all and sundry, even to the mongoose, who doesn't deserve to be remembered.

I will write.

Yours entirely,

A. Chekhov

[1] For reasons known only to bureaucrats and to scholars who come under their influence, the section in brackets was omitted in the new Soviet edition of Chekhov's complete works.

To MARIA CHEKHOVA

March 20, 1891, Vienna

My Czech friends,

I write this from Vienna, where I arrived yesterday afternoon at four. The trip came off very well. From Warsaw to Vienna I traveled like a railway Nana in a luxurious compartment of the "International Sleeping Car Company"; beds, mirrors, huge windows, carpets and so on.

Ah, my good Tungus friends, if you could only know how fine Vienna is! Comparing it with any of the cities I have seen in my lifetime is out of the question. The streets are broad, elegantly paved, there is a quantity of boulevards and squares, the apartment houses are all six or seven storeys high, and the shops—they are not shops but utter dizziness, dreams! They have millions of neckties alone in the windows! What stunning things of bronze, china, leather! The churches are huge, yet they do not overpower one with their immensity, but caress the sight, because they seem to be spun out of lace. Particularly exquisite are St. Stephen's Cathedral and the Votivkirche. They are not buildings, but petits fours. The Parliament, the Town Hall and the University are splendid. . . . Everything is splendid, and only yesterday and today have I truly realized that architecture is an art. And here this art doesn't show up in isolated examples, as it does at home, but extends miles on end. There are numerous monuments. Every little side-street is sure to have its bookshop. You can see Russian books, too, in their windows, but alas! not the works of Albov, or Barantsevich, or Chekhov, but of assorted anonymities who write and get their stuff printed abroad. I saw "Renan," "The Secrets of the Winter Palace," etc. Funny, you can read and say whatever you like.

Try to realize, O ye of little faith, what the cabs are like here, devil take them! They don't have droshkis, but spic-and-span, pretty little carriages drawn by one, or oftener by two horses. The horses are admirable. In the coachman's seat repose dandies in jackets and derbies reading newspapers. The soul of courtesy and service.

The meals are superlative. There is no vodka, but people drink beer and very decent wine. One thing grates: you have to pay for the bread served. When you get your bill you are asked, "Wieviel Brödchen?" i.e., how many rolls did you gobble? And they charge you for every roll you've eaten.

The women are beautiful and elegant. On the whole I would say everything is fiendishly elegant.

I haven't entirely forgotten my German; I understand what people say and people understand me.

Snow was falling as we crossed the border, but there is no snow in Vienna, though it remains cold.

I am lonesome for home and miss you all; besides, my conscience bothers me for having deserted you. Though it's not so terrible, for when I return I'll sit glued to one spot a whole year. My regards to all and everyone!

Papa, be so good as to buy for me at Sytin's or anywhere you like a popular print of St. Varlaam in which the saint is depicted riding on a sleigh, and on a little balcony in the distance stands the bishop; underneath the drawing is a picture of St. Varlaam's dwelling. Please put it on my desk. . . .

My very best wishes. Don't forget this miserable sinner. My deepest respects to all, I embrace you, bless you and remain,

Your loving
A. Chekhov

Everybody we meet recognizes us as Russians and doesn't look at my face but at my grizzly-furred cap. From it they probably figure I am a very wealthy Russian count. . . .

My compliments to handsome Levitan.

To IVAN CHEKHOV

March 24, 1891, Venice

I am now in Venice, where I arrived the day before yesterday from Vienna. I can say one thing: never in my life have I seen a more remarkable town than Venice. It is full of enchantment, glitter, the joy of life. There are canals instead of streets and lanes, gondolas instead of cabs, the architecture is amazing, and there isn't a spot that doesn't stir either historical or artistic interest. You skim along in a gondola and gaze upon the palaces of the doges, the house where Desdemona lived, the homes of celebrated artists, temples of religion. . . . These temples contain sculptures and paintings magnificent beyond our wildest dreams. In a word, enchantment.

All day long, from morning to night, I loll in a gondola and float through the streets or else wander about the famous St. Mark's Square, which is as smooth and clean as a parquet floor. Here is St. Mark's Cathedral—something impossible to describe —the palaces of the doges and buildings that give me the same feeling I get listening to music; I am aware of astounding beauty and revel in it.

And the evenings! Good God in heaven! Then you feel like dying with the strangeness of it all. You move along in your gondola. It is warm, calm, the stars gleam. . . . There are no horses in Venice, and so the silence is that of the countryside. All about you drift other gondolas. . . . Here is one hung about with little lanterns. In it sit bass viol, violin, guitar, mandolin and cornet players, two or three ladies, a couple of men—and you hear singing and instrumental music. They sing operatic arias. What voices! You glide on a bit farther and again come upon a boat with singers, then another; and until midnight the air is filled with a blend of tenor voices and violin music and sounds that melt one's heart.

Merejkowski, whom I met here, has gone wild with rapture. It is not hard for a poor and humble Russian to lose his mind in this world of beauty, wealth and freedom. You feel like remaining here forever, and when you go to church and listen to the organ you feel like becoming a Catholic.

The tombs of Canova and Titian are superb. Here eminent artists are buried in churches like kings; here art is not despised, as it is with us; the churches offer a refuge to statues and pictures, no matter how naked they may be.

There is a picture hanging in the palace of the doges that portrays about ten thousand human figures.

Today is Sunday. A band is to play on St. Mark's Square.

At any rate, keep well, and my best wishes to you all. If you ever happen to be in Venice, you will consider it the best time of your life. You should have a look at the glass manufactures! . . .

I'll write some more, but so long for now.

> Your
> **A. Chekhov**

To MARIA CHEKHOVA

March 29 or 30, 1891, Florence

I am in Florence and have exhausted myself running through museums and churches. I saw the Medici Venus and find that if she were dressed in modern clothing she would look ugly, especially around the waist. I am well. The sky is overcast, and Italy without sunshine is like a person in a mask. Keep well.

> Your
> **Antonio**

The monument to Dante is beautiful.

To MARIA KISELEVA

April 1, 1891, Rome

The Pope of Rome directs me to congratulate you on your birthday and wish you as much money as he has rooms. And he has eleven thousand of them! Staggering through the Vatican

I almost dropped with weariness, and when I got home I felt my legs were stuffed with cotton.

I dine at a table d'hôte. Just picture it, opposite me sit two Dutch girls, one of them looking like Pushkin's Tatiana, and the other like her sister Olga.[1] I stare at them all through dinner and visualize a clean little white house with a little turret, excellent butter, prime Dutch cheese, Dutch herrings, a good-looking pastor, a sedate teacher . . .and I feel like marrying the little Dutch girl and then having both of us painted on a tray as we stand by the clean little house.

I have seen and climbed into everything as ordered. When I was told to smell, I smelled. But meanwhile I experience nothing but weariness and a desire to eat cabbage soup with kasha. Venice fascinated me, infatuated me, but after I left it, on came Baedeker and bad weather.

Goodbye for now, Maria Vladimirovna, and the Lord God protect you. A most respectful bow from me and the Pope of Rome to His Honor, Vasilissa and Elisaveta Alexandrovna.

Neckties are wonderfully cheap here. Terribly cheap, so that I daresay I'll start eating them. A franc a pair.

Tomorrow I leave for Naples. Please hope I meet a handsome Russian lady there, if possible a widow or divorcée.

The guidebooks state that a love affair is indispensable in contemplating a trip to Naples. Well, I don't care—I'm ready for anything. If it's to be a love affair, let's have it.

Don't forget your miserably sinning, sincerely devoted and respectful,

A. Chekhov

To MIKHAIL CHEKHOV

April 15, 1891, Nice
Monday of Holy Week

. . . We are living at the seaside in Nice. The sun shines, it is warm and green and the air is like perfume, but it is windy.

---

[1] Tatiana and Olga are characters in Pushkin's *Eugene Onegin*.

We are one hour away from the celebrated Monaco with its town of Monte Carlo, where roulette is played. Just imagine the ballrooms of our House of Nobles, but even more beautiful, high-ceilinged and even larger. These rooms are furnished with large tables with roulette wheels placed on them, which I will describe to you upon my return. I played there three days ago and lost. The game tempts one terribly. After counting our losses, Suvorin fils and I began putting on our thinking caps and after due thought devised a system whereby we couldn't help winning. Last night we went there again, each of us with 500 francs; my first bet netted me a couple of gold pieces, and then I won more and more; my vest pockets were weighted down with gold; I was even handed some 1808 French coins, Belgian, Italian, Greek and Austrian coins. . . . I had never seen so much gold and silver. I started playing at five in the afternoon and by ten at night there wasn't a single franc left in my pocket and the only satisfaction left was the thought that I had previously purchased a return ticket to Nice. So there you have it, my friends! You will of course say, "What baseness! We are poverty-stricken and he plays roulette." You are absolutely right and have my permission to kill me. But personally I am very well satisfied with myself. At any rate I can now tell my grandchildren I have played roulette and experienced the sensation that this game arouses.

Next to the casino where roulette is played there is another form of roulette—the restaurants. They fleece you here unmercifully and feed you magnificently. Whatever dish you order is a regular composition before which one should bend the knee in reverence, but by no means have the daring to consume. Every mouthful is abundantly garnished with artichokes, truffles, an assortment of nightingales' tongues. . . . Yet good God, how contemptible and loathsome is this life with its artichokes, palms and the aroma of orange blossoms! I like luxury and wealth, but the local roulette type of luxury affects me like a luxurious toilet. You feel there is something in the air that offends your sense of decency, vulgarizes the charm of nature, the roar of the sea, the moon.

This past Sunday I attended the local Russian church. Peculiarities: palm branches instead of pussy willows, women in the choir instead of boys, so that the singing has an operatic tinge, people put foreign money in the collection plates, the verger and beadle speak French, etc. They sang Bortnianski's Cherubim No. 7 splendidly, and a plain Our Father.

Of all the places I have visited up to now, my loveliest memories are of Venice. Rome bears a general resemblance to Kharkov, and Naples is filthy. The sea does not fascinate me, though, as I had already wearied of it in November and December. The devil only knows what goes on, I seem to have been on the go for a whole year. I hardly managed to get back from Sakhalin when I left for St. Pete, then another trip to St. Pete and to Italy. . . .

If I don't manage to return by Easter, when you celebrate remember me in your prayers, and accept my good wishes sight unseen and the assurance that I shall be terribly lonesome without you on Easter eve.

Are you saving the newspapers for me?

. . . Do keep well, and may the Heavens preserve you. I have the honor to give an accounting of myself and remain,

Your homesick
Antonio

To MARIA CHEKHOVA

April 21, 1891, Paris

It is Easter today, so Christ has risen! This is my first Easter spent away from home.

I arrived in Paris Friday morning and immediately went to the Exposition.[1] The Eiffel Tower is really very, very high. I

1 The Exposition of 1891.

saw the other exposition buildings only from the outside, as the cavalry was stationed inside in case of riots.[2] Disorders were expected on Friday. People surged through the streets, shouted, whistled, flared up and were dispersed by the police. A dozen policemen are enough to break up a big mob. They rush them in a body and the crowd runs like crazy. During one of these rushes I had the honor of being grabbed by the shoulder by a policeman and shoved forward.

The streets swarm and seethe with continual movement. . . . The noise and uproar is general. The sidewalks are set out with little tables, behind which sit the French, who feel very much at home on the streets. An excellent people. However, there's no describing Paris, so I'll postpone descriptions until I get home.

I heard midnight mass at the Embassy church. . . .

We leave for Russia tomorrow or the day after. I will be in Moscow either Friday or Saturday. I am returning via Smolensk and so if you want to meet me, go to the Smolensk station. . . .

I am afraid you have no money.

Misha, I implore you by all that's holy to have my glasses repaired, using the same lenses as in yours. I am simply a martyr without eyeglasses. I was at a picture exhibition (The Salon) and didn't see half of them on account of my short-sightedness. I may say in passing that Russian artists are far more serious than the French. In comparison with the local landscapists I saw yesterday, Levitan is a king.

This is my last letter, so goodbye for now. I left with an empty trunk and am returning with a full one. You will all receive something according to your merits.

Good health to you.

Yours,

A. Chekhov

---

[2] Chekhov referred to the demonstrations of the First of May. He used the old Russian calendar.

To ALEXEI SUVORIN

May 10, 1891, Alexin

. . . Yes, you are right, my soul needs balm. I would with pleasure, even with joy, read something weighty not only about myself but about things in general. I yearn for serious reading; Russian criticism of the present time does not help me. It irritates me. I would be delighted to read something new about Pushkin or Tolstoy—that would be balm for my idle mind.

I also miss Venice and Florence and would be ready to climb Vesuvius again; Bologna has been wiped out and become a dim memory, and as for Nice and Paris, when I think of them "I look with loathing upon my life."[1]

The last number of the *"Foreign Literature Herald"* contains a story by Ouida translated from the English by our Mikhail, the assessor. Why don't I know languages? It seems to me I would translate fiction superbly; when I read other people's translations I am always changing and shifting the words around mentally, and I get something light and ethereal, like lace.

Mondays, Tuesdays and Wednesdays I work at my book on Sakhalin, the rest of the week, except Sunday, on my novel,[2] and on Sundays I write short stories. I work enthusiastically but alas! my family is a numerous one, and here I am, a writing man, resembling a crayfish in a net along with others of the species: quite a crowd. Every day the weather is glorious, our country place stands on dry, healthy ground, with lots of woods. . . . There are plenty of fish and crayfish in the Oka. I can see trains and steamers passing. On the whole I would be very, very content if only we weren't so cramped. When will you be in Moscow? Please write.

You won't like the French Exposition—be prepared for that reaction. . . .

I have no intention of getting married. I would like to be a

[1] A line from Pushkin's "Remembrances."
[2] The novel turned into the long short story called "The Duel."

little bald old man and sit at a big desk in a well-appointed study.

Keep well and calm. My respectful compliments to your family. Please write.

Yours,
A. Chekhov

To ALEXEI SUVORIN

May 20, 1891, Bogimovo

. . . The carp here bite with all their might. Yesterday I forgot all my woes. First I sat beside the brook reeling in carp and then alongside the deserted mill catching perch. Details of everyday life are also of interest.

The last two proclamations—on the Siberian railway and exiles—I liked very much. The Siberian railway is called a national matter and the tone of the proclamation assures its speedy completion; while prisoners who have served their terms either as transported criminals or peasant exiles will be permitted to return to Russia, without the right to live in Moscow or St. Petersburg provinces. The newspapers just haven't paid any attention to this, but actually it is something that has never happened in Russia, a serious step toward the abolition of the life sentence, which has for so long weighed upon the public conscience as being to the highest degree unjust and cruel. . . .

I shall expect you. You would do well to hurry, as the nightingales will soon stop singing and the lilacs blooming. . . . I can find rooms and beds for an entire division.

Keep well.

Yours,
A. Chekhov

To LYDIA MIZINOVA

June-July 1891, Bogimovo

Dear Lida,

Why the reproaches?

I am sending you my ugly face. We'll be seeing each other tomorrow. Don't forget your little Pete. A thousand kisses!!!

I have bought Chekhov's stories: how delightful they are! You buy them, too.

My regards to Masha Chekhova.

What a sweetheart you are!

To LYDIA MIZINOVA

June-July 1891, Bogimovo

Dear Lydia Stakhievna,

I love you passionately, like a tiger, and offer you my hand.

Leader of Mongrel Breeds[1]

Golovin-Rtishchev.

P. S. Give me your answer in gestures, as you squint.

To ALEXEI SUVORIN

August 18, 1891, Bogimovo

I sent you a letter today with my story, and now here is another in reply to the one just received from you. Speaking of Nikolai and the doctor who is attending him you keep stressing that "all this is done without love, without self-sacrifice, even as regards his little comforts." You are right to say this about people in general, but what would you have the doctors do? If, as our nurse puts it, "his bowel busted," what are you going to

---

[1] A "Leader of Nobility" was a chosen representative of well-born country families and a title of distinction. The Russian words for "nobility" and "mongrel breeds" are similar at first glance.

do, even if you want to give up your life for the patient? As a rule, when the household, relatives and servants take "all possible measures" and practically crawl out of their skins, the doctor just looks like a fool, the picture of discouragement, blushing gloomily for himself and his science and striving to maintain outer calm. . . . Doctors go through execrable days and hours, God protect you from anything like them. Among physicians, it is true, ignorant fools and cads are no rarity, as is also the case amongst writers, engineers and people generally; but those odious days and hours I mention occur only to doctors, and because of them, in all conscience, you must forgive them a great deal. . . .

My teacher-brother has received a medal and an appointment in Moscow for his conscientious efforts. He is stubborn in the good sense of the word and will get what he aims for. He is not yet thirty but is already considered a model pedagogue in Moscow.

I woke last night and started thinking of the story I sent you. My head was in utter confusion while I wrote it in fiendish haste, and it wasn't my brain that functioned, but a rusty wire. Hurrying is no good, for what results is not creative writing but muck. If you don't reject the story, defer its publication until autumn, when it will be possible to read proof. . . .

A peasant woman was carting some rye and fell out of her wagon, head first. She was horribly injured: concussion of the brain, dislocation of the neck vertebrae, vomiting, acute pains and so on. She was brought to me. She groaned, moaned, prayed God to let her die, but at the same time she turned to the mujik who had brought her and mumbled, "Cyril, don't bother with the lentils, you can thresh them afterward, but you'd better thresh the oats right now." I told her she could worry about the oats afterward, but now there were more serious things to consider, and she comes back with, "But his oats are so good!" A bustling peasant woman, to be envied. That type doesn't find it hard to die.

I am leaving for Moscow the fifth of September as I have to look for a new apartment.

Best wishes!

Yours,
A. Chekhov

To ALEXEI SUVORIN

September 8, 1891, Moscow
M. Dmitrovka, c/o Firgang

I have already moved to Moscow and am staying indoors. . . .

"The Lie," the title you recommended for my long story, won't do. It would be appropriate only in cases where the lie is a conscious one. An unconscious lie really isn't a lie, but an error. Having money and eating meat Tolstoy calls a lie—which is going too far.

Yesterday I was informed that Kurepin is hopelessly ill with cancer of the neck. Before he dies the cancer will have eaten up half his head and torment him with neuralgic pains. I was told his wife has written you.

Little by little death takes its toll. It knows its job. Try writing a play along these lines: an old chemist has concocted an elixir of immortality—a dose of fifteen drops and one lives eternally; but the chemist breaks the vial with the elixir out of fear that such carrion as he and his wife will continue to live forever. Tolstoy denies immortality to mankind, but good God, how much there is that's personal in his denial! The day before yesterday I read his "Epilogue."[1] Strike me dead, but this is stupider and stuffier than "Letters to a Governor's Wife."[2] which I despise. The hell with the philosophy of the great of this world! All eminent sages are as despotic as generals, as discourteous and lacking in delicacy as generals, because they know they are safe from punishment. Diogenes spat into peo-

---

[1] The "Epilogue" to Tolstoy's *Kreutzer Sonata*.
[2] Gogol's *Letters to a Governor's Wife*.

ples' beards, sure that nothing would happen to him; Tolstoy abuses doctors as scoundrels and shows his ignorance in regard to weighty questions because he is another Diogenes, whom you can't take to the police station or call down in the newspapers. And so, the hell with the philosophy of the great of this world! All of it, with all its beggarly epilogues and letters to governors' ladies isn't worth a single filly in his "Story of a Horse." . . .

Keep well and don't forget this miserable sinner. I miss you very much.

Yours,

A. Chekhov

To ELENA SHAVROVA

September 16, 1891, Moscow

So we old bachelors smell like dogs? Very well, but let me dispute your thesis that specialists in women's diseases are Lotharios and cynics at heart. Gynecologists are concerned with a kind of violent prose you have never even dreamed of, and to which, were you aware of it, you would attribute an odor even worse than that of dogs, with the harshness characteristic of your imagination. He who always sails the seas loves dry land; he who is eternally absorbed in prose passionately pines for poetry. All gynecolologists are idealists. Your doctor reads verses, and your instinct has served you well; I would add that he is a great liberal, something of a mystic, and muses of a wife along the lines of Nekrasov's Russian Woman. The eminent Snegirev never speaks of "the Russian woman" without a tremor in his voice. Another gynecologist I know is in love with a mysterious unknown who wears a veil, and whom he has seen from a distance. Still another attends all the first nights—and stands next to the coatroom swearing loudly and assuring people that authors haven't the right to depict women who aren't ideal, etc.

You have also lost sight of the fact that a good gynecologist cannot be stupid or a mediocrity. His mind, even if it has had only moderate training, shines more brightly than his bald spot; you, however, noticed the bald spot and stressed it and threw the mind overboard. You noted and stressed as well that a kind of grease oozes out of this fat man—brrr!—and completely lost sight of the fact that he is a professor, i.e., has thought and done things for some years that set him above millions of people, above all the little Veras and Taganrog Greek young ladies, above all meals and wines. Noah had three sons, Shem, Ham and, I think, Japheth. The only thing Ham noted was that his father was a drunkard, he completely lost sight of the fact that Noah was a genius, that he built an ark and saved the world. Writing people ought not imitate Ham. Put that in your pipe and smoke it. I don't dare ask you to be fond of gynecologists and professors, but I venture to remind you of justice, which is more precious than air to the objective writer.

The little girl in the merchant's family is done beautifully. The passage in the doctor's speech where he talks of his disbelief in medicine is good, but it isn't necessary for him to take a drink after every sentence. The fondness for corpses shows your exasperation with your captive thought. You have not seen corpses.

Now to move from the particular to the general. Let me advise you to watch your step. What you have here is not a short story or a novel, not a piece of artistry, but a long row of heavy, dismal barracks.

Where is the architectural construction that once so enchanted your humble servant? Where is the airiness, the freshness, the grace? Read your story through: a description of a dinner, then a description of passing women and misses—then a description of a party—then one of a dinner . . . and so on and on—endlessly. Descriptions, descriptions and more descriptions—and no action at all. You should start right off with the merchant's daughter, stick to her, and throw out the little

Veras, throw out the Greek girls, throw out everything . . . except for the doctor and the merchant's spawn.

We must have a talk. So it seems you are not moving to St. Petersburg. I was counting on seeing you, as Misha assured me you intended settling there. Keep well, then. The heavenly angels guard you. Your imagination is becoming an interesting thing.

Forgive the long letter.

Yours,

A. Chekhov

To ALEXEI SUVORIN

October 25, 1891, Moscow

. . . Run "The Duel" only once a week, not twice. If you carry it twice a week you will be violating an old established custom and it will look as if I were usurping someone else's space in the paper; as a matter of fact it's all the same to me and my story whether it appears once or twice weekly.

Among the St. Petersburg writing fraternity the only topic of conversation is the impurity of my motives. I have just had the agreeable news that I am getting married to rich Madame Sibiryakova. I've been getting lots of good news generally.

I wake up every night and read "War and Peace." One reads with such curiosity and naïve enthusiasm as though one had never read anything previously. It is wonderfully good. Except that I don't care for the passages where Napoleon makes an appearance. Wherever Napoleon comes on the scene, you get a straining after effect and all manner of devices to prove that he was stupider than he actually was in reality. Everything that Pierre, Prince Andrei, or even the utterly insignificant Nikolai Rostov say or do—is good, clever, natural and touching; everything that Napoleon thinks and does is not natural, not clever but inflated and lacking in significance. When I live in the provinces (and I dream of it day and night), I intend to practice medicine and read novels.

To YEVGRAF YEGOROV [*1891*]

I won't be going to St. Petersburg.

If I had treated Prince Andrei I would have cured him. It is extraordinary to read that the wound of the prince, a rich man, with a physician in attendance all the time and Natasha and Sonia to look after him, should emit the odor of a corpse. How scurvy medicine was at the time! Tolstoy must have had an unconscious hatred of medicine while writing this tremendous novel.

Keep well. Auntie died.

Your
A. Chekhov

To YEVGRAF YEGOROV

December 11, 1891, Moscow

Dear Yevgraf Petrovich,

Here is the story of my trip to your place which did not come off. I intended visiting you not as a newspaper correspondent, but on a mission, or rather at the bidding of a small circle of people who wanted to do something for the famine-stricken. The fact of the matter is that the public has no faith in officialdom and therefore refrains from donating its money. There are thousands of fantastic tales and fables going the rounds of embezzling, outright thievery and so on. People keep away from the Diocesan Office and are indignant at the Red Cross. The owner of my unforgettable Babkino, the head of the community there, cut me short sharply and categorically, "The Moscow Red Cross people are thieves!" In the face of such a mood the officials can scarcely expect any serious aid from the public. Yet at the same time the public wants to do good and its conscience is aroused. In September the Moscow educated class and plutocracy met together, thought, spoke, bestirred themselves, invited people who knew the situation for advice; everybody discussed how to get around the officials and organize help independently. They decided to send their own agents to the famine-stricken provinces, to get acquainted with the state of affairs on the spot, set up soup kitchens and so on. Several leaders of these groups, people with a good deal of weight, asked Durnovo's permission to operate, but Durnovo turned them down, declaring that the organization of aid belonged wholly to the Diocesan Office and the Red Cross. In short, personal initiative was nipped in the bud. Everyone was crestfallen and depressed; some flew into a rage, others simply washed their hands of the project. It needed the daring and the authority of Tolstoy to act in defiance of bans and official sentiments and do what one's sense of duty directed.

Well, sir, now about myself. My attitude was one of complete sympathy with private initiative, as everyone ought to be free to do good as he wishes; but judging officialdom, the Red Cross and so on seemed to me inopportune and impractical. I assumed that with a certain amount of equanimity and good nature it would be possible to avoid whatever was unpleasant or ticklish, and that under such circumstances, approaching the Minister was unnecessary. I went all the way to Sakhalin without a single letter of recommendation, and yet accomplished whatever I deemed necessary; why then should I not do the same in the case of the famine-stricken provinces? I also recalled such administrators as you, Kiselev and all my community-leader friends and officials—people honorable in the extreme and deserving of the most implicit confidence. And I decided, starting with a small district, of course, to try to unite the two elements of officialdom and private initiative. I wanted to call upon you for advice as soon as possible. The public believes in me, it would also believe in you, and I could count upon success. I sent you a letter, you will recall.

Then Suvorin arrived in Moscow. . . . Suvorin had influenza; usually when he comes to Moscow we spend days on end together discussing literature, which he knows admirably. This time, too, we had discussions and it wound up with my catching his influenza, going to bed and coughing furiously. Korolenko was in Moscow and found me suffering. A lung complication kept me languishing indoors a whole month doing absolutely nothing. Now my affairs are looking up, but I am still coughing and am very thin. Here you have my story. If it were not for the influenza, perhaps we together would have managed to wrest two or three thousands, or even more, from the public, depending upon circumstances.

Your exasperation with the press is entirely understandable. The snap judgments of newspaper writers vex you, who are familiar with the true state of affairs, as much as the snap judgments of laymen on diphtheria vex me, a medical man. But what would you have one do, I ask you? Russia is not England, nor France. Our newspapers are not rich and have very few people at their disposal. Sending an academy professor or Engelhardt to the Volga is expensive; sending a well-equipped, gifted newspaperman is also impossible—he is needed in the home office. The "New York Times" could arrange for a census of the famine provinces at its own expense, could put a Kennan into every district, paying him forty rubles a day—and something purposeful would come of it; but what can "Russian Reports" or "New Times" do, newspapers that consider a hundred-thousand-ruble profit as the wealth of Croesus? As to the correspondents themselves, you know these are city folks who are acquainted with rural life solely through the works of Gleb Uspenski. Their position is untenable in the extreme. Make a quick dash into a district, sniff around, give it a writeup and get going to the next. The man has neither material means, freedom of action nor authority. For two hundred rubles a month he keeps dashing around and praying God people won't get mad at him for his unintentional and unavoidable misrepresentations. He feels he is to blame. But you know it is not he who should be blamed, but Russian black ignorance. At the service of the Western correspondent are excellent maps, encyclopedias, statistical studies; in the West you can write up your report without leaving your house. But here? Our cor-

respondent can dredge up information only from conversations
and rumors. Why, in all of our Russia only three districts have
been investigated thus far: Cherepov, Tambov and one other.
That is for all Russia! The newspapers lie that correspondents
are roisterers, but what can they do? *And not writing is impossible.* If our press were silent you will agree with me the situation would be even more horrible.

Your letter and your project regarding the purchase of cattle
from the peasants galvanized me into action. I am ready with all
my heart and all my energies to carry out whatever you propose.
I have given the matter much thought and here is my opinion.
You cannot count upon the rich. It is too late. Every rich man
has already shelled out the thousands he had set aside for the
purpose. All the power is now in the hands of the middle-class
man who will donate his half-rubles or rubles. . . . That means
only the average man is left. Let us set up a subscription list.
You write a letter to the editor and I will have it published in
"Russian Reports" and "New Times." In order to combine the
above-mentioned elements, we might both sign the letter. If
you find this unacceptable because of your official duties, the
letter might be written in the third person, stating that in Section 5 of Nizhni-Novgorod District, such and such work has
been organized, that, praise God, things are going well, and it
is requested that contributions be sent to the head of the community, Y. P. Yegorov, residing at such and such an address, or
to A. P. Chekhov, or to the editorial office of such and such
newspapers. But the letter must be a good long one. Write in as
much detail as possible, I will add a thing or two—and we can't
lose. We must ask for contributions, not loans. Nobody will go
along with a loan: it is horrible. It is hard to give, but it is
even harder to take back.

I know only one wealthy person in Moscow, and that is Mme.
Morozova,[1] the well-known philanthropist. I called on her yes-

[1] Varvara Morozova was an extremely wealthy woman who had a famous
salon in Moscow.

terday with your letter, talked and ate. At the moment she is keen on the Committee on Literacy, which is establishing soup kitchens for schoolchildren and she is giving everything to this group. Since literacy and horses are incompatible, the lady promised me the co-operation of her committee only in the event that you wished to set up soup kitchens for schoolchildren and sent detailed information. It was *awkward* for me to ask her for money then and there, since people keep taking money from her endlessly and flay her like a fox. My sole request to her was that in case she intended donating to other commissions and committees, she not forget us either, and she promised not to. Your letter and your idea have also been communicated to Sobolevski, editor of "Russian Reports"—just in case. I am busy shouting that the project is already under way.

If any rubles or half-rubles come my way, I shall send them on to you without delay. Please consider me at your disposal and believe me when I say I would be truly happy to do something, as I have thus far done nothing at all for the famine-stricken and for those helping them.

We are all in good health, except that Nick died of consumption in 1889. . . . Ivan is teaching in Moscow, Misha is an assessor.

Keep well.

Yours,
A. Chekhov

To VLADIMIR TIKHONOV

February 22, 1892, Moscow

Forgive me, my dear Vladimir Alexeyevich, for not having answered your letter for so long. To start with, I have only just recently returned from Voronej Province, and secondly, I am buying an estate (keep your fingers crossed) and spend entire days in assorted notary, bank, insurance and similar parasitical establishments. This purchase of mine has reduced me to a state of frenzy. I am like a person who has entered an inn just for some chopped beef with onions, but meeting good pals, has gone to work on the bottle, got as drunk as a pig and must settle a bill for 142 rubles and 75 kopeks. . . .

You mistakenly think you were drunk at Shcheglov's birthday party. You were fairly high, that was all. You danced when everybody danced and your jigging on the cabman's box gave nothing but general pleasure. As to the criticism, it couldn't have been severe, as I don't recall it. I only remember that Vedenski and I laughed long and loud at you.

So you need my biography? Here goes. I was born in Taganrog in 1860. In 1879 I graduated from the Taganrog Boys' School. In 1884 I graduated from the Medical School of Moscow University. In 1888 I received the Pushkin Prize. In 1890 I took a trip to Sakhalin across Siberia and returned by sea. In 1891 I made a European tour, during which I drank some first-rate wine and ate oysters. In 1892 I had a good time at V. A. Tikhonov's birthday party. I began my writing in 1879 for "Dragon Fly" magazine. Here in substance are my works: "Motley Stories," "In the Twilight," "Tales," "Gloomy People," and a novel, "The Duel." I have also sinned in the dramatic field, though in moderation. I have been translated into all languages except the foreign. Joking aside, I have long since been translated by the Germans. The Czechs and Serbs also approve of me. And the French belong to our mutual admiration society. At thirteen I probed the mysteries of love. With my colleagues, both medical and literary, I maintain the most excellent relations. I am a bachelor. I would like a pension. I still practice medicine, if you can call it that. Summers in the country I even perform an autopsy every couple of years. Among writers my preference goes to Tolstoy, among doctors—to Zakharin.

All this is nonsense, though. Write whatever you like. If you haven't the facts, substitute lyricism

Keep well and happy. My regards to your little daughters.

Yours,

A. Chekhov

To ALEXEI SUVORIN

March 3, 1892, Moscow

. . . Every day I find out something new. What a terrible thing it is to have business with liars! The artist who sold me the property lies and lies and lies—needlessly, stupidly, and the upshot is a series of daily disillusionments. Every moment I expect him to put over another swindle and so I am continually exasperated. We are accustomed to assuming that only merchants cheat in measuring and weighing, but people should have a good look at our upper class! They are an odious spectacle. They are not people but ordinary kulaks, even worse than kulaks, for a peasant-kulak goes ahead and does some work himself, while my artist just goes around guzzling liquor and swearing at the servants. Just imagine, from as far back as last summer his horses haven't seen a single grain of oats, or a wisp of hay, but have lived off straw exclusively, although they work hard enough for ten. The cow doesn't give any milk because she is starving. His wife and mistress live under the same roof. The children are dirty and ragged. There is a stench of cats. Bedbugs and enormous cockroaches abound. The artist pretends he is devoted to me heart and soul and at the same time gives the peasants lessons in the art of cheating. Since is is difficult to judge even approximately where my fields and woodlands reach to, the peasants had been coached to point out for my benefit an extensive stand of woods which actually belongs to the church. But they refused to do as they were told. On the whole I am involved in a lot of tommyrot and vulgarity. It is disgusting to realize that all this hungry and filthy riffraff thinks that I, too, tremble for the sake of a kopek just as it does, and that I too don't mind putting over crooked deals. The peasants are downtrodden, frightened and worried. I am sending you a circular on the estates and am going to conduct an enquiry on the spot. . . .

You want to build a theatre, while I want terribly to go to Venice and write . . . a play. How glad I am I'm not going to have an apartment in Moscow! This is a sort of comfort I have never had the pleasure of enjoying before.

How is Alexei Alexeyevich's health? I don't understand why he had to take showers.

All the best!

Your
A. Chekhov

To LYDIA AVILOVA

March 19, 1892, Melikhovo

Dear Lydia Alexeyevna,

. . . I read your "Along the Way." If I were the editor of an illustrated magazine I would publish this story with great pleasure. Only here is the advice of this particular reader: when you portray miserable wretches and unlucky people and want to stir the reader to compassion, try to be cooler—to give their sorrow a background, as it were, against which it can stand out in sharper relief. The way it is, the characters weep and you sigh. Yes, you must be cold.

But don't listen to me, as I am a poor critic. I don't have the ability to formulate my critical ideas clearly. Sometimes I just talk frightful nonsense. . . .

Your letter distressed and bewildered me. You mention certain "strange things" that I seem to have said at Leikin's, then you beg me in the name of respect for womankind not to speak of you "in that spirit" and finally you even say "for having been trustful just this once, I can find my name dragged into the mud . . ." What is this dreaming of yours all about? Mud—and me! . . . My self-esteem will not permit me to justify myself: moreover, your accusations are too vague to allow me to decide on what grounds I can defend myself. As far as I can judge, it is a question of gossip, isn't it? I earnestly implore you (if you trust me no less than you do the gossips), do not believe all the nasty things people say in your St. Petersburg. Or, if you find it impossible not to believe these rumors, then don't swallow them plain, but with a pinch of salt; both as to my marriage to someone with five millions and my affairs with the wives of my best friends, etc. Calm down, for heaven's sake. If I don't sound convincing enough, have a talk with Yasinski, who was with me at Leikin's after the jubilee. I recall that both of us, he and I, spoke at some length of what fine people you and your sister were. . . . We both were somewhat high after the jubilee, but even if I were as drunk as a sailor or had lost my mind, I would not have lowered myself to "that spirit" or "mud" (didn't your arm wither as you spelled out that little word!) as I would be restrained by my usual decency and devotion to my mother, sister and women in general. Imagine speaking ill of you and especially in Leikin's presence!

However, I wash my hands of the business. Defending oneself against gossip is like begging for a loan from [. . .]: useless. Think as you wish about me. . . .

I am living in the country. I throw snow into the brook and with satisfaction ponder upon my decision—nevermore to visit St. Petersburg.

My best wishes.

> Your sincerely devoted and respectful,
>
> A. Chekhov

To PYOTR BYKOV

May 4, 1892, Melikhovo

Dear Pyotr Vasilievich,

Ieronym Ieronymich wrote me that you are on very friendly terms with the editors of "World-Wide Illustration." If you have the opportunity would you be good enough to inform them that the announcement in which they praise me as "highly gifted," and the title of my story which they print in letters as big as a signboard, have produced a most unpleasant impression on me. The announcement resembles the advertisement of a dentist or masseur and in any case is lacking in taste. I realize the value of publicity and am not opposed to it, but for a man of letters, modesty and the literary approach in dealing with readers and colleagues alike constitute the very finest and most infallible publicity. On the whole I have had no luck with "World-Wide Illustration": I requested an advance and am regaled with publicity. They didn't send the advance—all right, that's bad enough, but they should have had mercy on my literary reputation. This, my first letter to you, is a peevish one and is bound to irk you. Forgive me.

I beg you earnestly to excuse me and to believe that I have turned to you with a complaint only because I hold you in the sincerest esteem.

A. Chekhov

To ALEXEI SUVORIN

August 1, 1892, Melikhovo

My letters chase after you, but you are elusive. I have written often, and to St. Moritz, by the way. Judging by your letters, you haven't had anything from me. To start with, cholera is raging in and near Moscow, and will reach our area any day now. In the second place, I have been appointed cholera doctor, and my section includes twenty-five villages, four factories and one monastery. I organize, put up barracks, etc., and feel like a lonely soul, as everything connected with cholera is alien to my nature, and the work, which requires me to take trips continually, deliver talks and attend to petty details, is exhausting. There is no time for writing. Literature has long ago been cast aside, and I am poverty-stricken and wretched, as I found it proper, in the interests of independence, to turn down the compensation that section doctors usually receive. I am bored, yet there is a great deal that is interesting in cholera, looking at it objectively. It's a pity you are not in Russia. Material for those short letters of yours is falling by the wayside. The situation is more good than bad, and in this respect cholera differs sharply from famine. . . . Everybody is at work now, and working feverishly. At the Nizhni Fair miracles are performed which may cause even Tolstoy to adopt a more respectful attitude toward medicine and toward the general participation of educated people in life. It looks as if a lasso had been thrown over cholera. The number of cases has not only been lowered, but the percentage of mortality as well. In a huge place like Moscow it won't go beyond fifty cases a week, though on the Don it will fasten upon thousands every day—an imposing difference. We country doctors are ready: we have a definite program of action and perhaps we will lower the percentage of fatalities from cholera in our districts.

We have no assistants, and have to act as doctors and orderlies at the same time; the mujiks are crude, filthy, mistrustful; but the thought that our labors won't be wasted makes all these things practically unnoticeable. Of all the Serpukhov doctors I am the sorriest specimen; I have a scurvy horse and carriage, don't know the roads, can't see at night, haven't any money, get tired very easily, and most important of all—I cannot forget for a moment that I must write, and I feel very much like spitting on the cholera and getting down to my work. And I would like to have a talk with you. I am utterly lonely.

Our farming efforts have been crowned with complete success. The harvest is a solid one, and when we sell our grain, Melikhovo will net us more than a thousand rubles. The truck garden is a brilliant success. We have regular mountains of cucumbers, and wonderful cabbage. If it weren't for the damned cholera I could say I had never spent as good a summer as this one. . . .

Nothing is heard of cholera riots any more. There is talk of arrests, proclamations and so on. They say Astyrev,[1] the literary man, has been sentenced to a fifteen-year prison term. If our socialists actually exploit cholera for their own ends, I shall

[1] Astyrev was a sociologist.

despise them. Using vile means to attain worthy ends makes the ends themselves vile. Let them ride on the backs of doctors and medical assistants, but why lie to the people? Why assure the people they are right in their ignorance and that their crude prejudices are sacred truth? Can any splendid future possibly justify this base lie? Were I a politician, I could never make up my mind to shame my present for the sake of the future, even though I might be promised tons of bliss for a pinch of foul lying.

Shall we see each other in the fall, and will we be together in Feodosia? You, after your trip abroad, and I, after the cholera, might have a good deal that is interesting to tell each other. Let's spend October together in the Crimea. It wouldn't be boring, honestly. We can write, talk, eat. . . . There is no more cholera in Feodosia.

Write me if possible more often. . . . I can't be in very good spirits now, but your letters do tear me away from worries over the cholera and carry me briefly into another world.

Keep well. My regards to my classmate, Alexei Petrovich.

Yours,

A. Chekhov

I am going to treat cholera by the Cantani method: lots of enemas with tannin at 40 degrees and injections under the skin of a solution of sodium chloride. The former have an excellent effect: they warm, and decrease the diarrhea. The injection sometimes produces miracles, but on other occasions causes a stroke.

To ALEXEI SUVORIN

August 16, 1892, Melikhovo

I won't write any more, not if you cut me down. I wrote to Abbazzio, to St. Moritz, wrote at least ten times. . . . It's mortifying, particularly so when, after a whole group of my letters on

our worries over cholera, you suddenly write from gay, tur-
quoise-hued Biarritz that you envy me my leisure! May Allah
forgive you!

Well, sir, I'm alive and well. The summer is an admirable
one, dry, warm, teeming with fruits of the earth, but all its
delight, from July on, was totally spoiled by news of a cholera
epidemic. During the time you were inviting me first to Vienna,
then to Abbazzio, I had already become the section doctor of the
Serpukhov community, was trying to catch cholera by the tail
and had organized a new section like a whirlwind. In my section I have twenty-five villages, four factories and one monastery. In the morning I hold office hours for patients, in the
afternoon I pay visits. . . . I have turned out to be a first-rate
beggar; what with my beggar-like eloquence, my section now
has two excellent barracks completely equipped and five that
are not excellent but miserable. I have even relieved the community council of expenditures for disinfection purposes. I have
begged lime, vitriol and assorted stinking junk from manu-
facturers for all of my twenty-five villages. . . . My soul is spent
and I am weary. Not to belong to yourself, to think only of
diarrhea, to tremble at night at the bark of a dog and knock
at the gate (haven't they come to get me out of bed?) to drive
scurvy horses along unknown roads, to read only about cholera
and wait only for cholera and at the same time to be completely
indifferent to the malady and the people you are treating—
my dear sir, you can't have even a bowing acquaintance with
the stew that is going on within me. Cholera has already hit
Moscow and Moscow District. We must expect it hourly. Judging by its progress in Moscow, we have reason to believe it has
already abated and the bacillus is beginning to lose its vigor.
We must also realize that it must readily give way before the
measures taken here and in Moscow. The educated class is working diligently without sparing its body or its purse; I see evidence of it every day and am moved, and then when I recall
how Inhabitant and Burenin poured forth their venom on this

class, I get a pretty choked feeling. In Nizhni the doctors and educated people generally have performed wonders. I was overcome with delight when I read about the handling of cholera. In the good old days, when people sickened and died by the thousands, people couldn't even have dreamed of the astounding victories that are now being won before our eyes. It is a pity you are not a physician and cannot share my gratification, i.e., properly feel, recognize and value all that is being done. However, it is not possible to talk of this in a brief paragraph.

The method of treating cholera requires that the doctor, above all else, take his time, i.e., give five to ten hours to each patient, and sometimes more. As I mean to use the Cantani method—enemas of tannin and injections of a solution of sodium chloride under the skin—my situation will be stupider than a fool's. While I am fussing around with one patient, ten others will manage to get sick and die. You know I am the only one serving twenty-five villages, aside from the medical assistant, who calls me Your Honor, is timid about smoking in my presence and won't take a step without my advice. If we have isolated cases, I will be in full control, but if the epidemic spreads to even as few as five cases a day, I will lose my temper, worry and feel I am to blame. . . .

When you learn from the papers that the cholera has abated, you will know I have again taken up writing. While I serve the community, don't consider me a literary man. I can't try to catch two rabbits at once.

You write I have abandoned "Sakhalin." No, I cannot abandon my big baby. When boredom with fiction gets me down, I find it pleasant to take up with non-fiction. I don't think the question of when I shall finish "Sakhalin" and where I shall publish it is important. While Galkin-Vraski is king of the prison system I am strongly disposed against publishing the book. Though if I am forced to it, that will be another matter.

In all my letters I have insistently put one question to you which you don't have to answer, however: where will you be in the fall and don't you want to pass a part of September and October in Feodosia and Crimea with me. I feel an irresistible desire to eat, drink, sleep and talk about literature, i.e., do nothing and at the same time feel I am a decent person. But if you find my indolence distasteful, I can promise to write a play or novel with or near you. How about it? You don't want to? Well, the hell with it. . . .

. . . Picture to yourself my cholera boredom, my cholera solitude and forced literary idleness and write me more and oftener. I share your squeamish feeling toward the French. The Germans are very much above them, though for some reason we consider them stolid. And I care for Franco-Russian understandings as much as I do for Tatishchev. There is something low and suggestive in these understandings. . . .

We have raised some very delicious potatoes and wonderful cabbage. How can you get along without cabbage soup? I don't envy you your sea, or your freedom or the good mood you enjoy abroad. There is nothing like the Russian summer. And I may add incidentally, I don't particularly care about going abroad. After Singapore, Ceylon and our Amur, I daresay Italy and even Mt. Vesuvius don't seem enticing. When I was in India and China, I did not see any great difference between the rest of Europe and Russia.

My neighbor, Count Orlov-Davidov, the owner of the celebrated estate Consolation, who ran away from the cholera, is now living in Biarritz; he gave his doctor only five hundred rubles for the cholera campaign. When I went to visit his sister, the countess, who lives in my section, to talk about building a barracks for her workingmen, she treated me as if I had come to ask her to take me on as a hired hand. She just made me sick, and I lied to her that I was a man of means. I told a similar lie to the head of the monastery, who refused to give me any space for patients, of whom there will probably be quite a few. In answer to my question as to what he would do with those that fell ill in his hostel he replied that they were substantial people who would pay all charges themselves. Do you get it? I flared up and said I didn't need a fee, as I was rich, and all I wanted was for the monastery to be safe. Sometimes you get into the most stupid and insulting situations. . . . Before Count Orlov-Davidov's departure, I had an interview with his wife. Complete with enormous diamonds in her ears, a bustle and an inability to comport herself properly. A millionairess. With such personages you experience a stupid schoolboy reaction, when you feel like saying something vulgar for no good reason.

I often have visits, and long ones, from the local priest, a fine young fellow, a widower with illegitimate children.

Write, or there will be trouble.

Yours,
A. Chekhov

To ALEXEI SUVORIN

November 25, 1892, Melikhovo

You are not hard to understand and you abuse yourself needlessly for expressing yourself vaguely. You are a hard drinker and I treated you to sweet lemonade; after downing it wryly, you remark with entire justice that it hasn't an alcoholic kick. That is just what our works haven't got—the kick that would make us drunk and hold us in their grasp, and this you set forth clearly. And why not? Leaving me and my "Ward No. 6" out of it, let's talk in general terms, which are more interesting. Let's talk of general causes, if it won't bore you, and let's embrace the whole age. Tell me in all conscience, what writers of my own generation, i.e., people from thirty to forty-five, have given the world even one drop of alcohol? Aren't Korolenko, Nadson, and all today's playwrights lemonade? Have Repin's or Shishkin's paintings really turned your head? All this work is just amiable and talented, and though you are delighted, you still can't forget you'd like a smoke. Science and technical knowledge are now experiencing great days, but for our brother-

hood the times are dull, stale and frivolous, we ourselves are
stale and dreary. . . . The causes for it are not to be found in
our stupidity or lack of gifts and not in our insolence, as
Burenin holds, but in a disease which in an artist is worse than
syphilis or sexual impotence. Our illness is a lack of "something," that is the rights of the case, and it means that when you
lift the hem of our Muse's gown you will behold an empty void.
Bear in mind that writers who are considered immortal or just
plain good and who intoxicate us have one very important trait
in common: they are going somewhere and call you with them;
you sense, not with your mind but with all your being, that
they have an aim, like the ghost of Hamlet's father, who had a
reason for appearing and alarming the imagination. Looking
at some of them in terms of their calibre you will see that they
have immediate aims—the abolition of serfdom, the liberation
of their country, political matters, beauty, or just vodka, like
Denis Davidov; others have remote aims—God, life beyond the
grave, the happiness of mankind and so on. The best of them are
realistic and paint life as it is, but because every line is saturated
with juice, with the sense of life, you feel, in addition to life
as it is, life as it should be, and you are entranced. Now what
about us? Yes, us! We paint life such as it is—that's all, there
isn't any more. . . . Beat us up, if you like, but that's as far as
we'll go. We have neither immediate nor distant aims, and you
can rattle around in our souls. We have no politics, we don't
believe in revolution, we don't believe in God, we aren't afraid
of ghosts, and personally I don't even fear death or blindness.
He who doesn't desire anything, doesn't hope for anything and
isn't afraid of anything cannot be an artist. It doesn't matter
whether we call it a disease or not, the name doesn't matter, but
we do have to admit that our situation is worse than a governor's. I don't know how it will be with us ten or twenty years
hence, perhaps circumstances may change by then, but for the
time being it would be rash to expect anything really good
from us, regardless of whether or not we are gifted. We write

mechanically, in submission to the old established order whereby some people are in government service, others in business and still others write. . . . You and Grigorovich hold that I am intelligent. Yes, I am intelligent in that at least I don't conceal my illness from myself, don't lie to myself and don't cover my own emptiness with other people's intellectual rags, like the ideas of the sixties and so on. I won't throw myself down a flight of stairs, like Garshin, but neither will I attempt to flatter myself with hopes of a better future. I am not to blame for my disease, and it is not for me to cure myself, as I have to assume this illness has good aims which are obscure to us and not inflicted without good reason. . . . "It wasn't just the weather that brought them together. . . ."

Well, sir, now as to the intellect. Grigorovich believes the mind can triumph over talent. Byron was as brilliant as a hundred devils, but it was his talent that made him immortal. If you tell me that X spoke nonsense because his intellect triumphed over his talent, or vice versa, I will reply that X had neither intellect nor talent. . . .

. . . The Heavens guard you!

Yours,
A. Chekhov

To LYDIA MIZINOVA

November 1892, Melikhovo

Trofim![1]

You son of a bitch, if you don't stop showering attentions on Lika, I will drill a corkscrew into you, you cheap riffraff, in the place that rhymes with brass. You—you piece of filth! Don't tell me you don't know that Lika belongs to me and that we already have two children! You pig's tail! You toadstool! Go out into the barnyard and wash yourself in the mud puddle,

---

[1] Trofim was an imaginary lover of Lydia Mizinova.

you'll be cleaner than you are now, you son of a bitch. Feed your mother and respect her, but leave the girls alone. You rat!!!

Lika's Lover

To ALEXEI SUVORIN

February 24, 1893, Melikhovo

. . . Heavens! What a magnificent thing "Fathers and Sons" is! It is beyond words. Bazarov's illness is done so powerfully that I could feel myself getting weak and experiencing a sensation as though I had caught his infection. And Bazarov's death? And the old folks? And Kukshina? The devil knows how he did it. It is simply a work of genius. I do not like anything about "On the Eve" except Elena's father and the conclusion. This finale is tragic. "The Dog" is very good and the language he uses is striking. Please read it, if you have forgotten it. "Asya" is nice, "The Lull Before the Storm" is a hotchpotch which leaves one dissatisfied. "Smoke" I don't like at all. "A Nest of Gentlefolk" is weaker than "Fathers and Sons," but its finale is also in the nature of a miracle. Except for the old lady in Bazarov, i.e., Eugene's mother, and mothers generally, particularly ladies in good society, who by the way are all alike (Lisa's mother, Elena's mother), as well as Lavretski's mother, a former serf woman, and also the plain country types, all of Turgenev's women and young girls are insufferable in their artificiality and, if you will excuse it, their falseness. Lisa, Elena —these are not Russian girls, but a species of female pythons, crystal-ball gazers, crammed with high-flown notions out of harmony with their place in society. Irina in "Smoke," Odintsova in "Fathers and Sons," give the general impression of being lionesses; they are caustic, insatiable, appetizing wenches all looking for something or other—and they are all trash. When you recall Tolstoy's Anna Karenina, all these Turgenev ladies with their enticing shoulders aren't worth a hoot. His negative

[174]

female types—where Turgenev deftly caricatures (Kukshina) or pokes fun (description of balls) —are remarkably drawn and so superbly managed that there isn't a flaw in the fabric, as they say. The descriptions of nature are good, but ... I feel we have outgrown that sort of descriptiveness and something quite different is needed.

My sister is getting better, my father also. We are expecting cholera but we do not fear it because we are prepared; not to die, however, but to spend the community's funds. If there is an outbreak of the disease it will take away a great deal of my time.

Keep alive, well and serene. Special regards to Anna Ivanovna.

Yours entirely,
A. Chekhov

We have been sent a lot of Little Russian lard and bologna. Heavenly fare! ...

To MARIA CHEKHOVA

Tuesday.   *March 9, 1893, Melikhovo*

Buy a plain copper coffeepot, something like a receptacle for holy water, the kind we used to have, holding six or seven cups. The coffee is always undrinkable in those scientific coffeepots.

1 lb. epsom salts.

I am sending 25 rubles just in case.

It is snowing. ...

A quarter pound of onion and horseradish.

We are slaughtering a pig the week before Easter.

5 lbs. coffee.

Evening: Misha has arrived. He will be back on Thursday and will carry half the baggage for you.

Yours,
A. Chekhov

To ALEXEI SUVORIN

April 26, 1893, Melikhovo

Greetings and happy homecoming!

... First of all, let me tell you about myself. I'll begin by informing you that I am ill. A vile, despicable malady. Not syphilis, but worse—hemorrhoids ... with pain, itching, tension, no sitting or walking and such irritation throughout the entire body that one feels like lying down and dying. It seems to me that nobody wants to understand me and that everybody is stupid and unjust; I am in a bad temper and speak nonsense; I believe my people at home breathe easier when I go out. What a business! My malady cannot be explained either by sedentary living, for I was and am lazy, nor by my depraved behavior, nor by heredity. I once had peritonitis; in consequence the lumen of the intestines has constricted because of the inflammation. Sum total: an operation is necessary. ...

Well sir, here is a page right out of a novel. This I am telling you in confidence. My brother Misha fell in love with a little countess, wooed her with gentle amours, and before Easter was officially accepted as her fiancé. Ardent love, dreams of splendor. ... Eastertime the countess wrote she was leaving to visit her aunt in Kostroma. Up until these last few days there had been no letters from her. The languishing Misha, upon hearing that she was in Moscow, went to her home and—will wonders never cease?—saw people hanging about at the windows and gates of the house. What was happening? Nothing less than that a wedding was taking place within—the countess was marrying a gold-mine owner. How do you like that? Misha came home in despair and has been poking the countess' tender and loving letters under my nose and begging me to solve this psychological problem. A woman can't wear out a pair of shoes without deceiving someone five times over. However, I think Shakespeare has already spoken adequately on the subject. ...

I probably will not go to America, as I have no money. I haven't earned anything since spring, have been ill and exasperated by the weather. What a good idea it was to put the town behind me! Tell all the Fofanovs, Chermnis and tutti quanti who exist on literature that living in the country is immeasurably cheaper than in town. I experience this every day. My family doesn't cost me anything now, since lodgings, bread, vegetables, milk, butter and horses are all my own, not boughten. And there is so much work that time does not suffice. Out of the entire Chekhov family it is only I who may lie down or sit at the table, all the rest toil from morning until night. Drive the poets and fiction writers into the country! Why should they exist as beggars, and on the verge of starvation? Surely city life in the sense of poetry and art cannot offer rich material to the poor man. People live within four walls and only see others in editorial offices and beer houses.

There are many sick people about. For some reason, many consumptives. But keep well, old fellow.

The drought has begun.

Yours,
A. Chekhov

To ALEXEI SUVORIN

March 27, 1894, Yalta

Greetings!

Here I have been living in Yalta for almost a month in superboring Yalta, at the Hotel Russia, Room No. 39, with your favorite actress, Abarinova, occupying No. 38. The weather is springlike, it is warm and sunny, and the sea is behaving properly; but the people are utterly dull, drab and dismal. I was an ass to have set aside all of March for the Crimea. I should have gone to Kiev and there devoted myself to the contemplation of the holy places and the Little Russian spring.

My cough has not left me, but still I am heading north to my penates on the fifth of April. I cannot remain here longer and besides I haven't any money, as I took only 350 rubles with me.

If you calculate round-trip traveling expenses, you have 250 rubles left, and you can't do anything rash on that kind of money. If I had a thousand or fifteen hundred, I would go to Paris, which would be desirable for many reasons.

I am healthy generally speaking, but am ailing in several particulars. As an example, I have the cough, palpitations of the heart and hemorrhoids. This business with my heart went on for six days without a stop, and the sensation was a vile one. After cutting out smoking I no longer get into a gloomy or anxious mood. Perhaps because of my no longer smoking, the Tolstoyan morality has stopped stirring me, and in the depths of my soul I feel badly disposed toward it, which is, of course, unjust. Peasant blood flows in my veins, and you cannot astound me with the virtues of the peasantry. From childhood I have believed in progress and cannot help believing, as the difference between the time when I got whipped and the time when the whippings ceased was terrific. I liked superior mentality, sensibility, courtesy, wit, and was as indifferent to people's picking their corns and having their leg puttees emit a stench as to young ladies who walk around mornings with their hair done up in curl papers. But the Tolstoyan philosophy had a powerful effect on me, governed my life for a period of six or seven years; it was not the basic premises, of which I had been previously aware, that reacted on me, but the Tolstoyan manner of expression, its good sense and probably a sort of hypnotic quality. Now something within me protests; prudence and justice tell me there is more love in natural phenomena than in chastity and abstinence from meat. War is evil and the court system is evil, but it does not therefore follow that I have to walk around in straw slippers and sleep on a stove alongside a workman and his wife, etc., etc. This, however, is not the crux of the matter, not the "pro and contra"; it is that somehow or other Tolstoy has already passed out of my life, is no longer in my heart; he has gone away saying, behold, your house is left unto you desolate. I have freed myself from lodging his ideas in my brain. All these theories have wearied me, and I read such whistlers in the dark as Max Nordau with revulsion. A sick man with a temperature won't feel like eating, but has a vague desire for something or other, which he expresses by asking for "something sort of sour." I want something sort of sour, too. I am not an isolated case, as I have noted just this kind of mood all about me. It is as though everybody had fallen in love, had got over it and was now looking for some new distraction. It is very possible and very likely that Russians are again becoming enthusiastic over the natural sciences and that the materalistic movement will once more be fashionable. The natural sciences are now performing miracles; they can advance upon the public like Mamai, and subject it to their massiveness and grandeur. However, all this is in God's hands. Once you philosophize your brain starts whirling.

A German from Stuttgart sent me fifty marks for a translation of my story. How do you like that? . . .

Keep well and calm. How is your head? Does it ache more or less than it used to? My head doesn't ache as much—because I don't smoke.

My profound respects to Anna Ivanovna and the children.

Your

A. Chekhov

To LYDIA MIZINOVA

March 27, 1894, Yalta

Sweet Lika,

Thank you for the letter. Though you scare me by saying you are going to die soon, and you twit me for throwing you over, thanks anyway. I know perfectly well you aren't going to die and nobody threw you over.

I am in Yalta and at loose ends, very much so. The local aristocracy or whatever you call it is putting on "Faust" and I attend rehearsals, delight in gazing upon a regular flower bed

of charming black, red, flaxen and auburn heads, listen to singing and eat; I dine upon deep-fat fried lamb, onion fritters and
mutton chops with kasha in the company of the directress of the
girls' school; I eat sorrel soup with well-born families; I eat at
the pastry shop and at my own hotel as well. I go to bed at ten,
get up at ten and rest after dinner, but still I am bored, sweet
Lika. I am not bored because I don't have "my women" around,
but because the northern spring is better than this one, and the
thought that I must, that I am obliged to write, won't leave me
a single instant. I must write, write and write. I am of the
opinion that real happiness is impossible without idleness. My
ideal is to be idle and love a plump young girl. My most intense
pleasure is to walk or sit doing nothing; my favorite occupation
is picking useless stuff (leaves, straw and so on) and doing useless things. Meanwhile I am a literary man and must write, even
here in Yalta. Sweet Lika, when you become a great singer and
are paid enormous fees, be charitable: marry me and support me,
so that I will find it possible to live without work. If you really
are going to die, then give the job to Varvara Eberle, whom, as
you know, I love. I have worked myself into such a state by
continual worry over my obligations and the tasks I can't get
out of that I have been tormented for a week without letup by
palpitations of the heart. It is a loathesome feeling.

I sold my fox coat for twenty rubles! It cost sixty, but as forty
rubles' worth of fur has already shed, twenty rubles was no
bargain. The gooseberries haven't ripened yet but it is warm
and bright, the trees are in bloom, the sea has a summery look,
the young ladies pine for sensations, but still the north is better
than the Russian south, at least in spring. . . . Because of the
palpitations I haven't had wine now for a week, and because of
the lack of wine the local atmosphere strikes me as even sorrier.
You were lately in Paris? How are the French? Do you like
them? Fire away, then!

Mirov gave a concert here and made a net profit of 150 rubles.
He roared like a lion but had an enormous success. How ter-

ribly sorry I am I didn't study voice; I could have roared, too, as my throat is full of husky notes and people say I have a real octave. I would earn good money and be popular with the ladies.

I won't go to Paris this June, but want you to come to us in Melikhovo—homesickness for Russia will drive you to it. There's no way of getting out of a visit to Russia, even if it's only for a day. You run into Potapenko occasionally. Well, this summer he too is returning to Russia. If you make the trip with him it will cost less. Have him buy your ticket and then forget to pay him (you won't be the first). But if you won't make the trip, I'll go to Paris. Though I am sure you are coming. . . .

Keep well, Lika, and calm and happy and content. I wish you success. You're a bright girl.

If you want to spoil me with a letter, direct it to Melikhovo, where I shall soon be going. I will answer your letters regularly. I kiss both your hands.

Yours,
A. Chekhov

To ALEXANDER CHEKHOV

May 21, 1894, Melikhovo

Ungrateful brother!

I haven't answered for all this time, first, because I am a snob with property of my own, and you are poor; and second, because I didn't know how to reply to the thing you wanted most to know. That's because the same upheavals experienced by "The North" are now taking place at the "Artist" office, and there is no way of figuring who the editor is. Kumanin, who was editing it, has left, handing over the reins to Novikov; and the office itself has moved to Arbat St. Whatever has happened, the paper is still in existence and it is possible to get work on it (I even get my forty rubles monthly) but you won't overeat; all the new contributors are paid a fiver, i.e., fifty per sixteen pages.

The weather is fine. If you are thinking of visiting us, I shall be very much indebted to you; I'll put you to work looking after the young bull and shooing the ducks to the pond. I won't give you a salary, but the board will be on me.

All are in good health. Father philosophizes and grumbles at Mother because "something stuck right here in her throat," etc.

Greetings to the family and keep well. On the other hand, try not to act like a nincompoop.

Your

A. Chekhov

I have put twenty-three rubles in the savings bank. My wealth is accumulating. But you won't get a single kopek of it because you are not mentioned in my will.

To ALEXEI SUVORIN

July 11, 1894, Melikhovo

You wrote you would be here one of these days, so I waited. . . . I don't feel drawn toward Yasnaya Polyana.[1] My brain functions feebly and doesn't want to get any more weighty impressions. I would prefer some sea bathing and nonsensical talk.

Here is my plan. The twentieth or twenty-second of July I am going to Taganrog to treat my uncle, who is seriously ill and insists on my services. He is a truly fine person, the best of men, and I would feel bad about denying him this service although I know it will be futile. . . . After finishing my "Sakhalin" here, and offering thanks to heaven, I will declare my freedom and readiness to go wherever I please. If there is money I will go abroad, or to the Caucasus, or to Bukhara. But I shall doubtless have some financial difficulties, so that a change of plan is not to be avoided. It would be nice to speak to Witte, the Minister of Finance, and tell him that instead of scattering sub-

---

1 Yasnaya Polyana was the Tolstoy estate.

sidies right and left or promising 100,000 to the fund, he ought to arrange for literary people and artists to travel free on the state railways. Except for Leikin (blast his hide!) all Russian men of letters exist in a virtual state of chronic hunger, for all of them, even those who turn out a couple of thousand pages a year, by some quirk of fate are weighed down by a fiendish heap of obligations. And there is nothing more irksome or less poetic, one may say, than the prosaic struggle for existence which takes away the joy of life and drags one into apathy. However, all this has nothing to do with the matter in hand. If you go to Taganrog with me—a very nice city—so be it. In August I am at your service; we'll take off then for Switzerland.

The play can be written somewhere on the shores of Lake Como or even left unborn; there's no sense getting hot and bothered over it and if we do—then the hell with it.

Now as to leeches. What you need, mainly, is to be in good spirits, and not leeches. In Moscow you impressed me as being cheerful and healthy and as I looked at you I certainly didn't think you would be reminding me of leeches. But once you did bring them up, very well. Leeches won't do you any harm. It is not a matter of bloodletting, but rather a nervous counter-reaction. They suck but little blood and don't cause pain. . . .

Write me what's new. Write about our Taganrog project, too.

. . . About ten years ago I went in for spiritualism and once got this message from Turgenev, whose spirit I had evoked at a session, "Your life is nearing its decline." I want so keenly to enjoy everything as if life were a perpetual Shrove Tuesday. I seem to have tried everything: life abroad, a good novel . . . And some inner force, like a presentiment, nudges me to make haste. Perhaps it is not a presentiment but simply sorrow that life flows on in such a monotonous and pallid way. A protest of the soul, one might say. . . .

I send my respects and pray heaven for the forgiveness of your sins and the showering of blessings upon you.

Prior Antoni

To MARIA CHEKHOVA

About September 14, 1894, Odessa

I have been to Yalta and am now in Odessa. Since I probably won't reach home until October I consider it not amiss to tell you the following:

1. Get the money on the first of October by presenting the enclosed note.

2. Dig up the sword lilies and have the tulips covered with leaves. I shall be grateful if you set out some more tulips. You can buy peonies and such on Truba Square.

3. Handicraft courses are being given in Taganrog where young girls from fifteen to twenty are taught the art of sewing in the latest styles (modes et robes). Sasha, our deceased uncle's daughter, a very sweet and good girl, took these courses and according to the mayor was considered the star pupil. And she really does sew beautifully. She has a great deal of taste. It so happened that in a conversation with me the mayor complained it was utterly impossible to find a teacher for these classes, that they had to send to St. Petersburg for one and so on. I asked him if I took this cousin of mine whom he praised so highly to Moscow and had her apprenticed to the very best modiste there, whether he would give her the teaching post afterward. He replied he would be delighted to hire her. A teacher ordinarily gets a salary of fifty rubles a month and this money could not be more welcome in uncle's family, which will now be in real need. So please think it over: isn't it possible to do something for the little girl? She could stay in Moscow one winter; I would give her fifteen or twenty rubles a month for her lodgings. She might live with you, which would put you out only slightly since, I repeat, she is a fine young girl. The important thing is that she should be helped. Consider the matter before my return and then we'll talk it over.

4. On the fourteenth of September, Ascension Day, the policeman ought to get a ruble. Give it to him if you have not already done so.

[184]

5. When you send the horses to call for me, don't forget to take along a warm cap. . . .

My best regards to all. Keep well and don't get lonesome.

Your
A. Chekhov

To ALEXANDER CHEKHOV

December 30, 1894, Melikhovo

My Lord!

I received the book and find extremely impertinent your desire to compete with me in the literary market. Nobody will buy it because everybody knows of your immoral behavior and chronically drunken condition.

You are not worthy of contributing to the "Russian News," since the man who signs himself "Letter" (Vasilievski)—a dignified man of character—is already writing for it from St. Petersburg. However, I'll talk to them. I suppose they will print the stories without doing it as a favor to me.

I have not yet received the cigars and don't need your gifts. When I get them I'll throw them down the toilet.

Our Papa was groaning all night. When asked why, he replied that he had "seen Beelzebub." . . .

Three days ago I was at a Christmas party for the insane, held in the violent ward. Too bad you weren't there.

Since the New Year will soon be with us, may I wish your family a Happy New Year and all the best—as for you, may you see Beelzebub in your dreams.

The money has been given to the French girl, the one you liked so much, in payment for your immoral conduct with her. . . .

All the best, sir. Is everyone well, my good man?

Your, sir,
A. Chekhov

To ALEXEI SUVORIN

January 21, 1895, Melikhovo

I will telegraph you without fail. Please come, but don't "kiss the feet of [name omitted, ed.]." She is a gifted young girl but I doubt that you will find her attractive. I am sorry for her because I am annoyed with myself, but half the time I can't abide her. She is as foxy as the devil, but her motives are so petty that she turns out to be a rat rather than a devil. As for [name omitted, ed.], she's another matter. She is a very good woman and a good actress who might perhaps have developed into someone worthwhile if she hadn't been spoiled by her schooling. She is a bit gross, but that doesn't matter.[1]

Heavens, I hadn't the slightest intention of putting Kundasova[2] into the story! To begin with, Kundasova looks upon money in an entirely different light; secondly, she has never had a home life; thirdly, regardless of all else, she is a sick woman. Nor does the old merchant resemble my father, for my father will remain until the end what he has been all through life—a man of average calibre and limited imagination. As for religion, the young merchants are disgusted with it. If you had had beatings as a child because of religious matters, you would understand why. And why is such disgust labeled stupidity? Perhaps the sentiment is stupidly expressed, but in itself it is not as stupid as you think. It has less need for justification, for instance, than the idyllic attitude toward religion of those who worship it in feudal fashion, leisurely, as people enjoy a snowstorm or cloudburst while seated comfortably in their studies. I am writing to the lady astronomer [Kundasova] today to tell her you want to see her. She will be touched and will probably try to meet you. . . .

Phew! Women take away one's youth, only not in my case. My life has been that of the store clerk, not of the proprietor,

[1] It has been impossible to identify these ladies.

[2] Suvorin thought that he recognized Chekhov's father and Kundasova in the story "Three Years."

and fate hasn't often been kind to me. I have had few romances and am as much like Catherine as a nut is like a battleship. Silk nightgowns means nothing to me except that they are comfortable, that is, soft to the touch. I am well disposed toward the comfortable life, but debauchery does not attract me. . . .

My health requires me to go far away somewhere for eight or ten months. I'm going to leave for Australia or the mouth of the Yenisei—I'll croak otherwise. Very well then, I'll settle for St. Petersburg instead, but would there be a room where I might hide away? This is an extremely important question, because I ought to be writing all of February to earn enough for my trip. How much I need to get away! My chest rattles all over, my hemorrhoids are so bad that the devil himself would be nauseated. I must have an operation. No, the hell with literature, I should be busy with my medical practice. I shouldn't be making comparisons, though. I owe the best days of my life and my deepest-felt emotions to literature.

My profound salutations to Anna Ivanovna, Nastya and Borya.

Yours entirely,
A. Chekhov

I'll be in Moscow on the twenty-sixth. Grand Moscow Hotel.

To ALEXEI SUVORIN

April 13, 1895, Melikhovo

. . . I am making my way through Sienkiewicz's "The Polanetskis." This book is like a Polish cheese pudding flavored with saffron. Add Potapenko to Paul Bourget, sprinkle them with Eau de Cologne from Warsaw, divide in two and you get Sienkiewicz. "The Polanetskis" was undoubtedly composed under the influence of "Cosmopolis," Rome and marriage (Sienkiewicz recently got married); he has the catacombs, an elderly eccentric professor breathing idealism, the saintly Leo XIII with

a visage not of this earth, advice to return to prayer and asper-
sions on a decadent character dying of morphinism after going
to confession and taking communion, i.e., repenting his errors
in the name of the church. A devilish heap of scenes of family
happiness and discourses on love have been dragged in, and the
hero's wife is so extremely faithful to her husband and understands God and life so thoroughly "by intuition" that the final
result is sickeningly cloying and clumsy, just as though you had
got a wet, slobbery kiss. Sienkiewicz apparently hasn't read
Tolstoy, is not familiar with Nietzsche, discusses hypnotism like
a middle-class householder, but still every one of his pages is
brightly colored with Rubenses, Borgheses, Correggios, Botti-
cellis—all neatly done to show off his culture to the bourgeois
reader and to make faces at materialism. The novel's aim is to
lull the bourgeoisie into golden dreams. Be faithful to your
wife, pray alongside her before the altar, make money, love
sport—and you're all set both in this world and the next. The
bourgeoisie is very fond of so-called "practical" types and novels
with happy endings, because this kind of writing soothes it into
believing that it can make lots of money and preserve its innocence, act like a beast and stay happy all at the same time.

This spring is a pitiful affair. The snow still lies on the fields,
driving on runners or wheels is impossible and the cattle pine
for grass and for freedom. Yesterday a drunken old peasant undressed himself and went bathing in the pond, his decrepit old
mother beat him with a stick and everybody else stood around
and laughed boisterously. After finishing his bath the peasant
went home barefoot through the snow, his old mother behind
him. One day this old lady came to me for treatment of her
bruises—her son had beaten her up. What baseness it is to postpone enlightenment of our dark masses! . . .

I wish you all happiness. I congratulate you on the Sino-
Japanese peace and trust we may acquire the eastern shore for
an ice-free Feodosia as soon as possible, and lay out a railroad
to it. The old lady had nothing to worry about, so she bought

herself a pig. And it seems to me we are laying up a heap of troubles for ourselves with this ice-free port. It will stand us dearer than if we had made up our minds to conquer all of Japan. However, futura sunt in manibus deorum. . . .

Yours,

A. Chekhov

To ALEXEI SUVORIN

October 21, 1895, Melikhovo

Thanks for the letter, for the cordial words and the invitation. I will come, but most likely not until the end of November, as I have a fiendish amount of stuff to take care of. To start with, next spring I am putting up a new school in the village, of which I am a trustee; before going about it I must work up a plan and budget, go here and there and so on. In the second place, just imagine, I am writing a play[1] which I probably will not finish until the end of November. I am writing it with considerable pleasure, though I sin frightfully against the conventions of the stage. It is a comedy with three female parts, six male, four acts, a landscape (view of a lake), lots of talk on literature, little action and tons of love.

I read about Ozerova's flop and felt sorry, as there is nothing more painful than failure. I can imagine how this [. . .] wept and grew stony as she read the "St. Petersburg Gazette," which called her playing downright ridiculous. I read about the success of "The Power of Darkness" at your theatre. . . . When I was at Tolstoy's in August he told me, as he wiped his hands after one of his washings, that he wouldn't rewrite his play. And now, in recalling his remark, I believe he already knew his play would be passed in toto for public presentation. I stayed with him a day and a half. A wonderful impression. I felt as carefree as I do at home and the talks we had were in that easy vein. I will give you full details when we meet. . . .

1 *The Seagull.*

I am in a state—and this is why. There is a first-rate magazine published in Moscow called "The Annals of Surgery," which even enjoys popularity abroad. It is edited by the eminent surgeon-scientists Sklifasovski and Diakonov. The number of subscribers has grown annually, yet there is always a deficit at the end of the year. This deficit has been made up hitherto (until this coming January) by Sklifasovski; but as he has been transferred to St. Petersburg, he has lost his practice and so has no extra money. Now neither he nor anyone else in the world knows who will meet the 1896 debt, if there is one; and on the basis of analogies with past years a deficit of from a thousand to fifteen hundred rubles can be expected. When I learned the magazine was in peril I got hot under the collar; how absurd to witness the ruin of so essential a publication, and one that would show a profit in three or four years, and all on account of a paltry sum! This absurdity hit me in the face and at white heat I promised to find a publisher, as I was firmly convinced I could do so. And I did look diligently, begged, lowered myself, drove all over town, God only knows with whom I didn't dine, but couldn't find anybody. . . . How sorry I am your printing plant is not in Moscow! Then I wouldn't have had to take on this grotesque role of unsuccessful broker. When we meet I will draw you a true picture of the emotional upheavals I went through. Were it not for the building of the school, which is costing me about fifteen hundred rubles, I would undertake to publish the magazine out of my own funds, so difficult and painful do I find it to reconcile myself to a clearly ridiculous situation. On the twenty-second of October I am going to Moscow to see the editors and as a last resort will propose that they ask for a subsidy of fifteen hundred or two thousand a year. If they agree, I'll dash to St. Petersburg and begin hammering away. How does one go about it? Will you instruct me? To save the magazine I am prepared to interview just about anyone and hang around in just anyone's outer office; if I succeed I will heave a sigh of relief and enjoy a feeling of satisfaction, because saving a good surgical magazine is as useful as performing twenty thousand successful operations. At any rate, give me some advice on what to do.

Write me in Moscow after Sunday, c/o Grand Moscow Hotel, No. 5. . . .

My profound respects. Write, I implore you.

Yours,
A. Chekhov

To ALEXEI SUVORIN

October 26, 1895, Moscow

. . . Tolstoy's daughters are very nice. They adore their father and have a fanatic faith in him. That is a sure sign that Tolstoy is indeed a mighty moral force, for if he were insincere and not above reproach, the first to regard him skeptically would be his daughters, because daughters are shrewd creatures and you can't pull the wool over their eyes. You can fool a fiancée or mistress as much as you please, and in the eyes of a loving woman even a donkey may pass for a philosopher, but daughters are another matter. . . .

As for "The Annals of Surgery," the magazine itself, all the surgical instruments, bandages and bottles of carbolic acid send their most profound and humble greetings to you. Their joy, of course, is unconfined. This is what we have decided to do: if the idea of a subsidy seems feasible, I am to take up the matter and when we get the subsidy, we return the fifteen hundred to you. I am going to see Sklifasovski in November and, if possible, will actually see Witte[1] in an attempt to save these very artless people. They are like children. It would be hard to find any with less practical sense. At any rate, your fifteen hundred will be returned to you sooner or later. In gratitude for my endeavors they are operating on my hemorrhoids—an operation I cannot avoid and which is already beginning to worry me. They will sing your praises and when you come to Moscow will

[1] Witte was the Minister of Finance.

show you the new clinics in the neighborhood of Novo-Deviche Monastery. They're as much worth looking at as a cemetery or a circus.

Write. Send the fifteen hundred care of me, and, if possible, not through the mails but via your store. . . .

Yours,

A. Chekhov

To ELENA SHAVROVA

November 18, 1895, Melikhovo

I will be in Moscow around the twenty-eighth, too, and remain six to ten days. We'll be seeing each other, I am going to ask your pardon and perhaps will manage to convince you that I was very, very far from consciously wishing to wound your self-esteem. I agree I ought to be sent up for hard labor for losing your manuscript, but I assure you even a halfhearted apologist could find cause for going easy with me. . . .

I have finished my play. It is called "The Seagull." It's nothing to ooh and ah about. On the whole I would say I am an indifferent playwright.

I will be stopping at the Grand Hotel in Moscow, opposite the Iverskaya clock tower, last entrance. The telephone is at your service, messengers also. If you will let me know of your presence in Moscow, by messenger or otherwise, I shall be most grateful.

All my best wishes . . .

Your guilty and repentant

cher maître,

A. Chekhov

To ALEXEI SUVORIN

December 6, 1895, Moscow

The young lady with the Remington has done me a cruel turn. In leaving for Moscow I had counted upon my play's having been typed long since and sent to its destination—why, two full weeks had elapsed since I had sent it to the young lady. But the typing job turned out to be far from finished. I took back the manuscript and the young lady was most apologetic. You will have the play tomorrow, but in manuscript. If it is to be typed, we shall have to wait again, which annoys me for my patience has been exhausted. Read the play and tell me what to do with it and how. There is still plenty of time until next season, so that the most radical revisions can be undertaken. . . . So you will get the play on Friday. Order all flags at full mast on that day.

You write you are arriving in Moscow ten days hence. Shall I wait for you there? Write without fail. I am anticipating your visit with the keenest pleasure, if only you don't disappoint me! If you are not coming I will get out of Moscow say around the tenth or twentieth. The Moscow weather is fine, there is no cholera and no Lesbianism either. Br-r-r! The recollection of those people of whom you write turns my stomach, as if I had eaten a rotten fish. So now there aren't any in Moscow—splendid. . . .

Today is St. Nicholas Day and there is a delightful sound of bells in Moscow. I rose early, lit the candles and sat down to write; outside the bells were ringing and very agreeable it was.

I wish you health. Salutations to Anna Ivanovna, Nastya and Borya. Happiness to you all.

Yours,
A. Chekhov

To MIKHAIL CHEKHOV

October 18, 1896, St. Petersburg

The play fell flat and flopped with a bang.[1] The audience was bewildered. They acted as if they were ashamed to be in the theatre. The performances were vile and stupid.

[1] The first performance of *The Seagull* was a sensational flop; the second performance was a great success.

The moral of the story is: I shouldn't write plays.

Nevertheless and just the same I am alive and well and my innards are in good spirit.

Your pappy,
A. Chekhov.

To ALEXEI SUVORIN

October 22, 1896, Melikhovo

In your last letter (dated October 18) you thrice call me an old woman and say I was a coward. Why the libel? After the play I dined at Romanov's, as was fitting, then went to sleep, slept well and the next day left for home without pronouncing a single syllable in complaint. If I had acted the coward I would have dashed from one editor to another, from one actor to another, nervously begged their condescension, nervously introduced useless changes and would have spent another two or three weeks in St. Petersburg, running back and forth to performances of my "Seagull," in a dither, drenched in cold sweat, complaining. . . . Why, when you visited me the night after the show, you yourself said it would be better for me to leave; and the next morning I had a letter from you saying goodbye. So where is the cowardice? I acted just as reasonably and coolly as a man who has proposed, been turned down and has nothing left to do but leave. Yes, my vanity was wounded, but certainly the thing wasn't a bolt from the blue; I expected a flop and had prepared myself for it, as I told you in advance in entire sincerity.

Back home I gave myself a dose of castor oil, took a cold bath—and now I wouldn't even mind doing another play. I no longer have that tired, irritated feeling. . . . I approve your revisions—and thank you a thousand times. But please don't be sorry you weren't at the rehearsals. Actually there was only one genuine rehearsal, at which it was impossible to tell what was going on; the play was completely lost in a fog of vile acting.

I had a telegram from Potapenko:[1] a colossal success. I had a letter from Veselitskaya (Mikulich) [2] whom I haven't met, expressing her sympathy in the tone she would use had someone died in my family—which was hitting pretty wide of the mark. All this is nonsense, though.

My sister is enchanted with you and Anna Ivanovna and I am very glad, because I am as fond of your family as of my own. She hurried home from St. Petersburg, probably feeling that I would hang myself.

We are having warm, damp weather, and many people are ill. Yesterday I stuck a huge enema into a rich peasant whose intestine had become clogged with excrement and he got better at once. Please forgive me, I went off with your "European Herald" deliberately, and with Filippov's "Collected Works" unintentionally. I will return the first, and the second after I have read them. . . .

I wish you all the blessings of heaven and earth, and thank you with all my heart.

Yours,

A. Chekhov

To ELENA SHAVROVA

November 1, 1896, Melikhovo

Esteemed lady, if, as "one of the audience" you are writing about the first performance, permit me—yes, permit me—to doubt your sincerity. You hurry to pour healing balm on the author's wounds, assuming that under the circumstances this would be better and more needed than sincerity; you are kind, sweet Mask, very kind, and the feeling does honor to your heart. I did not see everything at the first performance, but what I did see was vague, dingy, dreary and wooden. I had no

1 Ignati Potapenko, as mentioned previously, was a novelist and playwright.
2 Lydia Veselitskaya was a writer.

hand in assigning the parts, I wasn't given any new scenery, there were only two rehearsals, the actors didn't know their parts—and the result was general panic, utter depression of spirit; even Kommisarjevskaya's performance was nothing much, though her playing at one of the rehearsals was so prodigious that people in the orchestra wept and blew their noses.
. . .

Well ma'am, how are you getting along? Why don't you try your hand at writing a play? You know, creating a play is like wading into a mineral bath, certain that it will be warm, and then being shocked by the fact that it is cold. Do drop me a line.
. . .

. . . Send me another two or three lines, for I do find life a bore. I have a sensation of nothingness, past and present.

My best wishes, and again my thanks.

Yours,
A. Chekhov

To ANATOL KONI

November 11, 1896, Melikhovo

Dear Anatol Fedorovich,

You cannot imagine how happy your letter made me. I saw only the first two acts of my play from the front, after that I kept in the wings, feeling all the time "The Sea Gull" would be a failure. The night of the performance and the day after people asserted I had created nothing but idiots, that my play was clumsy from the standpoint of staging, fatuous, unintelligible, even senseless, etc., etc. You can imagine my situation—it was a flop worse than a nightmare! I was ashamed and annoyed and left St. Petersburg brimming with doubts. I figured that if I had written and staged a play so obviously crammed with monstrous defects, I had lost all my senses and my machinery had apparently broken down for good. I was back home when I heard from St. Petersburg that the second and third performances were successful; I got several letters, signed and anonymous, praising the play and scolding the critics; I read them with a sense of pleasure but still I was ashamed and peeved, and the thought lodged itself in my head that if good people found it necessary to console me, my affairs must be going badly. But your letter had a galvanizing effect on me. I have known you for a long time, esteem you profoundly and have more faith in you than in all the critics put together—you must have felt that when you wrote your letter and that is why it is so fine and convincing. I am quite calm now and can already think back on the play and the performance itself without revulsion.

Kommisarjevskaya is a marvelous actress. At one of the rehearsals many people were teary-eyed as they watched her and remarked that she was the best actress in Russia at the present time; but at the performance she too succumbed to the prevailing mood of hostility toward my "Sea Gull" and was intimidated by it, as it were, and her voice failed her. Our press treats her coldly, an attitude she does not merit, and I am sorry for her.

Permit me to thank you with all my heart for your letter. Please believe that I value the feelings prompting you to write it more profoundly than I can express in words, and the sympathy that you entitle "unnecessary" at the end of your letter I will never, never forget, whatever the future may hold.

Your sincerely respectful and devoted

A. Chekhov

To ALEXANDER CHEKHOV

November 16, 1896, Melikhovo

Your parents are sick at heart that you are not doing anything. I beg of you, mend your ways! Get up early in the morning, wash yourself well and go to Klochkov's bookstore at 55 Liteinaya and buy:

658. Peterson, O. The Bronte Family (Currer, Ellis and Anton Bell) St. Petersburg, 1895, 8°, covers (1 r.) With a portrait of C. Bronte! 50 k.

752. Renan, Historical and Religious Studies, 3rd Ed., St. Petersburg, 1894, covers, 16°, 75 k.

943. Rules of the St. Petersburg Slavonic Philanthropic Society, St. Petersburg, 1877, 8°, covers, 10 k.

945. Rules and Memoranda of the Society for the Care of Poor and Sick Children, St. Petersburg, 1892, 16°, covers, 15 k.

All these are taken from their Catalogue No. 214. Wrap them in a package and if they don't weigh too much send them registered parcel post, sticking on two kopeks' postage for each 2 oz. If you can get the second two books for nothing, so much the better, especially as 943 is probably out of date already. The errand is not for me but for your benefactor, His Honor the Mayor and Chief Magistrate of Taganrog, with all his medals. . . . I have already written you that an information section has been opened at the Taganrog City Library. Needed are the rules and regulations of all learned, philanthropic, bicycle, Masonic and other societies to which you would not be admitted on account of your unseemly appearance. (Vukov knows all.)

I'll pay any expenses incurred. Can't I send trifling sums (up to three or five rubles) in current postage stamps? . . .

In your last letter you called me a fool. I am amazed that your despicable hand has not withered away on you. However, to your abuse I reply with a general pardon. No use paying any attention to a retired office boy with illegitimate children!

A. Chekhov

To VLADIMIR NEMIROVICH-DANCHENKO

Dear friend,   *November 26, 1896, Melikhovo*

This is in reply to the main point of your letter—why we have so few serious talks generally. When people are silent it is because they have nothing to talk about or are shy. What can we discuss? We have no political interests, we haven't any social, club, or even street life, our urban existence is poor, monotonous, wearisome and uninteresting—and talking about it is as tedious as corresponding with Lugovoi. You say we are men of letters, which in itself enriches our life. But is that right? We are stuck in our profession up to the ears and it has gradually isolated us from the outer world; as a result we have little free time, little money, few books, we read little and reluctantly, hear little, seldom go places. . . . Should we talk about literature? But we've taken that up already, you know. . . . Every year it's the same thing over and over again and whatever we usually take up leads inevitably to who wrote better and who worse; talks always flag on more general or broader themes, because when tundras and Eskimos surround you, general ideas, so unsuited to the moment, quickly spread thin and slip away like thoughts of everlasting bliss. Should we talk of personal life? Yes, sometimes this can be interesting, I daresay we might talk about it, but in this area we become shy, evasive, insincere, the instinct of self-preservation restrains us and we get fearful. We are afraid that some uncivilized Eskimo may overhear us, somebody who doesn't like us and whom we don't like; personally I am afraid my friend Sergeyenko,[1] whose intelligence you find pleasing, will blatantly reach a decision on why I live with A when B is in love with me, shaking his finger in the air meanwhile through the length and breadth of the land. . . . To put it briefly, don't blame yourself or me for our silence and the lack of seriousness and interest in our talks, put the blame on what the critics call "the times" or the climate, or the vast expanses, on whatever you wish and let circumstances take their own fateful, inexorable course, while we put our hopes in a better future. . . .

I thank you with all my heart for your letter and press your hand cordially. . . . Write when you are in the mood. I will answer with the very greatest pleasure.

Yours,
A. Chekhov

1 A writer who had gone to school with Chekhov in Taganrog.

To VLADIMIR YAKOVENKO

January 30, 1897, Melikhovo

Dear Vladimir Ivanovich,

Having read your letter in "The Physician," I wrote to Moscow to have them send you my "Sakhalin Island." There you will find a bit about corporal punishment and transportation for crime, and some comments, incidentally, on Yadrintsev, which I recommend to you. . . .

It may be pointed out, relevantly, that jurists and penologists consider as corporal punishment (in its narrow, physical sense) not only beating with birch rods, switching or hitting with the fist, but also shackling, the "cold" treatment, the schoolboy "no dinner," "bread and water," prolonged kneeling, repeated touching of the forehead to the ground and binding the arms.

This inventory has made me suffer. Never yet have I had so little time.

I wish you all the best and warmly clasp your hand.

Yours,

A. Chekhov

. . . The reaction of corporal punishment upon physical health can be noted in the doctors' records, which you will find in the proceedings on tortures.

III

1897-1904

"Since 1884 I have been spitting blood every spring. . . ." In the spring of 1897, as Chekhov sat down to dinner with Suvorin in a Moscow restaurant, he suddenly collapsed. He was carried to Suvorin's room, became critically ill during the night and was taken to a hospital the following morning. The diagnosis was tuberculosis of the upper lungs. For several weeks he lay in bed barely able to move or speak. His sister, Maria, and his brother, Ivan, came immediately—Chekhov forbade them to tell his mother and father the nature of the illness—but friends and admirers were barred from the room. Tolstoy, however, managed to get by the nurses: he came to soothe the patient with sickroom small talk, but he stayed to argue that a work of art only fulfilled its function if an uneducated peasant could understand it. That must, indeed, have been a scene: the great man pacing the floor, the sick man trying to answer from his bed. By the time Tolstoy left, the patient had had a dangerous relapse.

When he recovered enough to travel, Chekhov went to Nice. (From now on he was to live not where and how he chose, but where and how the disease dictated.) All of France, even the refugees and pleasure lovers of the Riviera, was in ferment over the Dreyfus case. Chekhov was convinced of Dreyfus' innocence and his warm defense of Zola's brave position got him into a fight with Suvorin. For many years Chekhov had disliked the politics and the anti-Semitism of Suvorin's newspaper, but he had managed to avoid an open row with Suvorin. Now he could no longer stomach Suvorin's position in the Dreyfus case, and he said so in sharp words. They were never again to be close friends.

The months of invalid exile in Nice were not lonely—the south of France has always had a large Russian colony—and one has the feeling that France was good for Chekhov. But, as always, the time came when he was desperate to go home. The doctors would not allow him to live in Moscow: they insisted that he move to a milder climate. And so began the last years, the Yalta years.

The Moscow Art Theatre was founded in 1895 by Nemirovich-Danchenko and Konstantin Stanislavski in revolt against a theatre of stale domestic plays and foreign fripperies, of rhetoric and rant, a theatre where the star actor manipulated everything to suit his own style and fancy. These two men and their associates believed in a more natural style of acting—they called it "spiritual realism." They believed that every side of stage production, direction, costuming, lighting, music, was of equal importance and should be carefully integrated into an artistic whole. The ideas of this new group were so fresh, their methods so interesting, and their productions so remarkable that the Moscow Art Theatre became the greatest theatre influence in modern times. Our stage still works from the prompt books of Stanislavski, although it sometimes treats the books as if they were the Bible in bad translation. Whenever and wherever it is curtain time in the Western world, Stanislavski and Nemirovich-Danchenko are still in the theatre.

Chekhov was attracted by this new theatre group and when they came to him he was pleased at the possibility of working with them. Nemirovich-Danchenko had always been a great admirer of *The Seagull* and now he proposed to include it in the opening repertory program. But he had a hard time persuading Chekhov to allow the performance and an even harder time persuading Stanislavski and the other actors. Stanislavski said he didn't like the play and, at the first few meetings, didn't like the playwright, either. He thought Chekhov arrogant and insincere, which are two quite remarkable words from Stanislavski about Chekhov. The actors of the company, in the early meetings, were also bewildered and irritated by Chekhov. When one of them asked him how a part should be played Chekhov said, "As well as possible." This remark is still quoted as the charmingly naïve statement of a writer who didn't know anything about the stage. It is, of course, the statement of a writer who knew a great deal about the stage but who refused to deal in the large words of stage palaver.

The Moscow Art Theatre opened its door with an initial success, but then went financially down hill. As the group approached the Nemirovich-Danchenko production of *The Seagull* they were at the end of their resources. Nemirovich-Danchenko had never intended the play to carry that much of a burden. The rehearsals and the opening night were as dramatic as they were comic. The company had enough trouble without the sudden appearance of Maria Chekhova, who came to plead with them to cancel the performance: she said the almost certain failure of the play would be dangerous to her brother's health. Fortunately, Nemirovich-Danchenko was a man of sense who knew more about Chekhov than his sister and he refused to cancel the performance. But the sister's last-minute dramatic plea, thrown at people who were already frightened that their theatre was about to collapse, was enough to cause a panic. Stanislavski said that "an inner voice"—an inner voice is as much a part of every theatre as is the curtain or the lights—told the cast that if they did not act well, if the play should fail, they would be the executioners of their beloved Chekhov. (This was, indeed, a romantic picture of a writer who had always taken failure and success with calmness and serenity.) The cast fortified their inner voices with valerian drops, and got ready. Stanislavski's left foot, which had taken to violent and mysterious jerkings all on its own, was finally put under control, and Olga Knipper and the other actors throttled down the hysterics in plenty of time to get dressed. The curtain went up, the curtain came down. The play was a great success. *The Seagull* had saved the Moscow Art Theatre. To this day, a seagull is painted on the curtain of their theatre, in gratitude to Chekhov.

Chekhov had rewritten—the date of rewriting is not clear—*Wood Demon* and renamed it *Uncle Vanya*. Provincial repertory companies had already picked up the play and were performing it—Gorki wrote to Chekhov that he had seen it in Nizhni-Novgorod—before the Moscow Art Theatre was ready with its production in the autumn of 1899. Chekhov, who Stanislavski thought would be killed by the failure of *The Seagull,* went to bed in Yalta without realizing that *Uncle Vanya* was opening in Moscow. The new production of *Uncle Vanya* was not a brilliant success, although it was certainly not the failure that Olga Knipper made it in her excited report to Chekhov. It was enough of a success to convince the Moscow Art Theatre that their future lay in the hands of their new playwright and, because it was difficult for him to come to Moscow, they arranged a Crimean tour in the hope of encouraging him to write more plays. It was a gay and charming troupe that came south and the triumph of their tour and the pleasure of their company gave Chekhov a happy time. He sat down to write *The Three Sisters* for them.

I think *The Three Sisters* is a great play. It is a greater play than *Uncle Vanya* which, to me, is a greater play than *The Cherry Orchard*. But all three plays are of such importance that no easy and quick summary should be made of them.

It would be impossible here, and needless, since the letters speak for themselves, to make a full report of the last five years of Chekhov's life. They were crowded years. Chekhov, as usual, moved around a great deal. Sometimes he was happy at Yalta, often he fumed and yawned in the dull, provincial life of the town. These were the years during which a new edition of his works was published, an edition that is now considered incomplete and badly annotated, but which was of great importance in its day; the years of his warm and generous and loyal relations with Maxim Gorki—Chekhov resigned from the Academy when Gorki was refused admission and he invited Gorki to live in his house when Gorki was under police supervision; the years of his complex relations with the Moscow Art Theatre; the years of his greatest powers as a writer, and of his greatest rewards.

And, at the age of 41, he got married. Chekhov biographers offer us a picture of Olga Knipper as a charming and intelligent woman deeply in love with, and deeply loved by, a brilliant and famous man. There is, of course, no tape measure for in-loveness, but the biographers' picture cannot be the whole truth because many of the facts do not support it. There has been a strange lack of speculation about the relationship between Chekhov and Knipper—every other aspect of Chekhov's life has been rather overexplored—and it is difficult to know the reason why. Perhaps because both people are, in a sense, of our generation, we wish to accept Chekhov's letters to Knipper at their charming face value. Perhaps most of us do not wish to see trouble in the marital relations of people we admire, not so much out of kindheartedness as out of fear that we will grow depressed about our own.

I think it is difficult to avoid the conclusion that the Chekhov marriage was not a good marriage. Indeed, it seems to me to have been a sad marriage. Knipper was a charming and talented young woman, but she was an ambitious woman who covered her ambition with self-righteous talk about duty to her art. She is one—and it is amazing how little she differs from the rest—in a long line of ladies who want love and all the good things that go with it, but who haven't the slightest intention of giving up much to get it. After the marriage she stayed on with her career in Moscow, her husband stayed on in Yalta, and they came together only occasionally like secret lovers on holiday trips. True, Chekhov urged her not to sacrifice her career to his invalid's life, but his words were laid over with loneliness and it seems that a warmer heart would have understood the isolation and the fears of a sick man. True, Knipper cried out in her letters that she did want to come to him, but she seldom came. Her letters are full of guilt, which is what makes them often so boring, and sometimes her guilt makes her sound angry with her husband. She was obviously a childish woman, not only crying to get her own way, but demanding to be assured that her own way was the best and only way for both of them. Her letters tell him of the grand parties she has been to in Moscow and then, catching herself, she says that she finds the parties dull and foolish. She never seems to notice that Chekhov, in answering, shows his own desire for a little pleasure, a little party gaiety. One biographer says, "It helped him (Chekhov) to know that despite the excitements of Moscow, Olga's thoughts were constantly with him." It may have helped him, but not very much. He was a man and not a saint. There have always been Knippers in the international theatre, and they do not change with the husband, the education, the century or the regime. It seems as foolish to glorify Knipper as it would be to condemn her.

It should be said that life with Chekhov at the time Knipper married him could not have been ideal for an attractive young woman. He was a very sick man, he was famous and she was not, his natural high spirits were completely circumscribed by sickness, and he had a doting and possessive family who, under the best circumstances, would have irritated any bride. A house of illness is always a gloomy house, and the house of a middle-aged bridegroom is set in its ways, and Yalta was a dull, provincial town filled with the aged and the complaining, and Knipper had a miscarriage of the child they both wanted, and so on down a long, long list of troubles. And it is doubtful if Chekhov was a man of passion. He was romantic and tender and he loved women, but if he ever had been a man of passion it was now too late.

The nature of the Chekhov marriage would not be of any great significance if everything in it—and everything lacking in it—were not such remarkable clues to his life and work. Here, in the mirror of the marriage, is all of him: the gentle pride—he would not beg or ask favors from Knipper, nor chastise her for not giving them; the ability to accept what life offered and to make the most of it; the sweetness of his nature, and the sadness; the refusal to fool himself. In the married Chekhov there are the thousand sides that make the work so wonderful. Conversely, what we miss in the marriage is exactly what we miss in the work: there is a lack of passion and of power. Chekhov was without that final spiritual violence which the very great creative genius has always had. And he knew it as he knew most things about himself.

In June, 1904, he went to Germany with Knipper. On the night of July 1st, for the first time in the history of his illness, he asked to see a doctor. His conversation with the doctor had a kind of noble humor. The doctor ordered an ice pack placed on his heart and Chekhov said, "You don't put an ice pack on an empty heart." Then the doctor insisted that he drink a glass of champagne. Chekhov's last words were, "It's a long time since I've had any champagne." They are perhaps the pleasantest last words ever spoken.

Chekhov's body, on its way home to Russia, traveled in a railroad coach marked "Fresh Oysters." This was an ending so pat-ironic, so ham, that while a lesser writer might have used it for the ending of "A Tiresome Tale," no writer as good as Chekhov would have touched it, and biographers should not be too sure that it would have amused him.

But Moscow paid him great honor: his death was a time of national mourning. He was more beloved than he ever knew. Years before, Tolstoy had said, "What a beautiful, magnificent man. He is simply wonderful."

To ALEXEI SUVORIN

April 1, 1897, Moscow

The doctors diagnosed tuberculosis in the upper part of the lungs and have prescribed a change in my way of life. I can grasp the first but not the second, which is just about impossible. I have been definitely ordered into the country, but certainly, continual living in the country presupposes continual trouble with peasants, animals, natural elements of various kinds, and it is as hard to protect yourself from fuss and trouble in rural areas as it is from burns in hell. Still, I shall try to change my life to the fullest possible extent and have already sent word through Masha that I am giving up medical practice. For me this will be both a relief and a severe deprivation. I am dropping official duties, am buying a dressing gown, will warm my bones in the sun and eat a lot. The doctors have ordered me to eat about six times a day and are in a state of indignation because I eat very little. I have been forbidden to do much talking, to swim and so forth and so on.

Except for my lungs, all my organs were found healthy. . . . Hitherto it seemed to me I drank exactly as much as would do me no harm; the latest checkup shows I drank less than I had a right to. What a pity!

The author of "Ward No. 6" has been moved from Ward 16 to 14. It is spacious here, with two windows, the lighting reminds one of a Potapenko play, and the room has three tables. I am not losing much blood. After the evening Tolstoy was here (we had a long talk), coughed a lot of blood at four in the morning.

Melikhovo is a healthy place; it happens to be in a water-shed and stands high, so fevers and diphtheria never visit it. At a consultation a decision was taken for me not to try a new spot, but to continue living in Melikhovo, except that the place would have to be made more comfortable. When I get tired of the house, I'll go next door to the cottage I rented for the use of my brothers, in case they should decide to visit.

People come and go continually, bring flowers, candies, good things to eat. In a word, bliss. . . .

I am not on my back, but am writing this sitting up, though the minute I'm through, I'll be back on my loge.

Yours,

A. Chekhov

Please write, I implore you.

To ALEXANDER CHEKHOV

April 2, 1897, Moscow

This is the story. Since 1884 I have been spitting blood every spring. That time when you accused me of being blessed by the Most Holy Synod, and didn't believe my denial, I was so upset that at a time when Mr. Suvorin was present I lost a lot of blood and was put into a clinic. My case was diagnosed as tuberculosis in the upper part of the lungs, i.e., I acquired the right, if I wished, to consider myself an invalid. My temperature is normal, I don't have night sweats or any weakness, but I dream of the saints, my future looks pretty dim and although the lung condition is not so very advanced, a will must be drawn up, without delay, so that you won't be able to grab all my property. I'm being dismissed from the clinic on Wednesday of Holy Week, will proceed to Melikhovo and then we'll see what happens next. I have been ordered to keep myself well nourished, so now it's me that has to be fed, not Papa and Mama. Nobody at home knows of my illness, so when you write don't shoot your mouth off with the malice peculiar to you. . . .

My kindest regards to your wife and children—with all my heart, of course.

Keep well.

Your benefactor,

A. Chekhov

To ALEXANDER ERTEL

April 17, 1897, Melikhovo

My dear friend Alexander Ivanovich,

I am home now. Just before the holidays I spent two weeks in Ostroumov's clinic, bleeding, and the doctor diagnosed tuberculosis of the upper part of the lungs. I feel fine all over, nothing aches, nothing disturbs me inwardly, but the doctors have forbidden me vinum, movement, talk, have ordered me to eat a lot, have forbidden me to practice medicine—and I am at loose ends, as it were.

I haven't heard a thing about a people's theatre. At the congress it was mentioned offhand and with no enthusiasm, and the group that had undertaken to write a charter and get work under way has evidently cooled off somewhat. This is probably due to the presence of spring. . . .

There is nothing new. There is a lull in literature. In the editorial offices people drink tea and cheap wine without relish, all as a result, evidently, of nothing to do. Tolstoy is writing a pamphlet on art. He visited me at the clinic and said he had tossed aside his novel "Resurrection" because he didn't like it, writes only on art and has read sixty books about it. His ideas on the subject are not new; all the wise old men have repeated them throughout the centuries in various keys. Old men have always been prone to see the end of the world, and assert that morality has fallen to its nec plus ultra, that art has been debased and is out at the elbows, that people have become weak and so on and so forth. Leo Nikolayevich's pamphlet would like to convince the world that art has now entered its final phase and is in a blind alley from which it cannot get out except by going backward.

I am not doing anything, am feeding the sparrows with hemp seeds and prune the roses, one a day. The flowers bloom luxuriantly afterward. I am not doing any farming.

Keep well, dear Alexander Ivanovich, thanks for your letter and friendly sympathy. Write me because of the infirmities of my flesh, and don't find too great fault with my irregularity in corresponding. From now on I will try to answer your letters right after reading them.

I cordially press your hand.

Yours,
A. Chekhov

To VASILI SOBOLEVSKI

August 19, 1897, Melikhovo

Dear Vasili Mikhailovich,

I have been looking for your address so as to get in touch with you and find out whether you would be going to Nice— and if you were, whether you couldn't take me along. From your yesterday's letter I learned you were in Biarritz. Excellent, I will go to Biarritz too. I can't get away from home before the end of August (around the twenty-sixth or twenty-seventh, I guess); furthermore, there is no need to rush, as the weather here is warm and dry. In the meantime please be so good as to let me know what is the best train for me to take out of Moscow, whether to Berlin or Vienna, what train out of Paris, what hotel you stopped at. I am asking you for this sort of detailed itinerary because this is my first time in Biarritz and I am somewhat shy. You know I talk all languages except the foreign ones; when I speak French or German abroad, the conductors usually laugh; and for me, transferring from one station to another in Paris is just like playing blind man's buff.

I count upon staying in Biarritz for a month, then will be off for some other warm spot.

So long! In anticipation of your reply let me shake your hand and wish you all the best.

Your
A. Chekhov

To LYDIA AVILOVA

October 6, 1897, Nice

. . . You deplore the fact that my characters are gloomy. Alas, it isn't my fault! This happens involuntarily, and when I write I don't think I am lugubrious; at any rate, I am always in a good mood while I work. It has been pointed out that sombre, melancholy people always write gaily, while the works of cheerful souls are always depressing. And I am a joyous person; at least I have lived the first thirty years of my life at my ease, as they say.

My health is tolerable in the morning and excellent at night. I am not doing anything, don't write and don't feel like writing. I have become frightfully lazy.

Keep well and happy. I press your hand.

Your
A. Chekhov

I shall probably remain abroad all winter.

To MARIA CHEKHOVA

October 27, 1897, Nice

Dear Masha,

. . . The weather is marvelous; so incredibly bright and warm. It is summer, really.

Here is a nice little treat for you: a French lesson. The accepted form of address is "Monsieur Antoine Tchekhoff" and not "à M-r Ant. Tchekhoff." You must write "recommandée" and not "recommendée." The French language is a very polite and subtle one and not a single sentence, even in conversation with servants, policemen or cab drivers lacks its monsieur, madame, or "I beg you" and "be so kind." It is not permissible to say, "Give me some water," you say rather, "Be so kind as to give me some water," or, "Give me some water, I beg of you." But this phrase, i.e., "I beg of you," should not be "Je vous en prie" (je vuzan pree), as they say in Russia, but unfailingly "S'il vous plaît" (if it please you), or, for variety, "ayez la bonté de donner" (have the goodness to give), "veuillez donner" (vuyay) —would you wish to give.

If someone in a shop says "Je vous en prie," you can tell he is a Russian. The Russians pronounce the word "les gens" in the sense of "servants" like *jans*, but this is not correct, one should say, "Jon." The word "oui" must be pronounced not "voóee" as we say it, but "ooee," so that you can hear the ee. In wishing someone a pleasant journey the Russians say, "bon voyage—bun vooayash," giving a distinct sound to sh, while it should be pronounced voayazh-zh . . . Voisinage . . . vooazinazh-zh . . . and not vooazhinash. Also "treize" (13) and "quatorze" (14) should be pronounced not tress and katorss, the way Adelaide says it, but trezzzz . . katorzzz—so that you get the z sound at the end of the word. The word "sens"—feeling, is pronounced sanss, the word "soit" in the sense of "so be it"— sooatt. The word "ailleurs"—elsewhere—and "d'ailleurs"— besides—are pronounced ayor and dayor, in which the eu sound approximates our ë.

Well, that will be enough for the first time. There is nothing new, my health is not bad. What's with Lika? Does she want to go to Milan?

Keep well. Kindest regards to all.

Yes, one more observation: Russians are recognized here by their frequent use of "donc" and "déjà." It sounds bad, trite. They also say "ce n'est pas vrai"—"that is not true." But for a Frenchman such an expression is too coarse, not an expression of doubt or incredulity, as it is with us, but opprobrious. If you wish to express doubt or incredulity you must say, "C'est impossible, monsieur."

I am doing a little writing.

Did Mama get the cards? If you wish me to bring or send any cosmetics or artists' supplies when the opportunity presents, write me what you need. I can bring in a whole box full of paints duty free and here all of this material is first-rate and not expensive.

Agréez l'assurance de ma parfaite considération.

Antoine Tchekhoff

To ANNA SUVORINA

November 10, 1897, Nice

Dear Anna Ivanovna,

Thank you very much for the letter, which I am answering immediately upon reading. You ask about my health. I feel extremely fit, outwardly (I believe) I am completely well, my misfortune is that I cough blood. I don't cough it in any quantity, but it persists for a long time and my last attack, which is still upon me, began about three weeks ago. Because of it I must subject myself to various deprivations; I don't leave the house after three in the afternoon, don't drink, don't eat anything hot, don't walk fast, am never anywhere except on the street, in short, I am not living but vegetating. This naturally annoys me and puts me in a bad temper; and it seems to me that at dinner the Russians here speak nonsense and banalities, and I have to control myself not to answer impertinently.

But for the Lord's sake, don't tell anyone about the coughing, this is between ourselves. I write home that I am entirely well; declaring anything to the contrary would not make sense, since I do feel fine—and if they find out at home about my losing blood, there will be loud outcries.

Now you want to know about that little affair of mine. In

Biarritz I picked up a young lady of nineteen, named Margot, to teach me French; when we bade each other farewell she said she would be in Nice without fail. She probably is here, but I just cannot find her and so—I am not speaking French.

The weather here is heavenly. It is hot, calm, charming. The musical competitions are under way. Bands march along the streets, which are full of excitement, dancing and laughter. I look at all this and think to myself how silly I was not to have lived abroad more. I now believe, if I remain alive, I will no longer spend winters in Moscow, no matter what the inducements. The minute October comes around, out I go from Russia. I am not inspired by the natural beauty hereabouts, which I find alien, but I passionately love warmth, and I love culture. . . . And culture here oozes out of every shop window, every willow basket; every dog has the odor of civilization.

. . . Don't be so proud and majestic, write me as often as you can. I need letters. I kiss your hand a hundred hundred times, wish you happiness and again thank you.

Yours heart and soul,

A. Chekhov

To ALEXEI SUVORIN

January 4, 1898, Nice

This is my program: the end of January (old style) or, more likely, the beginning of February, I am going to Algeria, Tunis, etc., then return to Nice, where I will expect you (you wrote you were coming to Nice), then after a stay here we will go to Paris together, if you like, whence on the "lightning" to Russia in time to usher in Easter. Your last letter arrived here unsealed.

I am very rarely in Monte Carlo, say once in three or four weeks. The first days, when Sobolevski and Nemirovich were here, I played a very moderate game (rouge et noir) and would return home occasionally with fifty or a hundred francs, but then I had to give it up, as it exhausts me—physically.

The Dreyfus affair has seethed and died down, but hasn't yet got back onto the right track. Zola is a noble spirit and I (a member of the syndicate and in the pay of Jews to the extent of a hundred francs) am in raptures over this outburst. France is a wonderful country, and its writers are wonderful. . . .

We have with us Hirshman, the Kharkov oculist, the well-known philanthropist and friend of Koni, a saintly man who is on a visit to his tuberculous son. I have been seeing him and talking with him, but his wife is a nuisance, a fussy dim-witted woman, as tedious as forty thousand wives. There is a Russian woman artist here who draws me in caricature about ten or fifteen times a day.

Judging from the extract published in "New Times," Leo Tolstoy's article on art doesn't sound interesting. It is all old stuff. Saying of art that it has grown decrepit, drifted into a blind alley, that it isn't what it ought to be, and so forth and so on, is the same as saying that the desire to eat and drink has grown obsolete, seen its day and isn't what it ought to be. Of course hunger is an old story, and in our desire to eat we have entered a blind alley, but still we have to do it and we will keep on eating, whatever the philosophers and angry old men may go to the trouble of saying.

Keep well.

Yours,

A. Chekhov

To ALEXEI SUVORIN

February 6, 1898, Nice

A few days ago I saw a striking announcement on the first page of "New Times" on the forthcoming issue of "Cosmopolis," which will contain my story, "On A Visit." To begin with, my story isn't called "On A Visit" but "Visiting with Friends." In the second place, this sort of publicity goes against the grain; let alone the fact that the story itself is far from unusual, being one of those things you grind out one per day.

You write you are provoked with Zola, while here the general feeling is as though a new, better Zola had come into being. In this trial of his he has cleaned off all his external grease spots with turpentine, as it were, and now gleams before the French in his true brilliance. He has a purity and moral elevation which no one had suspected. Just trace the whole scandal from the very beginning. The degradation of Dreyfus, whether just or otherwise, had a depressing, dismal effect on everyone (among others on you, too, as I recall). At the time of his sentencing Dreyfus conducted himself like an honorable, well-disciplined officer, while others present, the journalists, for instance, yelled at him, "Shut up, you Judas!" i.e., behaved scandalously. Everybody came away dissatisfied and left the courtroom with a troubled conscience. Particularly dissatisfied was Dreyfus' defense attorney, Démange, an honest man, who even during the preliminary hearing had felt something was wrong behind the scenes; then there were the experts, who, to convince themselves that they were not mistaken, spoke only of Dreyfus, of his guilt, and kept roaming through Paris, roaming. . . . Of the experts, one turned out to be crazy, the author of a grotesque, absurd scheme, two were eccentrics. The logic of the situation was such that one was bound to question the intelligence bureau of the War Ministry, that military consistory devoted to spy hunting and reading other people's letters; then people started saying that Sandher, the bureau chief, was afflicted with progressive paralysis; Paty de Clam turned out to be almost a counterpart of the Berliner, Tausch; and Picquart resigned, suddenly and mysteriously. A regular series of gross errors of justice came to light, as though purposely arranged. People became convinced, little by little, that Dreyfus had really been condemned on the basis of a secret document which had not been shown either to the defendant or to his attorney— and law-abiding people looked upon this as a basic breach of justice; had that letter been written even by the sun itself, not to speak of Wilhelm, it still should have been shown to Démange. Everyone had wild guesses as to the contents of this letter and cock-and-bull stories were current. Dreyfus was an officer, and so the military expected the worst; Dreyfus was a Jew—the Jews expected the worst. . . . All the talk was of militarism, of the yids. . . . Such profoundly distrusted people as Drumont held their heads high; an evil plant began growing in the soil of anti-Semitism, in a soil stinking of the slaughter-house. When something does not go well with us, we look for reasons outside of us and have no trouble finding them: "It's the French who are ruining us, the yids, Wilhelm. . . . Capital, bogeymen, Masons, the syndicate, the Jesuits—these are all spectres, but how they do assuage our uneasy minds! These things are a bad sign, of course. Once the French started talking about yids, or the syndicate, it was an indication that they felt all was not well, that some worm was gnawing underneath, that they needed such spectres to appease their troubled consciences. Then this Esterhazy, a brawler out of Turgenev, an insolent, doubtful character, a man despised by his comrades, the striking similarity of his handwriting with that of the document, the letters of the Uhlan, the threats he chose not to carry out for reasons of his own, finally the strange decision, made in absolute secrecy, that the document was written in Esterhazy's handwriting but not by his hand. . . . The gases were accumulating, and people began feeling acute tension, an oppressive closeness in the air. The scuffle in the court was a pure manifestation of nerves, simply a hysterical consequence of this tension. Zola's letter and his trial are also aspects of this same situation. What would you want? It is for the best people, always ahead of their nations, to be the first to sound the alarm—and this is just what happened. First to speak up was Scherer-Koestner, whom the French, knowing him, call (in Kovalevski's[1] words) a "Caucasian dagger"—he is so shiningly clean and flawless. Zola was the second. And now he is on trial.

[1] Kovalevski was a historian, sociologist and jurist. Because of his liberal views he lost his post as professor at Moscow University and emigrated to Paris, where he taught and lectured.

Yes, Zola is not Voltaire, nor are any of us Voltaires, but life sometimes produces such a chain of circumstances that it is very much out of place to reproach us for not being Voltaires. Think of Korolenko, who defended the Multan pagans and saved them from penal servitude. Nor was Doctor Haas a Voltaire, yet his wonderful life ran along to a good end.

I am acquainted with the affair from the stenographic report and it certainly is not what you read in the newspapers. I can see Zola plain. The important point is that he is sincere, i.e., he builds his judgments solely on what he sees, and not on spectres, as others do. Sincere people can certainly make mistakes—no doubt about that—but such mistakes cause less harm than well-advised insincerity, prejudices or political considerations. Suppose Dreyfus is guilty: Zola is right anyway, because it is the writer's business not to accuse and not to persecute, but to champion the guilty, once they are condemned and suffer punishment. People will say, what about politics and the interests of the government? But great writers and artists should engage in politics only to the extent necessary to defend themselves against politics. Even without political considerations there are plenty of accusers, prosecutors and policemen, and in any case the role of Paul suits them better than that of Saul. And no matter what the verdict may be, Zola nonethelesss will experience a vibrant joy after the trial is over, his old age will be a good old age and when he dies it will be with a serene or at any rate eased conscience.

The French people have sickened and they grasp at every word of comfort and at every well-intended reproach coming from without; that is why Björnstern's letter was so popular here, along with our Zakrevski's article (which people read in the "News"), and why the abuse of Zola was so obnoxious, i.e., the stuff the yellow press, which the French despise, dishes up for them every day. No matter how neurotic Zola may be, in court he still represents French common sense, and so the French love him and are proud of him, although they applaud the generals who, simple-minded as they are, frighten them first with the honor of the army and then with the threat of war.

See what a long letter this is. It is spring here and the mood is that of a Little Russian Easter: warmth, sunshine, the peal of bells, memories of the past. Do come! By the way, Duse will be playing here. . . .

Yours,
A. Chekhov

To OLGA HERMANOVNA CHEKHOVA

February 22, 1898, Nice

My dear daughter and protégée,

I congratulate you on the addition to the family and hope your daughter will be beautiful, clever, interesting, and to cap it all will marry a good man, if possible, a tender and patient one, who won't jump out of a window because of his mother-in-law. I had received word of this happy event in the family some time ago and heartily shared your joy, but haven't offered my congratulations until now because I haven't been up to it, I myself felt I had a young one in my belly, I've been having such acute pain. The dentist broke a tooth, took three sessions to extract it and probably caused an infection, as an infectious periostitis set in in the upper jaw, my countenance became distorted, and I crawled up the walls with the pain. I had a fever like typhus. The day before yesterday I had an operation and now the pain has eased. So saying, everything below concerns your husband. . . .

. . . You ask my opinion regarding Zola and his trial. I reckon first of all with the obvious facts: on Zola's side is the entire European intelligentsia and opposed to him is everything that is vile and of doubtful character. This is the way things are: just suppose a university administration expelled one student instead of another in error, you started protesting and people shouted at you, "You are insulting knowledge!" although the university administration and knowledge have only one thing in common, that both the administering officials and the professors wear blue frock coats; then you swear, assure, accuse, and people shout, "Proofs!"

"See here," you say, "let's go into the administrative office and have a look into its books."

"That's not allowed! That's an administrative secret! . . ."

Now, this is the wild-goose chase going on here. The psychology of the French government is transparent. Like a decent woman who has deceived her husband once, commits a number of gross mistakes, falls prey to insolent blackmail and finally kills herself—and all in order to conceal her initial fall from grace—so the French government, too, will stop at nothing, but shuts its eyes and reels to left and right, just to avoid acknowledging its mistake.

"New Times" is conducting a ridiculous campaign; on the other hand the majority of Russian papers, even though they are not for Zola, are against his persecution. The Court of Cassation will settle nothing, even with a favorable outcome. The question will resolve itself, in some casual fashion, as a result of the explosion of the steams now storing up inside of French heads. Everything will turn out all right.

There is nothing new. Everything is running along smoothly, if you don't count the periostitis. My countenance is still askew. Keep well. If Mama is still with you, give her my regards. I have sent home a lot of perfumed soap. If you were in Melikhovo you would get a piece.

Your papa,
A. Chekhov

To ALEXANDER CHEKHOV

February 23, 1898, Nice

Brother!!

. . . "New Times" behaved just abominably in the Zola affair. The old man and I exchanged letters on the subject (in an extremely moderate tone, though) and now both of us have shut up. I don't want to write to him or get his letters, wherein he justifies his paper's tactlessness by saying he loves the military—I really don't, as I have been sick and tired of the whole business for a long time. I am fond of the military, too, but if I owned a paper, I would not allow those cactuses to make a supplementary printing of a novel[1] of Zola's *without paying royalties* and then pour filth over the author—and what for?—for having qualities that not a single one of those cactuses could ever recognize—a noble impulse and purity of spirit. At any rate, abusing Zola when he is on trial is unworthy of literature.

I got your portrait and have presented it to a little French girl with this inscription: . . . She will think you are discussing one of your articles on the woman question.

Don't be bashful about writing. Greetings to Natalia Alexandrovna and the children.

L'homme des lettres,
A. Tchekhoff

To ALEXANDER CHEKHOV

August 14, 1898, Melikhovo

Your first-born, Nikolai, arrived the day before yesterday. He will live in Melikhovo until his studies in Moscow get under way. We have just had the following conversation:

I. I am going to write your father now. What shall I tell him about you?

He. Tell him I am sitting here eating apples and that's all.

He has been telling us about Valdaika and the estate it seems you have bought or intend to buy. If this is so, it's a good idea.

When you walk past the theatre office, go in and tell the young lady there that authors hafta eat. She owes me some money and you have every right to demand it. What do you

[1] Supplements were the extra section of newspapers or magazines given to readers as premiums for subscriptions. *New Times* was running Zola's novel *Paris* in its supplements without paying any royalties.

hear about Suvorin? Where is he? We are having hot weather and are melting away pleasantly. A general has taken up residence in the country home next door, which is very flattering to us. My greetings to Dr. Oldrogge, and write me in greater detail of your alcoholic undertakings. Regards to your pious family. In bad weather keep your pants dry and heed your elders.

Your benefactor,
Antonio

To ALEXEI SUVORIN

October 8, 1898, Yalta

You write that the public should not be pampered; so be it, but still there is no need to sell my books for more money than Potapenko's and Korolenko's. Here in Yalta my books are sold in large numbers and I have been told in the bookshops that the buying public is often ill-disposed toward me. I am in fear that the ladies I meet on the streets may thrash me with their parasols. . . .

The Crimean seashore is beautiful and comfortable and I prefer it to the Riviera, but it has one serious drawback—there is no culture. In the matter of civilization Yalta has even progressed beyond Nice with our splendid sewage system, but the outskirts are pure Asia.

I read a notice on Nemirovich's and Stanislavski's theatre and on their production of "Fyodor Ioannovich"[1] in "New Times" and I couldn't understand what the review was driving at. You had liked the production so much and it had been so cordially received that only some deep misunderstanding could have led to the writing of such a notice, something I know nothing about. What happened?

Before my departure, I may say in passing, I attended a rehearsal of "Fyodor Ioannovich." Its tone of culture had an

---

[1] *Czar Fyodor Ioannovich*—well-known play by Count Alexei K. Tolstoy (1817-1875). The role of Fyodor was played by the to-be-famous Ivan Moskvin.

agreeable effect on me and the performance was a truly artistic one, although no particularly dazzling talents were in evidence. In my opinion Irina[2] was admirable. Her voice, her nobility, her quality of warmth were so superb that I felt choked with emotion. Fyodor seemed to me not so good. . . . But Irina was best of all. If I had remained in Moscow I would have fallen in love with this Irina. . . .

Keep well and let me wish you all the best—I send my respects. I am on my way to the bath house.

Yours,
A. Chekhov

To VLADIMIR NEMIROVICH-DANCHENKO

October 21, 1898, Yalta

My dear Vladimir Ivanovich,

I am in Yalta and will continue here for some time to come. The trees and grass are wearing their summer green, it is warm, bright, calm, dry, and today, for example, it is not warm, but downright hot. I like it very much and may decide to settle here for good.

Your telegram affected me profoundly. My warm thanks to you, Konstantin Semyonovich and the company for remembering me. Please don't forget me and write, even though it isn't often. You are now a very busy person, and a director, but still do write now and then to this idle chap. Give me all the details, how the company reacted to the success of the first performances, how "The Sea Gull" is going, what changes have been made in the assignment of parts and so on and so forth. Judging by the newspapers, the start was brilliant—and I am very, very happy, happier than you can imagine. Your success is merely additional proof that both the public and the actors

2 Irina—this part was played by Olga Knipper. Knipper married Chekhov in 1901.

need a cultured theatre. But why is there no mention of Irina—
Knipper? Don't tell me some confusion has arisen? I didn't
like your Fyodor, but Irina seemed extraordinary; now people
talk more of Fyodor than they do of Irina.

I have become involved in the life of the community and
have been appointed a member of the board of trustees of the
girls' school. And now I walk along the school steps very sedately
and all the young girl students in their white caps drop me
curtsies. . . .

I am waiting for "Antigone"[1] and waiting because you promised to send a copy. I need it badly.

I am expecting my sister, who is coming here, according to
the wire she sent. We are going to decide what to do now. Now
that Father is dead my mother will scarcely wish to live alone
in the country. We'll have to think up something else for her.

My respects and regards to Ekaterina Nikolayevna, Roxanova
and Knipper, and my humble salutations to Vishnevski. I recall
them all with great pleasure.

Keep well and happy. Please write. A cordial handshake.

Yours,

A. Chekhov

To LYDIA AVILOVA

October 21, 1898, Yalta

I read your letter and could only throw up my hands in
despair. If I wished you happiness and good health in my last
letter it was not because I desired to discontinue our correspondence or, Heaven help us, avoid you, but simply because
I really wished and now wish you happiness and health. That
should be plain. And if you read things in my letters that are
not there, it is probably because I don't know how to express
myself. . . .

---

[1] Sophocles' tragedy was in rehearsal at the Moscow Art Theatre.

I am now in Yalta, will stay on for some time to come, even perhaps for the entire winter. The weather is marvelous, absolutely summerlike. . . . Perhaps I shall even make my home in Yalta. My father died this month and with his death the country place where I resided has lost all its delight for me; my mother and sister do not wish to live there either and now I must begin a new life. And since I am forbidden to spend my winters in the north, it behooves me to weave myself a new nest, in the south probably. My father died unexpectedly, after a serious operation—and it had a depressing effect on me and my whole family; I cannot pull myself together. . . .

At any rate, don't be angry with me and forgive me if in my last letters there was really anything stiff or disagreeable. I did not mean to cause you distress and if my letters don't please you, it is not intentional on my part, quite the contrary.

I cordially clasp your hand and wish you all the best. My address is Yalta. Nothing else is necessary. Just Yalta.

Yours,

A. Chekhov

To MIKHAIL CHEKHOV

October 26, 1898, Yalta

Dear Michel,

I had hardly mailed my postcard when I got yours. My heart ached when I found out what you had gone through at Father's funeral. I learned of Father's death from Sinani only on the evening of the thirteenth, as for some reason nobody had telegraphed me and if I hadn't dropped into Sinani's shop quite by accident I would have remained in the dark a long time.

I am buying a plot of ground in Yalta and intend building, so as to have a place to spend the winters. The prospect of a nomadic life with its hotel rooms, doormen, hit-or-miss cookery and so on alarms me. Mother could spend the winters with me. Yalta has no winter; here it is the end of October and roses and other flowers are blooming with all their might, the trees are green and the weather is mild. There is lots of water. The house by itself will take care of all my needs, without outbuildings, and everything under one roof.

The basement provides space for coal, wood, porter's quarters and everything. Hens lay all the year round and don't need special coops, as an enclosure is enough. The bakery and market are nearby. So life will be warm and very convenient for Mother. Incidentally, people pick various types of mushrooms all autumn in the outlying woods—and our mother would find this diverting. I am not going to undertake the building operations by myself but will let the architect take care of everything. By April the house will be ready. It is a sizeable plot for the city, with enough ground for orchard, flower bed and vegetable garden. Next year Yalta is to have a railway. . . .

As for your insistence on marriage—how can I explain it to you? Getting married is interesting only when one is in love; marrying a girl simply because she is attractive is like buying something you don't need just because it is nice. The most important thing that holds family life together is love, sexual attraction, "and they two shall be one flesh"—all the rest is dreary and unreliable, no matter how cleverly we may have calculated the factors. Accordingly it is not a question of an attractive girl but of a dearly loved one; so you see, delaying the matter doesn't make any difference. . . .

My "Uncle Vanya" is playing everywhere in the provinces with universal success. So you never can tell where you are going to find something good or where you may lose it. I certainly was not counting on that play. Keep well and write.

Yours,
A. Chekhov

It was a very good idea to have Father buried in Novodevichi Monastery. I wanted to telegraph about burying him there but thought I was too late; you anticipated my wishes.

To MAXIM GORKI

December 3, 1898, Yalta

Dear Alexei Maximovich,

Your last letter afforded me great pleasure. Thank you with all my heart. "Uncle Vanya" was written long ago, a very long time ago; I have never seen it on the stage. During these past few years it has been presented often on provincial stages—perhaps because a collection of my plays has been published. On the whole I react coolly toward my plays, have long ago lost touch with the theatre and don't feel like writing for it any more.

You ask for my opinion of your stories. My opinion? You have undoubted talent, truly a genuine, immense talent. In your story "On the Steppe," for example, your talent is shown as extraordinarily powerful, and I even experienced a moment of envy that it was not I who had written it. You are an artist and a brilliant man. You feel things magnificently; you are plastic, i.e., when you depict a thing, you see it and touch it with your hands. That is true art. There you have my opinion, and I am very glad that I can come out with it. I repeat, I am very glad, and if we could meet and chat for an hour or two, you would be convinced how highly I value you and what hope I have in your gifts.

Now shall I speak of your defects? This is not so easy, though. Referring to shortcomings in the way of talent is like talking of the defects of a fine tree in an orchard; in the main it is certainly not a question of the tree itself but of the tastes of those who look at it. Isn't that so?

I will begin by pointing out that in my opinion you have no restraint. You are like a spectator in a theatre who expresses his rapture so unrestrainedly that he prevents himself and others from hearing. This lack of restraint is especially evident in your descriptions of nature, which break up the continuity of your dialogues; one would like these descriptions to be more compact and concise, just two or three lines or so The frequent references to voluptuousness, whispering, velvet softness and so on lend a certain rhetorical quality and monotony to these descriptions, and they dampen one's enthusiasm and almost fatigue the reader. This lack of restraint is also evident in your characterizations of women ("Malva," "On the Rafts") and in love scenes. The effect you create is not of expansiveness nor of a broad sweep of your brush, but merely lack of restraint. Then, you make frequent use of words entirely unsuited to your kind of story. Accompaniment, disk, harmony—these words stand in the way of the narrative. You speak often of waves. There is a strained, circumspect effect in your portrayals of people of culture; it is not because you haven't observed them closely enough, for you do know them; it is that you don't exactly know how to tackle them.

How old are you? I don't know you or where you come from or who you are, but it seems to me that you should quit Nizhni while you are still young and really live for two or three years, lose yourself, so to speak, among literature and literary people; it would not be in order to learn to crow like the rest of our cocks or to acquire even more sharpness, but rather to plunge head over heels into literature and fall in love with it; in addition, the provinces cause one to age early. Korolenko, Potapenko, Mamin and Ertel are all excellent people; at the outset, perhaps, their company may seem somewhat dull, but after a year or two you will get used to them and esteem them according to their merits; their society will pay you back with interest for the unpleasantness and inconvenience of life in the capital.

I am hurrying to the post office. Keep well and happy, and let me clasp your hand cordially. I thank you again for your letter.

Yours,

A. Chekhov

To MAXIM GORKI

January 3, 1899, Yalta

My dear Alexei Maximovich,

I am answering both your letters right away. To begin with, I wish you a Happy New Year with all my heart and offer a friendly wish for your happiness, old or new—just as you would have it.

Apparently you misunderstood me somewhat. I didn't refer to crudity of style, but merely to the incongruity of foreign, not truly Russian or rarely used words. In other authors words like "fatalistically," for instance, pass unnoticed, but your things are musical and well proportioned, so that every rough spot stands out like a sore thumb. Of course we are here concerned with a matter of taste and perhaps I am only expressing the excessive fastidiousness or conservatism of a man who has long been rooted in definite habits. . . .

Are you self-taught? In your stories you are the true artist, a real man of culture. Least of all is coarseness a quality of yours, you are understanding and you feel things subtly and sensitively. Your best works are "On the Steppe" and "On the Rafts"—did I write you so? These are superb pieces, models of their kind, obviously by an artist who has gone through a very good school. I do not think I am mistaken. The only defect is the lack of restraint, of grace. When a person expends the least possible quantity of movement on a certain act, that is grace. There is a feeling of excess, though, in your outlay of words.

The descriptions of nature are artistic; you are a genuine landscapist. Except that the frequent use of the device of personification (anthromorphism) when you have the sea breathe, the heavens gaze down, the steppe caress, nature whisper, speak or mourn, etc.—such expressions render your descriptions somewhat monotonous, occasionally oversweet and sometimes indistinct; picturesque and expressive descriptions of nature are attained only through simplicity, by the use of such plain phrases as "the sun came out," "it grew dark," "it rained," etc. This simplicity is inherent in you to a degree rarely found among any of our writers.

I did not like the first number of the newly revived "Life" magazine. There seems to be a lack of seriousness in everything about it. . . . The tone of your "Little Cyril" is good, but the characterization of the local government administrator spoils the general effect. Never portray these people. There is nothing easier than depicting officialdom in its unattractive aspects; the reader loves this sort of thing, but he is the most disagreeable and banal type of reader. . . . But I happen to live in the country, am personally acquainted with all these people in my own and neighboring districts, have known them a long time and find that their characters and the things they do are altogether untypical, usually of no interest, and so I think I may be right.

Now as to vagabondage. It is a life that interests and entices one, but with the years a kind of heaviness sets in and one gets glued to a place. The literary profession itself draws one into its clutches. Time passes quickly with failures and disappointments, one fails to see life whole and the past, with its freedom, no longer seems to be mine, but someone else's.

The mail has arrived and I must read my letters and papers. Keep well and happy. Thank you for the letters, thank you for getting so easily into the swing of our correspondence.

Yours,

A. Chekhov

To ALEXEI SUVORIN

January 17, 1899, Yalta

. . . I have read Leo Tolstoy's son's story "The Folly of the Mir." The story construction is poor, and a straight article would have been more effective, but the idea is treated correctly and passionately. I myself am opposed to the commune. A commune makes sense when you have to deal with external enemies who are always raiding your lands, or with wild beasts, but today it is merely a crowd bound together artificially, like a gang of convicts. They say Russia is an agricultural country. That is so, but the commune has nothing to do with it, certainly not at the present time. The commune lives by farming, but once farming starts changing into scientific culture of the soil, the commune splits at all its seams, as the commune and scientific culture are incompatible ideas. I may add incidentally that the drunkenness and profound ignorance so widespread among our people are sins of the commune. . . .

The weather in Yalta is like summer. I leave the house evenings and go out on cold, rainy days—so as to get myself used to severe weather and be ready to spend next winter in Moscow and St. Petersburg. I'm weary of hanging around like this.

I am reading proof on the first volume, and doing over many of the stories completely. The volume will contain more than seventy stories in all. "Motley Stories" will make up the second volume, "In the Twilight" the third, etc. Except that here and there I have to add stories to make up the number of pages required by the censor.

Where will you be this spring? This summer? I would love to run away to Paris and most likely will do so. . . .

Keep well and happy.

Yours,
A. Chekhov

To VLADIMIR NEMIROVICH-DANCHENKO

January 29, 1899, Yalta

Dear Vladimir Nikolayevich,

. . . Here is what Mme. Just writes: " 'The Seagull' is being performed even better and more smoothly than it was at its second performance, although Stanislavski plays Trigorin as a novelist who is much too weak physically and morally, and the

Seagull herself (j'en conviens) might look a bit handsomer in the last act. But on the other hand Arkadina, Treplev, Masha, Sorin, the teacher (those wide trousers of his are a treat in themselves) and the steward—are magnificent, absolutely living people." Here you have a specimen of the reviews I have been receiving.

I think a radical change is taking place in my life; I have been negotiating with Marx and it seems the negotiations have been concluded and the sensation I feel is akin to being finally granted a divorce by the Most Holy Synod, after a long wait. No longer will I have any business with printing plants! I won't have to think of formats, prices, or book titles! . . .

How nice it would be for everybody in the cast of "The Seagull" to be photographed in their costumes and grease paint and the picture sent to me!

I am bored here. And so, keep well and happy.

Your

A. Chekhov

To ALEXEI SUVORIN

February 6, 1899, Yalta

Let me start by making a slight correction. I wired you just as soon as I was informed that Marx wanted to buy my works. And I wired Sergeyenko to get in touch with you. The offer wasn't any secret, nor was there any delay in getting in touch with you and, I assure you, the phrase you used in speaking to Sergeyenko and which you repeated in your last letter, "Chekhov didn't want to sell to me," is based, expressing myself in the language of classroom ladies, solely on a paradox of your own.
. . .

In the copy of the contract forwarded to me, a great number of all sorts of unnecessary items are set forth, but not a word said about royalties from the plays. I raised a rumpus and am now awaiting a reply. . . . The plays are the important thing, all the rest is not worth bothering about—I hold firmly to this old truth and consider the royalties from the plays my mainstay.

Out of sheer boredom I am reading "The Book of My Life" by Bishop Porphiri. Here is a passage on the subject of war: "Standing armies in peacetime are in essence a swarm of locusts devouring the people's bread, leaving behind a stench in society; as for their function in time of war they are artificial military machines which, as they increase and develop, sound a farewell to freedom, security and glory of the people! . . . They are lawless defenders of unjust and prejudicial laws, privilege and tyranny. . . ."

This was written back in the forties.

Please send me a calendar as a token of our thirteen-year-old association It is a bore not knowing when people's birthdays are. We'll each have to think up a fitting celebration for the occasion and then talk it over. . . .

I have just been given your second letter about Marx and the sale. I believe the sale will prove profitable if I don't live long, less than five or ten years; and unprofitable if I live longer.

Write me whether it is true that you are coming to Yalta.

Keep well and happy.

> Your
> A. Chekhov

To ALEXANDER CHEKHOV[1]

> *February 16, 1899, Yalta*

1. You don't have to rummage around for the material printed in 1885.

2. What isn't indicated in the letter does not have to be copied, for all of it has already been published in collections. . . .

---

[1] Chekhov's brother was looking for early Chekhov stories for the new edition about to be published by Marx.

3. I need "The Tale," "The Teacher," "Sister," "Difficult People," "Life's Tedium," and "Tales of Life." These are some of the first stories that were printed in "New Times," soon after "Requiem" and "The Witch."

4. There is still another "Tale" that is about millionaires. It was published at New Year's, or Easter, or Christmas.

5. What is "Bad Weather?" Let's have it.

6. Have someone else copy the folios and do the searching. You are no longer of an age to engage in such occupations. Here you are fifty-three years old and have for some time been suffering from impotentia senilis, if you will pardon the expression! I however am still a young man and I'm even on the lookout for a bride.

Your benefactor,

A. Chekhov

Have every story copied into a separate writing-paper notebook; indicate the year and the issue. Write on one side of the paper.

To IVAN ORLOV

February 22, 1899, Yalta

Greetings, dear Ivan Ivanovich,

. . . I have sold Marx everything—my past and my future, and have become a Marxist for the rest of my life. For every 320 pages of prose already published I will receive 5,000 from him; five years from now I will receive 7,000 and so on—with an increase every five years. Thus, when I am 95, I will be getting a fearful mess of money. I am getting 75,000 for my past. I drove a bargain in favor of myself and my heirs to retain royalties from the plays. But alas! I am still far from being a Vanderbilt. Twenty-five thousand is already on hand, but I won't be getting the remaining 50,000 in any hurry, but spread over two years; so I really can't set myself up in style.

There is no particular news. I am not writing much. During the coming season my play,[1] which has not thus far been put on in the big cities, is being produced at the Little Theatre: nice royalties involved, as you can see. My house in Autka has scarcely got under way because of the raw weather, which has stretched on for almost all of January and February. I'll have to leave before the completion of building operations. . . . I have hopes of constructing a house on the cheap side, but in European style, so as to be able to spend time there in winter as well. The present little two-storey place is adequate only for summer occupancy. . . .

Actually, Yalta in winter is a cross that not everyone can bear. It abounds in drabness, slanders, intrigue and the most shameless calumny. . . .

Your letter contains a text from the scriptures. To your complaint regarding the tutor and various failures, I will also reply quoting chapter and verse: put not your trust in princes, nor in the son of man. . . . And I recall yet another expression concerning the sons of man, those very ones who make life so difficult for you: they are children of the age. It is not the tutor, but the entire educated class that is at fault, all of it, my good sir. While they are just university students they are an honest, admirable group of people, they are our hope, the future of Russia; but no sooner do these university students, male and female, stand on their own feet and turn into adults than this hope for the future vanishes into smoke and in the filter are left nothing but doctors, owners of summer cottages, insatiable officials, thieving engineers. . . . I do not believe in our educated class, which is hypocritical, false, hysterical, poorly educated and indolent; I don't believe in it even when it suffers and complains, for its persecutors emerge from its own bosom. I believe in individuals, I see salvation in individual personalities scattered here and there throughout Russia—they may be

1 *Uncle Vanya.*

intellectuals or peasants—these are the ones with the power, however few they may be. A prophet is not honored in his own country; the individual personalities of whom I speak play an insignificant role in society. They do not dominate, but their work is apparent; at any rate, science is continually going forward, social consciousness is growing, questions of morality are beginning to cause uneasiness, etc., etc.—and all this is being done despite the public prosecutors, the engineers, the tutors, despite the intelligentsia en masse and despite everything.

. . . I clasp your hand cordially—keep well, happy and gay. Write!

Your
A. Chekhov

To LYDIA AVILOVA

February 26, 1899, Yalta

Dear Lydia Alexeyevna,

. . . Five or six days ago I sent you a letter and today I am writing again. What is new in St. Petersburg and in literature? Do you like Gorki? In my opinion he is genuinely talented, his brushes and colors are genuine, but his is a sort of unrestrained, devil-may-care gift. His "On the Steppe" is a magnificent thing. But I don't like Veresayev or Chirikov a bit. Theirs is not writing, but chirping; they chirp and then sulk. And I don't like the writer Avilova because she writes so little. Women authors should write a great deal, if they want to master the art; just take these Englishwomen as an example. What marvelous workers! But I seem to have gone in for criticism; I am afraid that in reply you are going to write me something edifying.

Today the weather is delightful, springlike. The birds are trilling, the almond and cherry trees are in blossom and it is hot. But still I should be going north. My "Seagull" is being performed in Moscow for the eighteenth time and I am told it is staged magnificently.

Keep well. I cordially clasp your hand.

Yours,

A. Chekhov

To MARIA CHEKHOVA

March 29, 1899, Yalta

Dear Masha,

I have already sent you word that on the first of January 1900 I will receive thirty thousand from Marx and will then be able to pay whatever amount you need for the house. If you like Yeremeyev's property, by all means buy it; perhaps Yeremeyev is agreeable to selling it before the first of January—in which event we can make out the title deed; if not, we can borrow. A mortgage can be raised, but not for a large amount, not above ten thousand, so that paying the interest won't be burdensome.

The house apparently will not pay for itself, but if we have a comfortable, decent and quiet apartment, it will fully compensate for all our losses; for the quieter (in the physical sense) our existence, the more lightly and gladly can work be done. Bestir yourself and make Yeremeyev take responsibility for the business of the title deed, i.e., all the expenses connected with the sale of the house, or else the house will certainly stand us thirty-two and a half thousand. You can just explain to him that it is easier for him to come down in the price than for us to add to it.[1]

As to "Uncle Vanya,"[2] I am not going to write or telegraph anything; I don't know the committee's address and therefore I don't know where to send a telegram; secondly, my letters go unanswered; I have already written Nemirovich-Danchenko a

1 The house in Moscow was never bought.
2 Chekhov had already had trouble with *Uncle Vanya.* He had refused to allow the Maly Theatre to make any changes in the play.

thousand times; thirdly, this whole business has annoyed me terribly, I just can't stand any more of it. Let me repeat, all this business with "Uncle Vanya" has annoyed me and I am not going to put on any of my plays with anyone or anywhere. And I won't write to anyone. . . .

The almond tree (with red blossoms) is blooming magnificently on our Autka property and it is a joy. The house is going up and work is at fever heat.

I will be arriving soon. Keep well. Greetings to Mama.

Your Antoine

To ANNA SUVORINA

March 29, 1899, Yalta

Dear Anna Ivanovna,

If St. Petersburg were not so remote and so cold, I would visit you in an attempt to bear off Alexei Sergeyevich [Suvorin]. I get a great many letters and listen to talk from morning to night and I know something of what is going on at your place. You reproach me for disloyalty. You write that Alexei Sergeyevich is good-hearted and disinterested and that I do not pay him back in kind; but what, as a sincerely well-disposed person, might I do for him? What? The present situation has not developed overnight, but has been going on for many years, and what people are saying now they have been saying for a long time, everywhere, and you and Alexei Sergeyevich were not aware of the truth, as kings do not know what goes on about them. I am not philosophizing but stating what I know. "New Times" is experiencing difficult days, but certainly it remains, and will remain, a force; a certain amount of time will elapse and everything will get back into its accustomed groove; nothing will change and everything will be as it was.

What interests me more is the question of whether Alexei Sergeyevich should remain in St. Petersburg; I would be very happy if he threw everything aside for a week and left town. I wrote him in this regard, asked him to wire me, but he hasn't sent me a single word and now I don't know what to do with myself, whether to stay in Yalta and wait for him or go north. . . . I will write Alexei Sergeyevich, but you speak to him as well and have him wire me.

Where will you be this summer? Are you taking a trip anywhere? It is spring here, my health is passable, but life is tedious, all this rigmarole has bored me. . . .

Hearty thanks to you for the letter and for remembering me. Keep well and happy. I kiss your hand and wish you all the very best.

Yours,

A. Chekhov

To ALEXANDER CHEKHOV

March 30, 1899, Yalta

Proletarian! My poor brother! Honest toiler, exploited by the rich!

When you get this letter I shall already be on the wing; the third of April I will be packing and the fourth or fifth will go north to Moscow and then to my own estate, where in the position of a man of wealth I will exploit the proletarians. And so you have not managed to swindle me out of part of my capital with flattering words! Your plans have crashed to earth.

If it is not warm by the fifteenth of April, I will remain in Moscow as late as the eighteenth; if you wish, stop in on your way back (M. Dmitrovka St., c/o Vladimirov) . . . .

Keep well and conduct yourself properly and moderately.

They write from home that Mother was ill, but that she is well now. There is nothing new. However strange it may appear, I am undergoing financial difficulties.

My benefactor Marx has only paid me a small part of what he owes, the rest will be handed over later on, after 1900, in the coming century, and little by little. This is certainly not England! . . .

Your brother, member of the Yalta Mutual Credit Society,

A. Chekhov

Sashechka, are you an atheist?

To MAXIM GORKI

April 25, 1899, Moscow

Dear Alexei Maximovich,

Not a sight or sound of you—where are you? What are you doing? Where are you off to?

The day before yesterday I was at Tolstoy's; he praised you highly and said you were a "remarkable writer." He likes your "The Fair" and "On the Steppe," but doesn't like your "Malva." He said, "You can invent anything you please, but not psychology, and Gorki is full of psychological inventions. He has described what he hasn't felt." There you are. I told him we would visit him together the next time you were in Moscow.

When will you be here? "The Seagull" is being performed on Thursday, a special performance for yours truly. I'll have a seat for you if you come. . . .

I have been getting grim, rather repentant letters from St. Petersburg[1] . . . and they trouble me, for I do not know how to answer them, or what attitude to take. Yes indeed, life is a complicated affair when it is not a psychological invention.

Drop me two or three lines. Tolstoy asked a great many questions about you—you have aroused his curiosity. It is evident you have stirred him.

So, keep in good health and let me clasp your hand. My compliments to your little Maxim.

Your

A. Chekhov

[1] From Suvorin. Chekhov very probably meant that Suvorin was repentant over his anti-Zola attitude in the Dreyfus Affair.

To MAXIM GORKI

My dear Alexei Maximovich,   *May 9, 1899, Melikhovo*

I am sending you a copy of Strindberg's play "Countess Julie." Read it and return it to its owner, Elena Just, 13/15 Panteleimon Street, St. Petersburg.

At one time I liked hunting, but now I am indifferent to it.[1] I saw "The Seagull" without the stage sets; I cannot judge the play dispassionately, because the Seagull herself[2] gave an abominable performance, kept sobbing violently; and the actor playing the part of the writer Trigorin walked and talked like a paralytic. He interpreted his part to be that of a man without a "will of his own" and in a way that absolutely nauseated me. But on the whole it was not so bad, it gripped me. In places I could hardly believe it was I who had written it.

I shall be very glad to make Father Petrov's[3] acquaintance. I have already read about him. If he is going to be in Alushta at the beginning of July it won't be difficult to arrange a meeting. I have not seen his book.

I am living here in comfort. It is hot, the rooks are croaking and the peasants pay me visits. For the time being life is not dull.

I bought myself a gold watch, but a very ordinary one.

When will you be here?

Do keep well, happy and gay. Don't forget, write me however seldom.

If you decide to write a play, do so and then send it to me for reading. But keep it a secret until you are done, otherwise you will get kicked around and your good spirits wiped out.

I cordially shake your hand.   Your

A. Chekhov

[1] Gorki had thanked Chekhov for the gift of a watch and asked if Chekhov liked hunting because he wanted to send him a gun.

[2] Roxanova played Nina and Stanislavski played Trigorin.

[3] Father Petrov was a priest who was later thrown out of the Orthodox Church for his heretical writings. Lenin called him "a Christian democrat, an extremely popular demagogue."

To ALEXANDER CHEKHOV

May 11, 1899, Melikhovo

My poor, indigent Sasha,

. . . I am going to be in St. Petersburg at the end of May. Get yourself dolled up.

At the moment all goes well at home. We feel fine. We entertain aristocratic guests, the Malkiels, for instance We serve tea as it is done in the finest homes, with little napkins. You would certainly be ordered away from the table, as people who smell are not permitted.

To have as few failures as possible in fiction writing, or in order not to be so sensitive to failures, you must write more, around one hundred or two hundred stories a year. That is the secret.

Is everyone still boycotting you and is it true that Diaghilev beat up Burenin? Where is Alexei Sergeyevich? Was there a court of honor? Write a lot more, don't cramp your style.

I wanted to send you my old pants but thought better of it; I was afraid you might put on airs.

Tuus frater bonus,
Antonius

To OLGA KNIPPER[1]

June 16, 1899, Melikhovo

What does this mean? Where are you? You are so stubborn about not sending news of yourself that we are absolutely at sea and have already begun thinking you have forgotten us and got married in the Caucasus. If you really are married, to whom is it? Haven't you decided to leave the stage?

The author is forgotten—and how terrible it is, how cruel and perfidious!

Everyone sends regards. There is nothing new. There aren't even any flies. Even the calves won't bite.

---

[1] By this date, Knipper and Chekhov were good friends and she had visited the Chekhovs at Melikhovo. This is the first letter Chekhov wrote to her.

I had wanted to accompany you to the station that time, but fortunately the rain prevented me from doing so.

I was in St. Petersburg and had my picture taken twice; I almost froze to death there. I won't be leaving for Yalta before the beginning of July.

With your permission, I press your hand cordially and send my best wishes.

Your

A. Chekhov

To MAXIM GORKI

June 22, 1899, Moscow

My dearest Alexei Maximovich,

Why are you depressed? Why do you abuse your "Foma Gordeyev" so violently? If you will permit me, I believe there are two reasons, in addition to the others, for your attitude. You started your career with success, with éclat, and now everything that appears commonplace and humdrum to you causes dissatisfaction and annoyance. That's one. Second, a literary man cannot live in the provinces with impunity. No matter what you may have to say on this score, you have partaken of literature and are already hopelessly infected. You are a literary man, and a literary man you will remain. His natural habitat is always close to literary circles, living among those who write, and breathing literature. Don't struggle against nature, yield to it once and for all and move to St. Petersburg or Moscow. Quarrel with literary people, don't recognize them, despise half of them, but live with them. . . .

Keep well, I firmly clasp your hand and wish you everything good. Don't give way to fits of despondency.

Yours,

A. Chekhov

To MARIA CHEKHOVA

July 22, 1899, Yalta

Dear Masha,

This is in answer to your letter. I am arriving in Moscow not later than the second of August. But why are you waiting for me to come? Certainly I left you the power of attorney, and we can't sell the property together—it must be sold by one of us alone. I do not propose to sell it and will not negotiate with Morel; if you cannot or will not go on with it (although it's not a complicated matter at all), let's give it to someone else. The price depends entirely on you. Go ahead and sell it for 15,000— I won't argue with you. Knipper is here, she is very sweet, but is depressed. The building is coming along nicely. Keep well. If you don't want to exercise the power of attorney, entrust it to someone, even a person like Vinogradov. Knipper likes your room very much. It isn't a room, but a bit of magic.

The packing job on the sideboard was schwach—everything was broken.

The armchair arrived in good condition.

To MARIA CHEKHOVA

August 29, 1899, Yalta

Dear Masha,

Here are the details. The kitchen is already done and Maryusha's room as well. The parquet is being laid in your room. They wanted to hang the wallpaper but I told them to wait with it until you arrived. Mother's and my rooms will be ready by the first of September, i.e., the flooring and wallpaper and window fittings will be in. . . . I am living in the wing and have fixed myself up cozily. The place is cramped with all the stuff and your cupboard, where I keep my underwear, has rendered great service.

All the things arrived intact. The table linen is in good condition, undamaged, and there are lots of towels. The cupboard reached here safely.

They are also not going to touch the walls in the entrance hall until your arrival. Only Mama and I will have wallpaper. The waterproofing is being rushed through. The water in the well is good. . . .

Bear in mind that there are a great many passengers on the train and steamboat. When you get to Sevastopol don't wait until the baggage is distributed, but hire a cabman immediately and then do your waiting seated in the carriage. . . . The tariff from the wharf is seventy-five kopeks including baggage. One cab will be enough, as they have two- and four-seaters here. I will meet you at the quay and Mustapha will take care of the luggage. . . .

It is morning now and I have had my coffee. The alcohol stove works very well. We get our milk from our neighbors at ten kopeks a bottle. Although our yard is not particularly large, we can find enough room for chickens.

I won't get any money until December and must get busy.

Our ground is fine for growing clover. If you can manage bring a pound of it with you and the same quantity of timothy and lucerne.

Yesterday I became a member of the Consumers' Society which runs a grocery and liquor store; I took out fifty rubles worth of shares. Now all our goods can be delivered to the house. In a few days I am installing a telephone. . . .

So—I hope you are well. Love to Mama. I am in good health.

Your Antoine

To OLGA KNIPPER

September 3, 1899, Yalta

Sweet actress,

I am answering all your questions. I arrived safely. My fellow travelers ceded me a lower seat, then matters were so arranged that only two of us remained in the compartment: I and a young Armenian. I drank tea a number of times a day, three glasses each time, with lemon, sedately and leisurely. I ate up everything in the basket. But I find that fussing with a basket lunch and dashing out at the stations for boiling water for tea is an unbecoming procedure that undermines the prestige of the Art Theatre.

It was cold until Kursk, then it warmed up gradually and by the time we reached Sevastopol it was quite hot. In Yalta I went straight to my own home, where I am now living, guarded by the faithful Mustapha. I don't have a regular dinner every day, since it is a long distance to the city and again my prestige inhibits me from fussing around with the oil stove in the kitchen; so I eat bread and cheese in the evenings.

. . . I am not drinking Narzan water. What more? I don't go to the park but stay home most of the time and think of you. Driving past Bakchisarai I thought of you and recalled our journey together. My precious, unusual actress, my wonderful woman, if you could only know how happy your letter made me! I bow down before you, bow low, so low that my forehead is touching the bottom of my well, which to date has been dug to a depth of forty feet. I have got used to you and miss you so much now that I cannot reconcile myself to the thought that I shan't be seeing you until spring; I am in a bad humor; and, in short, if Nadenka[1] only knew what is going on in my soul, there would be quite a scandal!

The Yalta weather has been splendid, but for no good reason we have had pouring rain for the past two days, now it is muddy and we must wear overshoes. The humidity is such that centipedes crawl along the walls and toads and young crocodiles disport themselves in the garden. The green reptile in the flowerpot you gave me which I carried here without mishap is reposing in the garden now and basking in the sun. . . .

---

[1] Nadenka was an imaginary lady, a joke between Chekhov and Knipper, sometimes she was a jealous fiancée, sometimes a stern wife.

Well, then, let me press your hand and kiss it. Keep in good health, be gay and happy; work, cavort, amuse yourself, sing, and if possible don't forget the minor author and your assiduous admirer,

A. Chekhov.

To MAXIM GORKI

September 3, 1899, Yalta

My dear Alexei Maximovich,

Greetings once again! This is in answer to your letter.

To start with, I am opposed in principle to dedicating books to living people, whoever they may be. I once did so and now feel maybe I shouldn't have. This is a general observation. Getting down to particulars, I could only consider your dedication of "Foma Gordeyev" to me as a pleasure and honor. But why do I deserve it? However, it's for you to make up your mind and for me just to thank you humbly. If possible don't put in anything fancy, i.e., just say "dedicated to so and so" and that's all. . . . Here is some more practical advice for you, if you want it: make it a big edition, not less than five or six thousand copies. The book will sell fast. You can have the second edition printed along with the first.

Here is more advice: when you read proof, take out adjectives and adverbs wherever you can. You use so many of them that the reader finds it hard to concentrate and he gets tired. You understand what I mean when I say, "The man sat on the grass." You understand because the sentence is clear and there is nothing to distract your attention. Conversely, the brain has trouble understanding me if I say, "A tall, narrow-chested man of medium height with a red beard sat on green grass trampled by passersby, sat mutely, looking about timidly and fearfully." This doesn't get its meaning through to the brain immediately, which is what good writing must do, and fast.

Now for one more thing: by nature you are a lyricist and

your spirit is tuned to melody. If you were a composer you would avoid composing marches. Being coarse and noisy, taunting, accusing frantically—such things are not characteristic of your talent. Consequently you will understand why I advise you in reading proof not to have any mercy on the sons of bitches and curs that flit here and there through the pages of "Life."

Shall I expect you at the end of September? Why so late? Winter begins early this year, the autumn will be a short one and you should hurry.

Well, sir, keep yourself nice and alive and in good health.

Your

A. Chekhov

Performances begin at the Art Theatre on the thirtieth of September. "Uncle Vanya" is being given on the fourteenth of October.

Your best story is "On the Steppe."

To OLGA KNIPPER

September 29, 1899, Yalta

Your sensible letter with a kiss for my right temple and your other letter with the photos have arrived. Thank you, sweet actress, thank you awfully. Your performances start today and so in gratitude for the letters and for remembering me I am sending you my congratulations on the season's getting under way—a million good wishes. I would have liked to send a wire to the directors and congratulate the whole company, but as nobody writes and I have apparently been forgotten, not even being sent the company's yearly report (which came out recently, according to the neswpapers), and as that same old Roxanova is playing in "The Seagull," I considered it best to appear offended and so my congratulations are for you alone.

We had some rain, but now it is bright and brisk. There was

a fire last night; I got up to watch it from the terrace and felt terribly alone.

We are occupying our own house now, use the dining room and have a piano.

I haven't a bit of money and am spending all my time hiding from my creditors. It will continue this way until the middle of December, when Marx sends some money.

I would like to make some more sensible remarks but can't think of a thing. My own season certainly has not begun, I have nothing new or interesting to talk about and everything is just as it has been. I am not expecting anything except bad weather, which is already around the corner.

"Ivanov" and "Uncle Vanya" are playing at the Alexander Theatre.

So keep well, sweet actress, remarkable woman, and may God preserve you. I kiss both your hands and bow all the way down to your little feet. Don't forget me.

Yours,
A. Chekhov

To OLGA KNIPPER

September 30, 1899, Yalta

At your bidding I am dashing off a reply to your letter, in which you ask me about Astrov's last scene with Elena.[1] You tell me that in this scene Astrov's attitude toward Elena is that of the most ardent man in love, that he "snatches at his feelings as a drowning man at a straw." But that is incorrect, absolutely incorrect! Astrov likes Elena, her beauty takes his breath away, but by the last act he is already aware that the whole business is futile, that Elena is vanishing forever from his sight—and so in this scene the tone he takes with her is the one he would use in discussing the heat in Africa, and he kisses her simply because that is all he has to do. If Astrov interprets this scene

---

1 Chekhov was speaking of *Uncle Vanya.*

tempestuously, the entire mood of Act IV—a quiet and languid one—will be ruined. . . .

It has suddenly grown cold here, as if a Moscow wind had blown upon us. How I should like to be in Moscow, sweet actress! However, your head is in a whirl, you have become infected and are held in a spell—and you have no time for me. Now you will be able to say, "We are creating a stir, my friend!"

As I write I look out of an enormous window with a very extensive view, so magnificent it cannot be described. I shan't send you my photograph until I get yours, you serpent! I wouldn't think of calling you a "snake," as you say; you are a great big serpent, not a little snake. Now, isn't that flattering?

Well my dear, I press your hand, send my profound compliments and knock my forehead against the floor in worship, my most respected lady.

I am sending you another present soon.

Yours,

A. Chekhov

To GRIGORI ROSSOLIMO

October 11, 1899, Yalta

Dear Grigori Ivanovich,

Today I sent Dr. Raltsevich eight rubles fifty kopeks for the photograph and five rubles for annual dues. I am sending my photograph to you registered, rather a poor one (taken when my enteritis was in full swing).

My autobiography? I have a disease called autobiographophobia. It is a real torment for me to read any details about myself, let alone prepare them for publication. On a separate sheet I am sending some extremely bare facts, and more than that I cannot give you. If you wish, add that my application to the dean for admission to the university was for the medical courses.

You ask when we are going to see each other. Probably not

before spring. I am in Yalta, in exile, a splendid one, maybe, but still exile. Life proceeds drably. My health is so-so: it is not every day that I am well. Besides all the rest, I have hemorrhoids, catarrh recti and there are days when I am utterly exhausted by frequent trips to the toilet. I must have an operation.
. . .

Please write if anything interesting occurs. I am lonesome here, really, and if it were not for letters I might even hang myself, learn to drink the poor Crimean wine or marry an ugly and stupid woman.

Keep well. I clasp your hand cordially and send my heartiest good wishes to yourself and your family.

Yours,

A. Chekhov

My name is A. P. Chekhov and I was born on the 17th of January 1860 in Taganrog. My education began at the Greek school connected with the Emperor Constantine Church, after which I attended the Taganrog Boys' school. In 1879 I entered the medical school of Moscow University. At that time I only had a vague idea of the various courses and cannot recall what considerations led me to choose the medical course, but I do not now regret the choice. During my first year at the university I was already having things printed in the weekly newspapers and magazines, and by the early eighties these literary pursuits had assumed a regular, professional character. In 1888 I was awarded the Pushkin Prize. In 1890 I visited Sakhalin Island to write a book on our penal colony and prison system there. Excluding court reports, reviews, articles, notes, all the items composed from day to day in the newspapers and which would now be difficult to unearth and collect, in twenty years of literary activity I have set down on paper and had published more than forty-eight hundred pages of tales and stories. I have also written plays for the theatre.

My work in the medical sciences undoubtedly had a great

influence on my writing; certainly it widened the area of my observations and enriched my knowledge, and only one who is himself a doctor can tell you how valuable that training has been. My medical background has also been a guide to me; I have probably managed to avoid many mistakes because of it. Familiarity with natural sciences and the scientific method has always kept me on my guard, and wherever possible I have tried to write on the basis of scientific data; where it was impossible, I preferred not to write. I may note incidentally that artistic considerations do not always allow me to write in complete harmony with scientific data; on the stage you cannot show death by poisoning as it actually occurs. But even in such a case one must be consistent with scientific data, i.e., the reader or spectator must clearly realize that certain conventions are responsible for what has been shown and that he is dealing with an author who knows what he is talking about. I am not in the same camp with literary men who take a skeptical attitude toward science; and I would not want to belong to those who handle every subject solely on the basis of their wits.

As to my medical practice, while still a student I worked in the Voskresensk Community Hospital (near New Jerusalem) with P. A. Archangelski, the eminent physician; later I spent a short period as doctor at the Zvenigorod Hospital. During the cholera years ('92, '93) I directed the medical work in Melikhovo Section of Serpukhov District.

To OLGA KNIPPER

October 30, 1899, Yalta

Sweet actress and good little fellow,

You ask whether I am excited. As a matter of fact it was only from your letter, received on the twenty-seventh, that I learned "Uncle Vanya" was being performed on the twenty-sixth. The telegrams started arriving the evening of the twenty-seventh, after I had already gone to bed. They were repeated to me over the telephone. I kept on waking each time and running barefoot to the telephone in the dark, giving myself a bad chill; I would hardly fall asleep before there would be another ring, and another. This is the first occasion my own personal glory has prevented my sleeping. Upon going to bed the next night I put my bedroom slippers and bathrobe next to the bed, but there were no more telegrams.

The telegrams contained nothing but words about the number of curtain calls and the brilliant success achieved, but I could sense something strained, something very elusive, about all of them, which led me to conclude that you were not all in such very good spirits. The newspapers received here today have confirmed this conjecture of mine. Yes, my dear actress, you Art Theatre performers are not satisfied any more with just ordinary, average success. You must have fireworks, cannonading and dynamite. You are utterly spoiled, deafened with these continual discourses on success, on full and empty houses; you are already infected with this dizzy whirl and in a couple of years you won't be fit for anything! So much for you people!

How are you getting along and how do you feel? I am still in the same place and everything remains the same: my program consists of literary work and setting out trees. . . .

Don't forget me and don't let our friendship fade, so that the two of us can take another trip somewhere next summer. So long! We shall probably not see each other before April. If you came to Yalta this spring, you could give some performances here and relax. That would be wonderfully artistic. . . .

I clasp your hand cordially. My respect to Anna Ivanovna[1] and your military uncle.

Yours,
A. Chekhov

[1] Anna Ivanovna was Olga Knipper's mother; She was a teacher of singing at a conservatory.

To OLGA KNIPPER [1900]

My dear actress, do write, in the name of all that is holy, or I shall be lonesome. It's as if I were in jail and my spirits are very low.

To OLGA KNIPPER

November 1, 1899, Yalta

I understand your mood, sweet little actress, understand it perfectly, but still in your place I wouldn't be in such a desperate dither. Neither the role of Anna[1] nor the play itself is entitled to impair your emotions and nerves to such an extent. The play is old and already outdated and has all sorts of defects; if more than half the performers just couldn't get into the swing of the thing the play is naturally to blame. That's the first point. Secondly, you've got to cut out worrying about successes and failures once and for all. They are not your affair. Your job is to jog along, day in, day out, like a quiet little creature, prepared for the mistakes that can't be avoided and for failures; in short, to do a job as an actress and let the others count the curtain calls. It is usual to write, or to act, and know all long that you are not doing the right thing—and for beginners this awareness is so useful!

In the third place, your director telegraphed that the second performance [of Uncle Vanya] came off magnificently, everybody played wonderfully and he was completely satisfied.

Masha writes that Moscow is unpleasant and I oughtn't to go there, but I would like so much to leave Yalta, where my lonely life has wearied me. I am a Johannes[2] without a wife, not a learned Johannes and not a virtuous one. . . .

Keep well! Write that you have already calmed down and that everything is going beautifully. I press your hand.

Your

A. Chekhov

---

[1] "Anna" must be a mistake. Chekhov was, of course, writing about Elena in *Uncle Vanya*. Knipper was also playing the part of Anna in Hauptmann's play *Lonely Lives* that season.

[2] Johannes is a character in *Lonely Lives*.

To MARIA MALKIEL

November 5, 1899, Yalta

Dear Maria Samoilovna,

I hereby inform you that I have been converted to the Mohammedan faith and have already been entered as a member of the Tatar Society of Autka Village near Yalta. Our laws do not permit us to enter into correspondence with such weak creatures as women and if, in complying with the inclination of my heart, I write to you, I am committing a grievous sin. I thank you for the letter and send hearty regards to you and your prophetic sister, and I hope you both get into the harem of an eminent gentleman, one who is as handsome as Levitan.

Write some more. Keep well and happy.

Osman Chekhov

To VLADIMIR NEMIROVICH-DANCHENKO

December 3, 1899, Yalta

My dear Vladimir Ivanovich,

An answer has come from Karpov.[1] He agrees to postpone the production of "Uncle Vanya" until next year (or more exactly next season). Now it remains for you to act on a "legal" basis, as good lawyers say. The play belongs to you, you can go on with it and I will pretend I am powerless to do anything about it, since I have already given it to you.

Are you afraid of Suvorin? We no longer correspond and I don't know what is going on there now. But I can tell you beforehand that very probably St. Petersburg won't like the Art Theatre. St. Petersburg literary men and actors are extremely jealous and envious, and superficial at that. . . .

I have read the criticisms of "Uncle Vanya" only in the "Courier" and "News of the Day." . . .

---

[1] Evtikhi Pavlovich Karpov (1859-1926), playwright, fiction writer and producer at various St. Petersburg theatres.

So you want definitely to have a play for next season. But suppose it doesn't get written? I will try, of course, but won't vouch for it and cannot promise a thing. However, we'll discuss it after Eastertime when, if I can believe Vishnevski and the newspapers, your troupe will be in Yalta. Then we'll really talk things over. . . .

Yes, you are right, Alexeyev-Trigorin[2] has to be done over for the St. Petersburg public, even if only slightly. Sprinkle a bit of thyroid extract over him, or something. Alexeyev, who plays Trigorin as a hopeless impotent, will puzzle them all in that town, the home of most of our men of letters. I find the recollection of Alexeyev's acting too dismal to shake off and cannot possibly believe he is good in "Uncle Vanya" although everybody writes that he is really very good, very, very good.

You promised to send me your picture and I am still waiting. I need two copies: one for myself, the other for the Taganrog library, of which I am a trustee. . . .

Do keep well. My compliments to Ekaterina Nikolayevna, Alexeyev and the entire company. I press your hand and embrace you.

Yours,
A. Chekhov

To OLGA KNIPPER

January 2, 1900, Yalta

Greetings to you, sweet actress,

Are you angry that I haven't written for so long? I have written you often but you haven't been getting the letters because a mutual acquaintance of ours has intercepted them at the post office.[1]

---

2 Stanislavski (whose real name was Alexeyev) played the part of Trigorin in *The Seagull.*

1 The mutual acquaintance was Nemirovich-Danchenko. This was, of course, a joke.

My best wishes for a very Happy New Year. I wish you all happiness and throw myself at your feet in worship. Be happy, prosperous, healthy and jolly.

We are getting along pretty well, eat a lot, chatter a lot, laugh a lot and your name comes up often in our talks. Masha will tell you how we passed the holidays when she returns to Moscow.

I am not congratulating you on the success of "Lonely Lives." I nurture the vague hope that all of you will be coming to Yalta, that I will see a performance of "Lonely Lives" and will then really and truly congratulate you. I wrote Meierhold to persuade him not to act the part of a nervous man with such abruptness. Most people are certainly nervous, and most of them suffer, and many feel acute pain, but where on earth do you see people throwing themselves around, hopping up and down or clutching their heads with their hands? Suffering should be expressed as it is expressed in life itself, not by action of arms and legs, but by a tone of voice, or a glance; not by gesticulation, but by a graceful movement. Subtle spiritual manifestations natural to cultivated people should be subtly expressed outwardly too. You are going to bring up considerations of staging. But no considerations can justify falsity.

My sister tells me you played Anna[2] marvelously. If only the Art Theatre would visit Yalta!

Your company has had high praise from "New Times." They have shifted their course; evidently they will praise all of you even during Lent. My long story—a very peculiar one—is appearing in the February number of "Life." The cast of characters is large, with scenery, a crescent moon and a bittern, the bird that cries boo-boo from off in the distance, like a cow locked in a barn. There is a little bit of everything.

Levitan is with us. Over my fireplace he has painted a picture of a moonlit night during haying season. There's a meadow, sheaves, woods in the distance and a moon reigning over all.

2 In *Lonely Lives.*

[258]

Well ma'am, stay healthy, my sweet, extraordinary actress. I have missed you very much.

Yours,

A. Chekhov

When are you sending your photo?
What cruelty!

To ALEXEI SUVORIN

January 8, 1900, Yalta

Happy New Year!

The holidays are over, today I bade my guests farewell, am alone again and feel like writing letters. . . .

What you tell me about the subscriptions to the paper is of interest. . . . Certainly the "Northern Courier" is widely read in the provinces. In judging Prince Baryatinski by his paper I must admit I was unfair, as my own picture of him was quite different from what he actually is. His paper won't last, of course, but he will long retain his reputation as a good journalist. Do you want to know why the "Northern Courier" is enjoying success? It is because our society is sick, hatred is making it decay and get sour like grass in a swamp, and it craves something fresh, light and free, craves it desperately. . . .

I often run into Kondakov, the academician. We have been discussing the Pushkin Section of Belles-Lettres. As Kondakov is taking part in the selection of future academicians I have been trying to hypnotize him into suggesting that they elect Barantsevich and Mikhailovski. The former is a worn-out, tired man, but unquestionably a man of letters; now that old age is upon him he is in need and holds a post with a horse-car company, just as he held the same job as a young man because of poverty. In his case a salary and repose would be very much to the point. The latter, Mikhailovski, would put the new section on a solid basis and his selection would satisfy three quarters of our literary brotherhood. But my hypnotism hasn't worked, and the project has not been successful. The addenda to the statutes are exactly like Tolstoy's epilogue to the "Kreutzer Sonata." The academicians have done their utmost to protect themselves from literary men, in whose company they are as shocked as the Germans were in the company of Russian academicians. A literary man can only be an honorary academician, which doesn't mean a thing, any more than being an honorary citizen of the town of Vyazma or Cherepovets; no salary and no voting rights. They've worked it pretty cleverly; they will elect professors to be the real academicians, and writers who do not live in St. Petersburg as honorary ones, i.e., those who cannot attend meetings and exchange abuse with the professors.

I can hear the muezzin calling from the minaret. The Turks are very religious; this is their fasting time and they eat nothing all day. They do not have religious ladies, that element in society which makes religion petty, as sand makes the Volga shallow. . . .

Thank you for your letter, and your indulgence. I give you a hearty handclasp.

Yours,
A. Chekhov

To PYOTR KURKIN

January 18, 1900, Yalta

Dear Pyotr Ivanovich,

. . . Thank you for the letter; I have long been wanting to write you, but haven't had time, as I am burdened with business and official correspondence. Yesterday was the 17th, my birthday and the day I was elected to the Academy. The telegrams I got! And the letters yet to come! And all these will have to be answered, else posterity will accuse me of ignorance of social amenities.

Do you see Masha? Have you drunk her wine? There is some

news though I won't tell it to you now (no time), but later on.
I am not very well, and was sick all day yesterday. I press your
hand cordially. Keep well.

Yours,

A. Chekhov

To FYODOR BATUSHKOV

January 24, 1900, Yalta

Dear Fyodor Dmitrievich,

Roche[1] requests you to send him the passages in "The
Peasants" that were deleted by the censor. There weren't any
such, though. There was one chapter that did not get into
either the magazine or the book; that was the peasants' conversation about religion and the authorities. But there is no need
to send this chapter to Paris, just as there wasn't any need at all
for translating "The Peasants" into French.

Thank you sincerely for the photograph. To be illustrated by
Repin is an honor I did not expect and for which I didn't dare
hope. Getting the original will be most gratifying; tell Ilya
Efimovich [Repin] I am awaiting it impatiently, and that he no
longer has a right to change his mind, since I have already willed
the original to the city of Taganrog, where I was born, incidentally.

Your letter mentions Gorki. How do you like him, by the
way? I don't like everything he writes, but there are some things
I like very, very much and there isn't the least doubt that
Gorki is kneaded out of the kind of dough from which genuine
artists rise. He is the real article. Personally he is a good, intelligent, reasonable and thoughtful man but he carries a lot of
dead weight around with him, his provincialism, for one thing.
. . .

Thank you very much for your letter and for remembering
me. I lead a solitary and boring life here and feel as though

1 Roche was Chekhov's French translator.

I had been pitched overboard. On top of it all the weather is miserable and I am ailing. I still keep on coughing.

I wish you the best of everything.

Devotedly,
A. Chekhov

To MIKHAIL MENSHIKOV

January 28, 1900, Yalta

Dear Mikhail Osipovich,

I cannot figure out what sort of ailment Tolstoy has. Cherinov[1] failed to reply and from what I read in the newspapers and what you now write me it is impossible to draw any conclusion. Stomach or intestinal ulcers would have been otherwise indicated; there is no ulcerous condition present, nothing but bleeding scratches caused by gallstones passing through and making lacerations. He doesn't have a cancer, either, which would be immediately reflected in lack of appetite, general condition and above all in his face. Most likely Tolstoy is in good health (apart from the stones) and will live another twenty years or so. His illness frightened me and kept me in a state of tension. I dread Tolstoy's death. His death would create a vacuum in my life. To begin with, I have never loved anyone as much as him; I am an unbeliever, but of all the faiths I consider his the nearest to my heart and most suited to me. Then again, as long as there is a Tolstoy in literature it is simple and gratifying to be a literary figure; even the awareness of not having accomplished anything and not expecting to accomplish anything in the future is not so terrible because Tolstoy makes up for all of us. His career is justification for all the hopes and expectations reposed in literature. In the third place, Tolstoy stands solid as a rock with his immense authority, and as long as he remains alive bad taste in literature, all vulgarity, be it insolent or tear-

1 Professor of medicine in Moscow to whom Chekhov had telegraphed to find out about Tolstoy's illness.

ful, all coarse, irascible vanities will be held at a distance, deep in the shadows. His moral authority alone is capable of keeping so-called literary moods and trends at a certain high level. Without him the literary world would be a flock without a shepherd or a hopeless mess.

To wind up the subject of Tolstoy, I have something to say about "Resurrection," which I did not read in fits and starts but all at one gulp. It is a remarkable work of art. The most uninteresting section is that concerned with the relations of Nekhludov and Katusha; the most interesting characters are the princes, generals, old ladies, peasants, prisoners and overseers. As I read the scene at the general's, the commandant of the Peter and Paul Prison, and a spiritualist, my heart beat furiously, it was so good! And Mme. Korchagina in her armchair, and the peasant, Feodosia's husband! This peasant calls his old lady a "crafty character." So it is with Tolstoy; he has a crafty pen. The novel has no end; what there is can hardly be called one. Certainly it is using a theological device when he writes on and on and then proceeds to resolve the problems raised on the basis of a Gospel text. It is as arbitrary to use such a solution as it is to divide criminals into five classes. Why five and not ten? Why use a text from the Gospels and not from the Koran? First you ought to make people believe in the truth of the Gospels and then you can go ahead and solve your problem with a Gospel text.

. . . I have been ailing for some weeks and have attempted to get over my indisposition. Now I am at home with a blister under my left clavicle and don't feel too bad. The blister doesn't bother me but the resulting red spot does.

I am certainly going to send you my photograph. I am pleased to have acquired the title of academician, since it is nice knowing that Sigma envies me. But I shall be even gladder when I lose this title after some misunderstanding. And there will undoubtedly be misunderstandings, because the learned academicians are very much afraid that we shall shock them. Tolstoy was elected with a gnashing of teeth. In their opinion he is a nihilist. At least that was how a lady, the wife of a very important person, entitled him, and I congratulate him upon it with all my heart. . . .

Keep well, and let me press your hand warmly. . . .

Yours,

Write!   A Chekhov

To MIKHAIL CHEKHOV

January 29, 1900, Yalta

Dear Michel,

This is in reply to your letter.

1. I was never in Torjok in my life and never sent anyone a telegram from there. I left St. Petersburg the day following the performance of "The Seagull" and was accompanied to the station by Suvorin's valet and Potapenko.

2. Suvorin knew in detail about the sale of my works to Marx and under what conditions it took place. When the straight question was put to him as to whether he wished to purchase them, he replied that he had no money, that his children would not permit him to do so and that nobody could offer more than Marx.

3. An advance of 20,000 would actually mean purchasing my works for 20,000, as I would never be able to wrest myself free from my debts.

4. When everything was concluded with Marx, A. S. wrote me he was very glad of it, because his conscience had always troubled him on account of the bad job he had made of publishing my work.

5. Nobody in Nice talked about the trend "New Times" was taking.

6. The "relations" I wrote you about (of course you shouldn't have been so frank with the Suvorins) began to change drastically when A. S. himself wrote me there was nothing more for us to write to each other.

7. His presses started printing a complete edition of my works but did not continue, as the printers kept losing my manuscripts and there was no reply to my letters; this careless attitude caused me to despair; I had tuberculosis and had to consider what steps to take to prevent dumping my works upon my heirs in a messy, practically valueless heap.

8. Of course I should not have told you all this, as it is much too personal and only a nuisance; but I have to tell you all this because they have got you in their clutches and have presented the affair to you in that light, so read these eight points and think them over carefully. Talk of reconciliation is out of the question, as Suvorin and I did not quarrel and are again corresponding as if nothing had happened. Anna Ivanovna is a nice woman, but she is very sharp. I believe she is kindly disposed, but when I talk with her I never forget for an instant that she is an artful character and that A. S. is a very good man and publishes "New Times." I am writing this for you alone.

Everything is all right here. Mother was slightly ill but has recovered. Did you see Masha in Moscow?

... I wish you both good health and all the best.

Yours,

A. Chekhov

To MAXIM GORKI

February 3, 1900, Yalta

Dear Alexei Maximovich,

Thank you for the letter and your words about Tolstoy and "Uncle Vanya," which I haven't seen on the stage; thanks generally for not forgetting me. You feel like lying down and dying in this blessed Yalta unless you get letters. Indolence, a silly winter with a constant temperature just above freezing, the utter absence of interesting women, the pigs' snouts you encounter along the boardwalk—such factors can drive one to wrack and ruin in no time at all. I am tired out, and it seems to me the winter has been ten years long.

Are you suffering from pleurisy? If so, why do you remain in Nizhni, why? What are you doing in this Nizhni, may I ask incidentally? What's the tar that keeps you sticking to this city? If you like Moscow, as you say you do, why don't you live in it? Moscow has theatres and all sorts of other things, and the main point is its handiness to the border, while if you continue living in Nizhni you will just get stuck there and never get any farther than Vasilsursk. You must see more and know more, you must have a wider range. Your imagination is quick to catch and grip, but it is like a big stove that isn't fed enough wood. You can feel this lack in general, and your stories reveal it in particular; you will present two or three strong figures, but they stand aloof, apart from the mass; it is evident that they are alive in your imagination, but it is only they who live—the mass is not grasped properly. I am excluding from this generalization your Crimean things ("My Companion," for example), where you get a feeling not alone of the figures but of the human mass from which they are derived, and of the atmosphere and perspective—in short, of everything that should be there. You see what a talking to I have given you—and all to get you out of Nizhni. You are a young, vigorous, hardy individual; in your place I would be off for India, for God only knows where, and I would get myself a couple of university degrees. I would indeed—you may laugh at me, but I am so exasperated that I am forty years old, am short of breath and suffer from all sorts of nonsensical ailments that prevent my living like a free soul. At any rate, be a good man and a good comrade, don't get angry at my reading you written sermons, like a churchman.

Do write. I am looking forward to "Foma Gordeyev," which I haven't yet read properly.

There is nothing new. Keep well and let me clasp your hand cordially.

Yours,

A. Chekhov

To MARIA CHEKHOVA

February 6, 1900, Yalta

Dear Masha,

Maria Abramovna Altshuller is now in Moscow. Her address is c/o Mirke, the Bakhrushin house, George Lane, Myasnitskaya Street. She has two bottles of wine for you. She will be in Moscow about five days. Give her some caviar, sausage from Belov's, smoked meat and some other stuff to take back with her. If for some reason you can't get to see her, send a messenger. Altshuller is treating Mother and there is no way for me to pay him back other than to give his wife the chance of seeing my play—once she expressed the desire. Arrange for her to see "Lonely Lives" and "Uncle Vanya." If you haven't time to get the tickets, write Vishnevski to send tickets for her to the above address and then you can pay him.

Mother is well, complains only of her shoulder; everything is in order. The weather was good, now it is miserable. The pavement hasn't been finished yet.

Keep well.

Your Antoine

To OLGA KNIPPER

February 10, 1900, Yalta

Sweet actress,

The winter is so long, I have been ailing, nobody has written for almost a month—and I had decided there was nothing left to do but to go abroad, where life is not quite so drab. But now the weather has become more balmy and life is more pleasant, and so I have made up my mind to leave for abroad only at the end of this summer, in time for the exposition.

Why, oh why have you got the blues? You are really living, working, hoping and singing, you laugh when your uncle reads aloud—what more do you want? It's another matter as far as I am concerned. I have been wrenched from my native soil, can't live a rounded life, can't drink, although I like to very much; I love sound but never hear any, in brief, I am now in the situation of a transplanted tree hesitating as to whether it will take root or wither away. I may have some basis for occasionally allowing myself to complain of boredom in my letters, but have you? Meierhold complains of life's dullness, too. My God! Incidentally, a word on Meierhold. He must spend all summer in the Crimea, his health requires it. And I mean all summer.

Well, ma'am, I'm in good health now. I am not doing anything, as I am getting ready to sit down to my work. I've been digging away in the garden.

You wrote not long ago that the future of you little people is shrouded in mystery. Recently I had a letter from your boss, Nemirovich. He tells me the company is going to perform in Sevastopol, and then in Yalta at the beginning of May. There are to be five performances in Yalta followed by evening rehearsals. Only the valued members of the cast are going to stay behind for the rehearsals, while the rest can have time off to rest wherever they wish. I hope you are valued. For the director you may be valued, but for the author you are beyond value. There you have a pun as a tidbit. I won't write more until you send your picture. I kiss your sweet hand.

Your Antonio, academicus

... Thanks for your good wishes on my marriage. I informed my fiancée[1] of your intention to visit Yalta in order to carry on with me behind her back. To this she said that when "that horrid woman" came here, she would not let me out of her embraces for an instant. I said that embracing for such a protracted period during hot weather was unhygienic. She became offended and went into a brown study, in an attempt to guess in what sort of circle I had acquired this façon de parler; after a brief pause she said that the theatre is evil and that my inten-

1 This is, again, the joke about the imaginary lady.

tion to give up play writing was most praiseworthy. Then she asked me to kiss her. To this I replied that it was not decorous to kiss so often in my position as academician. She cried, and I left.

To OLGA KNIPPER

February 14, 1900, Yalta

Sweet actress,

The photos are very, very good, especially the one in which you wear an air of dejection, with your elbows on the back of the chair and with a modestly sorrowful, quiet expression, behind which lurks a little imp. The other is also successful, but there you resemble somewhat a little Jewess, a very musical young lady who attends the conservatory and at the same time, just in case, is secretly studying the art of dentistry and is engaged to a young man from Moghilev,[1] the Manasevich[2] type. Are you angry? Really and truly angry? That is my revenge for your not having signed them. . . .

The willow tree is green all over; near the bench in the corner the grass has been a lush green for a long time. The almond tree is in blossom. I've set up benches all over the garden, not fancy ones with iron legs, but plain wooden ones, which I am painting green. I've put up three little bridges across the brook and am setting out some palms. . . . Not since autumn have I heard music, or singing, nor have I seen a single interesting female—can you wonder that I am blue?

I had decided not to write you, but since you have sent the pictures I have lifted the ban and here I am, obviously, writing. I'll even travel to Sevastopol to meet you, only, let me repeat, you are not to tell anyone, especially not Vishnevski. I'll go there incognito, and will sign the hotel register as Count Blackmugg.

1 Moghilev was a city within the Jewish settlement of Byelorussia.
2 Manasevich was the secretary of the Moscow Art Theatre.

I was just joking when I said you looked like a Jewess. Don't be angry, my precious one. Now let me kiss your sweet hand and be eternally your

A. Chekhov

To MAXIM GORKI

February 15, 1900, Yalta

Dear Alexei Maximovich,

Your article in the "Nizhni-Novgorod Blade" was balm to my soul. How gifted you are! I don't know how to write anything except fiction, while you are completely master of the newspaperman's pen as well. At first I thought I liked the article so much because you praised me . . .

Why am I not sent "Foma Gordeyev?" I have read it only in snatches, but I should have read it all together, at one sitting, as I read "Resurrection" not long ago. Except for the relations of Nekhludov and Katya, which are rather unclear and contrived, everything in this novel struck me with its vigor and richness, its breadth, and I was also struck with the insincerity of a man who fears death, won't admit it and clutches at texts from Holy Writ. . . .

"Twenty Six Men and a Girl" is a good story, the best of the stuff "Life" generally prints in its dilettantish magazine. You get a vivid sense of the place and can smell the hot bagels.

My story in "Life" was full of bad errors despite my having read proof. Their provincial pictures by Chirikov also annoy me, and their illustration entitled "Happy New Year!" as well as Gurevich's story.

I have just been handed a letter from you. So India is out? Too bad. When you have India in your past, and long sea voyages, you have something to recall when you can't sleep nights. And a trip abroad doesn't take much time, it won't interfere with your walking trip through Russia.

I am bored not in the sense of Weltschmerz, nor from any

loneliness of existence as such, but merely bored without people, without music, which I love, and without women, who just don't exist in Yalta. I am bored without caviar and sauerkraut.

I am very sorry you have evidently changed your mind about a visit to Yalta. The Moscow Art Theatre will be here in May, is giving five performances and is then staying on for rehearsals. Do come, you will learn all about the conventions of the stage at rehearsals and will then write a play in five to eight days which I would welcome joyfully, with all my heart.

Yes, I now have the right to expose the fact that I am forty, and no longer a young man. I was the very youngest of the fiction writers but you came on the scene and I immediately grew more sedate and now nobody calls me the youngest any more. I press your hand cordially. Keep well.

Yours,

A. Chekhov

To OLGA KNIPPER

March 26, 1900, Yalta

Black melancholy streams from your letter, sweet actress; you are gloomy, and frightfully unhappy, but not for long I should think, as soon, very soon, you will sit in a railway coach and eat snacks with great gusto. It's a good thing you are coming before the others, with Masha; at any rate we will manage to talk about things, take walks, visit places roundabout, eat and drink. But please don't bring Vishnevski along, or else he will trail at our heels and not let anybody get in a word edgewise; he won't let us live in peace, as he will keep on reciting stuff from "Uncle Vanya."

I haven't got a new play, the newspapers are just lying. Generally speaking, the papers have never written the truth about me. If I had begun a new play, naturally you would be the first I would have told of it.

We have a wind here, and real spring weather hasn't come into its own but still we can go out without galoshes and with regular hats. Soon, any day now, the tulips will be in bloom. I have a lovely garden, but it is rather messy and dusty, a sort of dilettante garden.

Gorki is here and praises you and your theatre very highly. I'll introduce you to him.

Goodness! Somebody has driven up. The visitor has just come in. Goodbye for now, actress!

Yours,

A. Chekhov

To OLGA KNIPPER

August 8, 1900, Yalta

Greetings, my sweet little Olya, joy of my life,

I got your letter today, the first since your departure, read it, then reread it and now I am answering, my actress. After seeing you off I drove to Kiest's Hotel, where I spent the night; the next day, out of boredom and for want of something better to do, I drove to Balaklava. There I spent my time dodging the ladies who recognized me and wanted to give me an ovation; after a night there I left for Yalta the next morning on the "Tavel." The crossing was fiendishly upsetting. Now I am back home, lonesome, out of sorts, and worn out. Alexeyev [Stanislavski] was here yesterday. We spoke of the play[1] and I gave him my word I would finish it not later than September. See what a bright boy I am.

I keep on thinking the door will open and you will walk in. But you won't, you are either attending rehearsals or are at home in Merzlyakovski Lane, far from Yalta and me.

Farewell, and the heavenly powers and guardian angels preserve you. Farewell, my good little girl.

Your Antonio

1 *The Three Sisters.*

To OLGA KNIPPER

August 18, 1900, Yalta

My sweet little pet,

Here are answers to the questions that pop out of your letters. I am not working in Gurzuf but in Yalta, and I am being hindered, cruelly, vilely and basely hindered. The play[1] is complete in my head, has taken form from where my imagination left off and is pleading to be set onto paper, but hardly do I place a sheet of paper in front of me than the door opens and some ugly mug intrudes. I don't know how it is going to turn out, but the start is not bad, pretty smooth, I think.

Shall we be seeing each other? Yes, we will, but when? The first part of September, in all probability. I am lonesome and in a bad temper. My money is disappearing devilishly fast; I am being ruined and will wind up in the poorhouse. Today we have a most fierce wind, a gale, and the trees are withering.

One crane has flown away.

Yes, my sweet bit of an actress, how joyfully, with what purely calflike pleasure would I disport myself in field and forest, beside a stream, amongst the herd. It does seem silly to bring up, but it has been two years since I have seen grass. My precious, how dull is life!

Masha is leaving tomorrow.

Do keep well. . . .

Your Antonio

Vishnevski doesn't write and is probably angry. Just for that I'll write in a bad part for him.

To OLGA KNIPPER

September 8, 1900, Yalta

You write that you find everything bewildering, in confusion. . . . It is good for things to be confused, my sweet little actress, very good! It indicates that you are a philosopher, a woman of parts.

1 *The Three Sisters.*

So the weather seems to have turned warm? No matter what, the twentieth of September I am leaving for Moscow to stay until the first of October. I'm going to spend all that time sitting in my hotel room and working on the play. Shall I write or make a clean copy? I don't know, dear old lady of mine. One of my lady characters just hasn't come off somehow, I can't do a thing with her and am in despair.

I just had a letter from Marx, who tells me my plays will be out in ten days.

I am afraid you may be disillusioned with me. My hair is falling out in terrible quantities, so fast that one fine day you'll take a look at me and a week later find me resembling somebody's grandpappy. Apparently it is the barber's fault, for I started losing my hair the minute I had it cut.

Is Gorki writing a play or isn't he? Whence the note in "News of the Day" about the title "The Three Sisters" not being appropriate? What stuff and nonsense! Perhaps it isn't suitable, but I have no intention of changing it.

I am terribly blue. Do you know what I mean? Terribly! My diet consists exclusively of soup. It is cold at night, and so I stay home. There are no handsome young ladies, less and less money, and my beard is turning gray. . . .

My little darling, I kiss your sweet hands, both the right and the left. Keep well and don't feel depressed and don't worry about being confused.

Goodbye for now, my good little Olya. You are a little crocodile who has crawled into my heart!

Your Antonio

To MARIA CHEKHOVA

September 9, 1900, Yalta

Dear Masha,

This is in reply to the letter in which you ask about Mother. In my opinion it would be better for her to go to Moscow now, this fall, rather than after December. Why, in Moscow she would get tired and lonesome for Yalta in a month, and if you take her to Moscow in the fall, she will be back in Yalta again at Christmas. That's how I look at it, and I may possibly be mistaken, but at any rate in reaching a decision you must bear in mind that it is much duller in Yalta before Christmas than after; incomparably duller. . . .

There is nothing new. There is no rain, either, and everything is parched. At home it is quiet, peaceable, very nice and, of course, dreary.

Writing "The Three Sisters" is very hard, harder than my earlier plays. But no matter, maybe it will come out all right, if not now, then next season. I may say in passing that writing in Yalta is a hard job: people bother me and in addition I seem to write without aim and I don't like today what I wrote yesterday. . . .

I have just had a telegram from Kommisarjevskaya, asking for a play for her benefit performance.

Well, keep in good health and happy. My deepest respects to Olga Leonardovna, and Vishnevski and the rest.

If Gorki is in Moscow, tell him I sent a letter to His Worship in Nizhni-Novgorod.

Yours,
A. Chekhov

To OLGA KNIPPER
September 27, 1900, Yalta
My sweet little Olya, my wonderful little actress,

Why this tone, why the querulous, petulant mood? Am I really so much to blame? Then do forgive me, my darling, my good girl, don't be angry, for I'm not so much at fault as your misgivings prompt you to assume. I assure you, my sweet, the only reason I have not yet left for Moscow is because I haven't been well, upon my word of honor. Honestly and truly! Won't you believe me?

To OLGA KNIPPER [*1900*]

I shall remain in Yalta until the tenth of October to work, after which I will leave for Moscow or abroad, depending upon my health. In any event I shall keep on writing you.

I haven't had any letters from my brother Ivan or sister Masha. Apparently they are angry, but I don't know why. . . .

Do keep your eyes open and write in detail how "The Snow Maiden"[1] went, how the shows have been going generally, what mood the company is in, the reaction of the audiences and so on and so forth. Certainly you aren't in my situation; you have a great deal of material for letters, more than you can handle; I have nothing to report, beyond the fact that I caught two mice today. . . .

You write that I have a loving, tender heart and ask why I have steeled it. When have I done so? Precisely how have I expressed this hardheartedness? I have always loved you tenderly with all my heart and never have I concealed my sentiments from you, never, never, yet here you accuse me of hardheartedness just to have something to put down in the exuberance of your health.

Judging from the general tone of your letter, you wish and expect some kind of explanation, some sort of lengthy conversation carried on with grave expressions on our faces and with momentous conclusions to be drawn. But I don't know what to tell you, except the one thing I have repeated ten thousand times and will probably continue to repeat for a long time to come, i.e., that I love you—that's all. If we are not together now, it isn't you or I who are to blame, but the demon that filled me with bacilli and you with love for art.

Goodbye once again, my charming little lady, and may the holy angels guard you. Don't be cross with me, dear one, don't be blue, be a good girl.

What's new in the theatre? Please write.

Your Antoine

1 *The Snow Maiden* was a play by A. N. Ostrovski. It was made into an opera by Rimsky-Korsakov.

To OLGA KNIPPER

September 28, 1900, Yalta

My sweet Olya,

I sent you a telegram today saying I would probably come to Moscow in October. If I do, it will be on or about the tenth, not sooner; I will remain there five days or so and then leave for abroad. In any event I shall inform you by telegram of the day of my arrival. I do not know whether express trains will be running after the fourth of October; will you find out about it so that you do not go to the station needlessly.

Today I read the first criticisms of "The Snow Maiden"—they like only the beginning and then they get tired of it, as of a game. I am of the opinion that your theatre should produce only contemporary plays, nothing but! You should treat of contemporary life, of life among the intelligentsia, which is neglected in other theatres because of their utter lack of intellectuality and, in part, want of talent.

I don't get letters from anybody. Nemirovich seems to have gotten angry and hasn't sent me a line all this time. My relatives do not write. How did "Lonely Lives" go off? It should be somewhat better than "The Snow Maiden."

And so, keep well and happy. Oh, what a role there is for you in "The Three Sisters!" What a role! If you give me ten rubles you'll get it, otherwise I'll give it to another actress. I won't offer "The Three Sisters" this season; let the play lie a bit and ripen, or, as certain good ladies say about a cake when they put it on the table—let it sigh.

There is nothing new.

Your own Antoine

To MAXIM GORKI

October 16, 1900, Yalta

My dear Alexei Maximovich,

. . . Well, my dear sir, the twenty-first of this month I am leaving for Moscow, and thence abroad. Just think, I've written a play. I haven't recopied it, though, as it won't be put on now, but only next season. I'll let it lie around and ripen. Writing "The Three Sisters" was terribly hard work. It has three heroines, you know, each one has to be a special type, and all three of them are a general's daughters! The action takes place in a provincial city, on the order of Perm, and the surroundings are military, an artillery unit.

The Yalta weather is glorious, the air is fresh, and my health has improved. I don't even feel like leaving here for Moscow, the work goes on so well and it is so nice not to feel the itching in my rear end that I had all summer. I am not coughing and even eat meat. I am all by myself, all alone. Mother is in Moscow.

Thank you for the letters, dear chap. I read them twice. Remember me to your wife and little Maxim, and give them my hearty regards. And so, until we meet in Moscow. I hope you won't disappoint me and that we'll be seeing each other.

God bless you!

Yours,

A. Chekhov

To OLGA KNIPPER

December 28, 1900, Nice

My sweet little pup, imagine this horrible situation!

I was just informed some gentleman had asked for me downstairs. I go down, look him over—an old fellow, who introduces himself as Chertkov. In his hands are a bundle of letters, and it turns out that he had received all these letters, addressed to me, because of the similarity of names. One of your letters (there were three in all—the first three you wrote) had been opened. How do you like that? Henceforward you should apparently write me thus: Monsieur Antoine Tchekhoff, rue 9 Gounod (or Pension Russe), Nice. But be sure you write Antoine—otherwise I won't get your letters for ten or fifteen days after you have posted them.

The letter of reprimand regarding Vienna, in which you call me "a Slavonic jellyfish," came very late; fifteen years ago, it is true, I would lose my way abroad and not get where I wanted to go; but when I was in Vienna this time I got everywhere; I went to the theatre, too, but all their tickets were sold out. However, upon leaving the city I remembered that I had forgotten to read the ads of what was being played—just like a Russian. I bought myself a magnificent wallet there, at Klein's. It seems he had opened his shop two days before. I also bought some straps for my luggage. So you can see what a practical person I am, my precious.

You lecture me for not writing Mother. My dear, I have written both my mother and Masha many times, but haven't had an answer and probably won't get one. So I've given up. I haven't had a single line from them, but have it your way—I always was and will be a jellyfish and will always be in the wrong, though I don't know why.

Thank you for the words about Tolstoy. . . . Vladimir Nemirovich and his spouse are in Nice. In comparison with other women here she seems utterly banal, like the wife of a small-town storekeeper. She is buying the devil knows what, as cheaply as she can get the stuff. I am sorry she is with him. He is as ever a fine person, and good company.

We had a cold spell but now it is warm and we are wearing our summer coats. I won five hundred francs at roulette. May I play, my love?

I was in such a hurry with the last act, thinking you people needed it. But it seems you won't begin rehearsing before Nemirovich's return. If I could only have kept this act another two or three days, I daresay it would have been much more meaty. . . .

Have you fully recovered? It's about time! Although you are a nice little girl even when you are ill, and write nice letters, just the same don't you dare get sick again.

I dine at the same table with a great many ladies, some of

them from Moscow, but I won't exchange even half a word with them. I sit there and sulk in silence, eat stubbornly or think of you. Once in a while the Moscow ladies turn the talk to the theatre in an obvious effort to draw me into the conversation, but I maintain my silence and keep on eating. I am always gratified to hear you praised. And you are very highly praised! They talk about you as a good actress. Well, little miss, keep healthy and happy. I am yours! Just take and eat me with olive oil and vinegar. A big kiss.

Your Antoine

To KONSTANTIN STANISLAVSKI

January 2, 1901, Nice

Dear Konstantin Sergeyevich,

I received the letter sent on the twenty-third of December only yesterday. . . .

I wish you a Happy New Year, and, if I may hope, a new theatre, which you will soon start building. And I wish you about five new and magnificent plays. As to that old play, "The Three Sisters," reading it at the Countess'[1] evening party is absolutely forbidden under any circumstances. For God's sake, I beg of you, don't read it, not by any means, nor in any manner, otherwise you will cause me a great deal of anguish.

I sent Act IV off long ago, before Christmas, addressed to Vladimir Ivanovich. I have made a great many changes. You tell me that in Act III, when Natasha makes the rounds of the house at night, she extinguishes the lights and looks for evil-doers under the furniture. But it seems to me it would be preferable to have her walk across the stage in a straight line without looking at anything or anybody, à la Lady Macbeth, with a candle—that way the scene would be shorter and more blood-curdling. . . .

---

[1] Tolstoy's wife, who was arranging a charity soirée.

Thank you with all my heart for the letter which gave me such joy. I warmly clasp your hand.

Yours,

A. Chekhov

To JOASAPH TIKHOMIROV[1]

January 14, 1901, Nice

Dear Joasaph Alexandrovich,

I have just received your letter—you have given me great pleasure and I thank you enormously. Here are the answers to your questions:

1. Irina does not know that Tuzenbach is having a duel, but surmises that something went wrong that may have grave, not to say tragic, consequences. And when a woman guesses, she says, "I knew it, I knew it."

2. Chebutykin only sings the words, "Would it not please you to accept this date . . ." These are words from an operetta which was given some time ago at the Hermitage. I don't remember its title, but you can make inquiries, if you wish, from Shechtel the architect (private house, near the Yermolayev Church). Chebutykin must not sing anything else or his exit will be too prolonged.

3. Solyoni actually believes he looks like Lermontov; but of course he doesn't—it is silly even to consider a resemblance. He should be made up to look like Lermontov. The likeness to Lermontov is immense, but only in the opinion of Solyoni himself.

Forgive me if I haven't answered as I should, or satisfied you. There is nothing new with me, all goes along in the old way. I will probably return earlier than I thought, and it is very possible that in March I will already be at home, i.e., in Yalta.

Nobody writes me anything about the play; Nemirovich-Danchenko never said a word about it when he was here and

[1] This letter refers, of course, to the characters in *The Three Sisters*.

it seemed to me it bored him and wouldn't be successful. Your letter, for which I thank you, helped to dispel my melancholy. . . . I wish you good health and all the best.

Yours,

A. Chekhov

To KONSTANTIN STANISLAVSKI

January 15, 1901, Nice

Dear Konstantin Sergeyevich,

Many thanks for your letter. Of course you are a thousand times right, it wouldn't do at all to show Tuzenbach's body. I myself felt it when I wrote the play and spoke to you of it, if you will recall. That the finale reminds one of "Uncle Vanya" is a minor evil. "Uncle Vanya" happens to be my own play, and not someone else's, and when you are reminiscent of yourself in your works, people will say that is the way it should be. Chebutykin doesn't talk, but sings the phrase, "Would it not please you to accept this date." It is from an operetta, I don't remember which one, not if my life depended on it. . . .

Many thanks for having written. My sincere compliments to Maria Petrovna and all the artists, and I wish you all the best. Keep well and happy.

Yours,

A. Chekhov

To MARIA ANDREYEVA

January 26, 1901, Nice

Dear Maria Fyodorovna,

It was not I who sent you the flowers, but please let us assume that I did, for otherwise my embarrassment and anguish will be boundless. I cannot express the joy your letter caused me. My heartiest thanks, and you can now consider me forever in your debt.

You write that I made you unhappy on my last visit, that I

was afraid of speaking frankly, as it were, about "The Three Sisters," etc., etc. Merciful Heavens! I wasn't afraid of speaking frankly, I was afraid of intruding on you and purposely said nothing and restrained myself as much as possible, so as not to interfere with your work. If I were in Moscow I would certainly not undertake to make remarks except after the tenth rehearsal, and then, as a matter of fact, only on minor points. People write me from Moscow that you are magnificent in "The Three Sisters," that your performance is downright marvelous, and I am glad—very, very glad—and may God give you strength! Consider me your debtor, that is all.

Today I am departing for Algiers, will remain there a couple of weeks and then leave for Russia. I very much regret that you will be performing in St. Petersburg, since I do not like the city and do not rate its tastes very high. My respects and regards to your husband and the children. Keep nice and healthy, and may the heavenly angels guard you.

Devotedly,
A. Chekhov

To OLGA KNIPPER

March 1, 1901, Yalta

My dear one,

Don't read the newspapers, don't read anything, or you will pine away altogether. Here is some sound advice for future reference: heed the words of your old holy hermit. Certainly I told you, I assured you, that things wouldn't go well in St. Petersburg—and you should have listened to me. At any rate, your theatre will never again visit the place—thank God.

Personally I am giving up the theatre entirely, and will never again write for it. It is possible to write for the stage in Germany, in Sweden, even in Spain, but not in Russia, where dramatic authors are not respected, are kicked around and are forgiven neither their successes nor their failures. You are being abused now for the first time in your life, which accounts for

[283]

your sensitiveness, but it will pass away with time, and you'll get used to such treatment. But imagine the divine, sublime feelings of Sanin.[1] He probably has his pockets crammed with reviews and looks upon the rest of you most superciliously. . . .

We are having remarkable weather here, with warmth and a brightly shining sun, and the apricots and almond trees are in bloom. I shall expect you during Holy Week, my poor abused little actress, and shall continue to wait for you, bear that in mind.

Between the twentieth and twenty-eighth of February I sent you five letters and eight telegrams; I asked you to telegraph me, but haven't had a word in reply. . . .

Tell me how long you are all staying in St. Pete. Write, little actress.

I am well—cross my heart.

I press you tenderly to me.

Your Holy Hermit

To OLGA KNIPPER

April 22, 1901, Yalta

My sweet, delightful Knippschitz,

I didn't detain you because I found Yalta revolting and had the idea we would soon be seeing each other anyway as free souls. Be that as it may, your anger is groundless, my darling. I haven't any concealed thoughts of any kind, and tell you everything that comes to mind.

I shall be arriving in Moscow early in May, and if it is possible we'll get married and take a trip along the Volga, or we can take the trip first and then get married—whichever you find more convenient. We can board the boat at Yaroslavl or Rybinsk and head for Astrakhan, thence to Baku, and from Baku to Batum. Or maybe you don't care for that route? We might take

---

[1] The Moscow Art Theatre opened its St. Petersburg repertory with Hauptmann's *Lonely Lives*. Sanin, apparently, was the only actor in the company who was praised by the critics.

one along the northern Dvina to Archangel, on the Solovka. We'll go wherever you decide. After that we can live in a Moscow apartment for all or the greater part of the winter. If only I keep my strength and stay well! My cough deprives me of every bit of energy, I take a dim view of the future and work quite without enthusiasm. Please think about the future for me, be my little manager, and I'll do whatever you say; otherwise we shan't really live, but gulp down a tablespoonful of life once every hour.

So you are left without a part now? That's very pleasant. Today I was sent a review of "The Three Sisters" from the "Revue Blanche." I also received a copy of the Tolstoy reply to the Synod's resolution.[1] Then there was a copy of the almanac called "Northern Flowers" with my story in it. I had a letter from my brother Ivan saying he was ill. I also had a telegram from the Olympia acting company in St. Petersburg asking permission to perform "The Three Sisters." Today we have rain and a desperate wind, but out of doors the air is warm and pleasant. My dog, Chestnut, whom you call Redhead, had her leg stepped on by a horse, and now I have to fuss over her and put on bandages; I am quite permeated with iodoform. . . .

What plays will I find on at your theatre? What rehearsals are under way? Rehearsals of "Mikhail Kramer"? "The Wild Duck"? At moments I experience an overwhelming desire to write a four-act farce or comedy for the Art Theatre. And I'm going to do so, if nothing interferes, except that I won't let the theatre have it before the end of 1903.

I will telegraph you, but don't tell anyone and come to the station alone. Do you hear? So long for now, my precious, my charming little girl. Don't go around moping and imagining God only knows what; honest to goodness, I haven't the slightest secret I would keep from you even for a moment. Be a good little creature, don't be cross.

Your Antoine

[1] The Synod had excommunicated Tolstoy from the Church.

To EVGENIA CHEKHOVA [Telegram]

May 25, 1901, Moscow

DEAR MAMA GIVE ME YOUR BLESSING AM GETTING MARRIED
EVERYTHING WILL REMAIN AS IT WAS LEAVING TO TAKE KUMISS
CURE ADDRESS AKSENOVO SAMARA ZLATOUST HEALTH IS BETTER

ANTON

To MARIA CHEKHOVA

June 2, 1901, Aksenovo

Greetings, dear Masha,

I have been intending to write you and have not got around
to it; I have lots of business to take care of, trivial matters, of
course. You already know I am married. I believe this action
of mine will in no wise change my life or the surroundings I
have always been in. Mother most likely is already saying God
knows what, but you tell her there will be absolutely no changes,
everything will continue as it has until now. I will keep on
going along as I have hitherto, and Mother as well; my relations
with you will remain as unalterably warm and good as they
always have been.

Here in Ufa Province life is dull and uninteresting; I am
drinking kumiss, which, apparently, agrees with me pretty well.
It is an acid drink similar to kvass. . . .

If your funds are running low send me a blank check, which
you can get out of my desk. I have put the receipts from the
government bank into one packet, have added another one for
3,700 rubles and have marked it "For M. P. Chekhova." The
packet is at Knipper's, and they will turn it over to you. Take
care of it, please, or I may lose it.

My health is tolerable at the moment, you might even say
good, and I hardly cough any more. I will be in Yalta at the
end of July and will stay there until October, then live in
Moscow until December and then back again to Yalta. It looks
as though my wife and I must live apart—a situation to which,
by the way, I am already accustomed. . . .

To MARIA CHEKHOVA [*1901*]

I shall write you again soon, and in the meantime keep well. I send my deepest respects to Mama. Her telegram was forwarded to me by mail from Moscow. . . .

There is no bathing here. It would be nice to go fishing, but the place is at some distance.

Christ be with you.

Your Antoine

To VASILI SOBOLEVSKI

June 9, 1901, Aksenovo

Dear Vasili Mikhailovich,

. . . Well, sir, I suddenly up and got married. I have already become accustomed, or practically so, to my new state, i.e., to deprivation of certain rights and privileges, and feel fine. My wife is a very decent person, and far from stupid, and a kindly soul.

And so, permit me to await a letter from you, my dear chap. We have a sanatorium here, and kumiss is drunk in quantity; at first life here seems tiresome and pallid, but then you don't mind it so much. Good luck and good health, give my regards to Varvara Alexeyevna and the children; and with all my heart I wish you the best of everything.

Yours,
A. Chekhov

To MARIA CHEKHOVA[1]

August 3, 1901, Yalta

Dear Masha,

I will to you for possession during your lifetime my home in Yalta, the money and royalties from my dramatic productions, and to my wife Olga Leonardovna the country home in Gurzuf

[1] Olga Knipper Chekhova delivered this letter to Maria Chekhova, after Chekhov died.

and five thousand rubles. If you wish, you may sell the real estate. Give our brother Alexander three thousand. Ivan is to get five thousand and Mikhail three thousand. One thousand rubles are to be given to Alexei Dolzhenko[2] and one thousand to Elena Chekhova[2] upon her marriage. After your death and Mother's death, everything that remains, except for the royalties from the plays, reverts to the Taganrog city administration for public education; royalties from the plays are for brother Ivan, and after Ivan's death are to be assigned to the Taganrog city administration for the same purpose mentioned above. I promised the peasants of Melikhovo Village one hundred rubles to pay for the highway; I also promised Gabriel Alexeyevich Kharchenko (private house, Moskalevka Street, Kharkov) to pay for his older daughter's secondary school education. . . . Help the poor. Take care of Mother. Live together peaceably.

Anton Chekhov.

To OLGA KNIPPER

August 21, 1901, Sevastopol

My sweet, my darling, my good wife,

I have just got out of bed, have had my coffee and am cocking an ear to the noise of the wind with a certain amount of alarm. I dare say the crossing will be a violent one. My darling, buy 1 lb. of raffia in some shop, even if it is only Lisitsin's and send it to me in Yalta. You can't get any here in Sevastopol. With it enclose about five cords for my pince-nez. Put in anything else you like, but try to manage not to have the parcel weigh more than two pounds.

I shall leave for Yalta and await your letter there. Don't be lonesome, little one, don't get sick or blue, don't be cross, but be gay and laugh—it suits you very well.

I love you very much and will always love you. My greetings to all your family. I kiss you firmly a hundred times, embrace

2 Cousins.

you tenderly and am sketching in my imagination various pictures in which you and I figure, and nobody and nothing else.

Goodbye, my darling, farewell!

Your boss Anton

To OLGA KNIPPER

August 28, 1901, Yalta

My kitten, my little kitten,

I just got your letter, read it through twice—and kiss you a thousand times. I like the plan of the apartment, and will show it to Masha (she left to see Dunya Konowitzer off on the boat) ; everything is very nice, only why did you put "Anton's study" next to a certain place? Want to get beaten up?

Here are answers to your questions. I am sleeping splendidly [. . .] my "innards" have been in running order thus far, and I haven't rubbed my neck with Eau de Cologne—forgot to. Yesterday I washed my head.

Yesterday I was at Orlenev's and was introduced to Mme Leventon;[1] they share an apartment.

Masha is bringing you some almonds from our tree.

You can see what kind of husband I am; I write you every day, in the most exemplary fashion. I am so lonesome without you! . . . It seems to me I have become a regular middle-class householder and cannot live without a wife. . . .

Behave yourself properly, or I'll beat you until it hurts. Write, sweetie, don't be a lazybones.

Your Ant.

To OLGA KNIPPER

September 4, 1901, Yalta

See all the trouble I go to for you!

With this passport you can live as you please wherever you please, with a husband or without such a character. Except that

[1] Mme. Leventon was Alla Nazimova.

you must: (1) sign "Olga Chekhova" on page 6, and (2) register with the Yalta police that you have received it; you can do this the next time you are in Yalta. So, you see, you are now a regular Yaltan, until the brink of the grave. At first I was inclined to put you down as the wife of an "honorary academician," but then decided it was incomparably pleasanter being the wife of a medical man.

Live placidly and generously, be a loving soul, and then I will kiss you every day. They tell me "The Three Sisters" was presented in Odessa with great success. I had my hair cut today, washed my head, trimmed by beard, took a walk along the promenade, then dined at home with Dr. Reformatski.

Write every day, or I'll take your passport away. Generally speaking, I intend keeping you strictly in line, so that you will fear and obey me. I'll give it to you!

Your severe husband,

A. Chekhov

Even though I haven't seen our apartment, you speak so well of it that I am satisfied with it sight unseen, very well satisfied, my sweet. Thank you for all the trouble you have taken, God bless you.

To MAXIM GORKI

October 22, 1901, Moscow

My dear Alexei Maximovich,

Five days have gone by since I read your play[1] and I haven't written you until now for the reason that I just couldn't get hold of Act IV; I kept on waiting—and still am. And so I have only read the three acts, but I think they are sufficient to judge the play. As I anticipated, it is very good, written with the true Gorki touch, a singular thing, very engrossing, and if I may begin by speaking of its defects, I have thus far noted only one,

1 The play was Gorki's *Small Folk*.

irremediable, like a redhead's red hair—and that is its conservatism of form. You force new, strange people to sing new
songs from a score that looks second-hand; you have four acts,
your characters deliver moral lectures, the long-drawn-out passages cause dismay, and so on. But all this is not basically important and is submerged, so to say, in the play's merits. How
alive Perchikhin is! His daughter is fascinating and so are
Tatiana and Peter, and their mother is an admirable old lady.
The play's central figure—Nil—is powerfuly done and extraordinarily interesting! In brief, the play grips one from the start.
Only, God save you from allowing anyone except Artem to play
Perchikhin, and have Stanislavski play Nil without fail. These
two people will do them exactly right. Peter should be played by
Meierhold. Except that Nil's part, a magnificent one, should be
made two or three times longer, the play should end with it
and be built around it. Don't contrast Nil with Peter and
Tatiana, though, just let him stand on his own feet, and them
on theirs; all these remarkable, splendid people, independent of
one another. . . .

Plenty of time remains before the staging, and you will manage to revise your play a good ten times over. What a pity that
I have to leave! I would sit in on the rehearsals and send you
word whenever it was needed.

On Friday I leave for Yalta. Keep well, and God keep you.
My deepest respects to Ekaterina Pavlovna and the children.
Let me give you a friendly handclasp and embrace you.

Yours,
A. Chekhov

To OLGA KNIPPER

November 2, 1901, Yalta

My sweet little pup, greetings!

. . . I am in good health, but yesterday and the day before,
since the day of my return, in fact, I have been out of sorts and

yesterday had to take some ol. ricini. But I am very happy that you are well and merry, my precious, it makes my heart easier. And how terribly I want you now to have a little half-German[1] to divert you, to fill your life. It should be so, my darling little one! What do you say?

Gorki will soon be passing through Moscow. He wrote me he was leaving Nizhni on the tenth of November. He has promised to revise your part in the play, i.e., give it broader range, has promised a lot generally, and I am extremely happy about it, because it is my belief revisions will not make his play worse, but much better, more rounded.

. . . I haven't been at Tolstoy's[2] yet, but am going there tomorrow. People say he is feeling well.

Olya, my dear wife, congratulate me: I have had a haircut!! Yesterday my boots were cleaned—the first time since my arrival. My clothes haven't yet had a cleaning. But on the other hand I have been changing my tie every day, and yesterday I washed my head. . . .

I am sending you the announcement from Prague on "Uncle Vanya." I keep on wondering what to send you and can't think of a thing. I am living like a monk and dream only of of you. Although it is shameful making declarations of love at forty, I cannot restrain myself, little pup, from telling you once again that I love you deeply and tenderly.

I kiss you, embrace you and press you close.

Keep healthy, happy and gay.

Your Antoine

To OLGA KNIPPER

November 9, 1901, Yalta

Greetings, my little darling,

Today's weather is amazing: warm, bright and dry, and quiet —like summer. The roses are blooming and the carnations and

---

1 Knipper's family were of German origin. Chekhov meant, of course, that he wanted her to have a baby.
2 Tolstoy was living in Yalta.

chrysanthemums, and some yellow flowers. Today I sat in the garden for a long time and thought of how splendid the weather is here but how much pleasanter it would be to ride in a sleigh. Forgive me this cynicism.

So Roxanova is again acting in "The Seagull"? Why, they took the play out of the repertory until they could get a new actress for the part and suddenly here's Roxanova in it again! What a beastly business! From the repertory list sent here I also noted that "Ivanov" is in rehearsal. To my way of thinking this is futile, unnecessary toil. The play will be a failure because it is going to get a dull production before an indifferent audience.

I'm going to get all the best authors to write plays for the Art Theatre. Gorki has already done so; Balmont, Leonid Andreyev, Teleshov and others are in the process of writing. It would be quite proper to assign me a fee, if only one ruble per person.

My letters to you don't satisfy me at all. After what you and I have experienced together, letters mean little; we ought to continue really living. How we sin by not living together! But what's the sense of talking! God be with you, my blessings upon you, my little German female, I am happy you are enjoying yourself. I kiss you resoundingly.

Your Antonio

To OLGA KNIPPER

November 17, 1901, Yalta

My sweet little spouse,

The rumors reaching you about Tolstoy, his illness and even death, have no basis in fact. There are no particular changes in his health and have been none, and death is evidently a long way off. It is true he is weak and sickly-looking, but he hasn't a single symptom to cause alarm, nothing except old age. . . . Don't believe anything you hear. If, God forbid, anything happens, I will let you know by wire. I will call him "Grandpa," otherwise I daresay it won't reach you.

Alexei Maximovich[1] is here, and well. He sleeps at my place and is registered with me. The local policeman was around today.

I am writing and working, but, my darling, working in Yalta is impossible, utterly, utterly impossible. It is remote from the world, uninteresting—and the principal point—cold. . . .

My lamp is burning now in the study. It's not too bad as long as it doesn't stink of kerosene.

Alexei Maximovich hasn't changed, he is the same decent, cultivated, kind man. The only thing in him, or on him, rather, that I find disconcerting is that Russian shirt of his. I can't get used to it any more than to the Court Chamberlain's uniform.

The weather is autumn-like, nothing to boast of.

Well, stay alive and healthy, light of my life. Thank you for the letters. Don't get sick, be a smart girl. Send my regards to the family.

I kiss and embrace you tenderly.

Your husband,
Antonio

I am in good health. Moscow had an astonishingly good effect on me. I don't know whether it was Moscow, or your doing, but I have been coughing very little. . . .

To OLGA KNIPPER

December 7, 1901, Yalta

Dear little miss actress,

How come you are not obeying your husband? Why didn't you ask Nemirovich to send the last act of "Small Folk"? Please ask him, my sweetheart. How disgusting, how unfortunate that you are not coming to Yalta for the holidays. It seems to me we shall be seeing each other only after many years, when we are both old folks.

---

1 Gorki was under constant police surveillance.

To VICTOR MIROLUBOV [1901]

I just spoke to Leo Tolstoy over the telephone. I have read the conclusion of Gorki's novel, "Three of Us." It is an extraordinarily queer thing. If it hadn't been Gorki who had written it, nobody would have read it. At least so it appears to me.

I haven't been well these last days, my lamb. I took some castor oil, think I have lost a lot of weight, cough and can't do a thing. Today I am better, so that tomorrow I shall probably get back to work again. . . . Solitude, apparently, reacts most perniciously on the stomach. Joking aside, my darling, when shall we get together again? When shall I see you? If only you could come here for the holidays, even for one day, it would be infinitely good. However, you know best.

I am writing this on the night of the seventh and will send it out tomorrow, the eighth. You are always attending dinners or jubilees—I am glad, puss, and commend you for it. You are a bright child, you are so sweet.

May the Lord be with you, my dear. I kiss you countless times.

Your Ant.

Don't spend too much money on the play—it won't be a success anyway. Twelve hundred rubles for dresses—for God's sake! I read Leonid Andreyev while I was still in Moscow, and on my way back to Yalta. Yes, he is a good writer; if he would write more, he would enjoy greater success. There is not much sincerity or simplicity in him, and so it is hard to get used to him. But still, sooner or later the audience will get accustomed to him and he'll make a big name for himself.

To VICTOR MIROLUBOV

December 17, 1901, Yalta

Dear Victor Sergeyevich,

I am not well, or not altogether well—that is more like it, and I cannot write. I have been coughing blood and now I feel feeble and ill-tempered as I sit with a hot compress on my side and take creosote and all sorts of trash. . . .

I read the article in "New Times" by that policeman Roza-nov,[1] which, incidentally, told me of your new activities. My dear fellow, I wish you knew how upset I was! It seems to me you ought to leave St. Petersburg right now—for Nervi or Yalta, it doesn't matter—but leave. What have you, a fine, up-standing man, in common with this Rozanov, or with that egregiously crafty Sergi, or, finally, with super-satisfied Merej-kowski? I would like to write you at great length but had better restrain myself, all the more so as letters are now read for the most part by those to whom they are not addressed. I will only say that the important thing about the problems engaging you are not the forgotten words, not the idealism, but the con-sciousness of your own decency, i.e., the complete freedom of your soul from all forgotten and unforgotten words, idealisms and the rest of those words that nobody understands. One should believe in God; if one doesn't have faith, though, its place should not be taken by sound and fury but by seeking and more seeking, seeking alone, face to face with one's conscience.

At any rate, keep well. If you decide to come, drop me a line. Tolstoy and Gorki are here and you won't find it dull, I hope.

There is nothing new. I clasp your hand firmly.

Yours,

A. Chekhov

To KONSTANTIN STANISLAVSKI

January 20, 1902, Yalta

Dear Konstantin Sergeyevich,

To the best of my knowledge (from information obtained by mail) the portraits of writers in the Taganrog library are hung in a row in one big frame. They probably want to put you, too, in the same sort of frame and therefore I believe it

---

1 Vasili Rozanov was on the staff of *New Times*. Chekhov considered him vain and hypocritical. He had organized a philosophic society with the approval of the St. Petersburg Church authorities and Chekhov is here attacking the hypocrisy of Rozanov and his friends.

would be best without further ado to forward a photograph of the usual studio format, without a frame. If a frame proves necessary, you can send it along afterward just as well.

As I read "Small Folk," I felt that the part of Nil was the central one. He is not a mujik, not a skilled workman, but a new man, an intellectualized worker. He doesn't seem to be a finished character, and it would not be a hard or lengthy job to fill him in, and it is a pity, a terrible pity, that Gorki is deprived of the possibility of attending the rehearsals.

May I say incidentally that Act IV is badly done (except for the ending) and since Gorki is deprived of the possibility of attending the rehearsals, it will be very bad.

I clasp your hand cordially and send hearty greetings to you and Maria Petrovna.

Yours,
A. Chekhov

To OLGA KNIPPER

January 20, 1902, Yalta
How stupid you are, my kitten, and what a little fool!

What makes you so sick, why are you in such a state? You write that life is hollow, that you are an utter nonentity, that your letters bore me, that you feel horror at the way your life is narrowing, etc., etc. You foolish creature! I didn't write you about the forthcoming play not because I had no faith in you, as you put it, but because I do not yet have faith in the play. It is in its faint dawn in my brain, like the first flush of day-break, and I still am not clear as to what sort of thing it is, what will come of it and whether it won't change from one day to the next. If we were together, I would tell you all about it, but it is impossible to write because nothing gets set down properly, I just write all sorts of trash and then become indifferent to the subject. In your letter you threaten never to ask me about anything, or to mix into anything; but what is your reason, my sweet? No, you are my own good girl, you will substitute mercy for wrath when you realize once again how much I love you, how near and dear you are to me, how impossible it is to live without you, my silly little goose. Quit having the blues, quit it! And have yourself a good laugh! I am permitted to be depressed, because I live in a desert, without anything to do, don't see people, am sick practically every week, but you? No matter what, your life is a full one.

I had a letter from Stanislavski. He writes a good deal and graciously. Hints that perhaps Gorki's play may not be put on this season. Writes about Omon, about "mesdames, ne vous décolletez pas trop."

Let me say in passing, Gorki intends working on a new play, about life in a cheap flophouse,[1] although I have been counseling him to wait a year or two, and to take his time. An author must produce in large quantities, but he must not hurry. Don't you think so, my good wife?

On my birthday, the seventeenth of January, I was in an abominable mood because I was ailing and because the telephone kept ringing all day with congratulatory telegrams. Even you and Masha did not spare me! . . .

You write me not to be sad, that we shall see each other soon. What do you mean? Will that be Holy Week? Or earlier? Don't get me excited, joy of my life. You wrote in December that you would be coming in January, got me all worked up, then wrote you would come during Holy Week—and I ordered my soul to becalm itself, withdrew into my shell and now you are again raising a gale on the Black Sea. Why?

The death of Solovtsov,[2] to whom I had dedicated my "Bear," was a most distressing event in my provincial life. I knew him well. The newspaper accounts implied that he had made some revisions of "Ivanov" and that I, as the playwright, had taken his advice, but it isn't true.

1 *The Lower Depths.*
2 Solovtsov was an actor.

And so, my wife, my enchanting creature, my adored, beloved girl, may God keep you, may you be healthy, gay and mindful of your husband, even if it is only when you go to bed at night. The important thing is not to get depressed. Why, your husband certainly is no drunkard, nor a spendthrift, nor a brawler. I am a regular German husband in my behavior, and even wear warm underdrawers.

I embrace you a hundred times, and kiss you infinitely, wife of mine.

Your Ant.

You write: wherever you poke your nose you hit a stone wall. And where did you poke it?

To OLGA KNIPPER

January 31, 1902, Yalta

Greetings, my sweet little Olya,

How are you? I am just so-so, for living otherwise is not possible. You are in raptures over L's[1] play, but actually it is the work of a dilettante, composed in solemn classical language because its author does not know how to write naturally of Russian life. It seems this L. has been writing for some time, and if you were to go poking around, I wouldn't wonder but what you might turn up some letters of his in my desk. Bunin's "In Autumn" is done with a constrained, tensed hand; at any rate Kuprin's "At the Circus" stands much above it. "At the Circus" is a free, artless, gifted work, in addition to being written by someone who knows the business. But why bother with either! How did we get talking about literature anyway? . . .

Tolstoy felt better yesterday, and now there is hope.

I've received your description of the evening and the placards and thank you, my darling. It made me laugh hilariously. The

[1] L. was Anatol Lunacharski and the play was a drama about life in the Renaissance. Lunacharski, after the Bolshevik Revolution, became the first People's Commissar of Education.

wrestlers, Kachalov in big boots, the orchestra under Moskvin's baton, amused me particularly. How jolly your life is and how dreary mine!

Anyway, keep well, my joy, God keep you safe. Don't forget me. Let me kiss and embrace you.

Your German,
Ant.

Tell Masha Mother is already walking about, and is fully recovered. I am writing this on the thirty-first of January, after tea, and wrote the letter to her in the morning. Everything is fine.

To PYOTR SERGEYENKO

February 2, 1902, Yalta

My dear Pyotr Alexeyevich,

Here are the details regarding Leo Nikolayevich.[1] One evening he suddenly felt ill. Angina pectoris set in, with intermittent heartbeats and agony. The doctors who are treating him happened to be visiting me at the time and were summoned by telephone. The next morning they let me know that Tolstoy was in a bad way, that there was scant hope he would pull through and that pneumonia had set in, the type that generally attacks old people before death. This tormenting, expectant mood continued for about two days, and then we got the information by telephone that the process in the lungs had been arrested and that there was hope.

Now Tolstoy is lying on his back, extraordinarily weak, but his pulse is good. Hope has not abated. He is being magnificently treated, among his doctors being Shchurovski of Moscow and Altshuller of Yalta. The fact that Tolstoy has remained alive and that there is hope for him I attribute at least in part to the good offices of these two doctors.

1 Tolstoy.

Thank you for the photograph. There is nothing new, all goes well for the time being. Keep well.

> Your
> A. Chekhov

To MARIA LILINA

February 3, 1902, Yalta

Dear Maria Petrovna,

You are very kind and I thank you very much for the letter. To my regret I cannot tell you anything interesting . . . we grow old, drink medicinal teas, walk around in felt boots. . . . However, there is one bit of news, and most agreeable at that— Leo Tolstoy's recovery. The Count was very seriously ill and had the beginnings of pneumonia, which such old fellows as he usually do not get over. For three days we expected the end and suddenly the old chap brightened up and started giving us hope. At present writing, our hopes have been enhanced considerably and when you read this letter, Leo Nikolayevich will probably be quite well.

As to Gorki, he doesn't feel too bad, maintains a cheerful attitude but is lonesome and is preparing to set to work on a new play, for which he has already found a theme. To the best of my understanding, about five years hence he will be writing magnificent things; right now he seems to be groping.

What you disclose in confidence about Konstantin Sergeyevich and my wife made me extraordinarily happy. Thank you, now I can take measures and will now proceed on the matter of a divorce.[1] I'm sending a statement to the Consistory today, to which I will attach your letter, and believe I will be free by spring; but before May I will give it to that spouse of mine properly. She fears me and I certainly don't handle her with kid gloves—she gets it wherever my foot lands!

[1] Lilina had jokingly written that her husband was paying attention to Knipper.

Greetings and hearty regards to Konstantin Sergeyevich. My congratulations to you both on the new theatre—I believe in its future success.

My profound compliments to you, I kiss your hand and greet you once more.

Your sincerely devoted
A. Chekhov

To OLGA KNIPPER

February 13, 1902, Yalta

Sweetie, pussy cat,

I will not meet you at the pier, as it will probably be chilly. Don't worry. I will meet you in my study, we will have supper together and then a good long talk.

Yesterday I suddenly and unexpectedly had a letter from Suvorin. This was after a silence of three years. He runs down your theatre but praises you, as it would be embarrassing to abuse you. . . .

It doesn't take three, but five days for letters to reach Yalta. This one, which I am mailing on the thirteenth of February, you will receive the seventeenth or eighteenth. So you see! Consequently I will write you one little bit of a letter tomorrow and then—enough! Then, after, a brief interval, I will enter upon my marital responsibilities.

When you arrive, please don't mention a word to me about eating. It is a bore, especially in Yalta. After Masha's departure everything changed again and goes along in the old way, as it did before her arrival, and it could not have been otherwise.

I am reading Turgenev. One eighth or one tenth of what he has written will survive, all the rest will be a mere matter of historical record twenty-five or thirty-five years from now. You don't mean to say you once liked Chichagov, the "Alarm Clock" artist? Heavens!

To VLADIMIR KOROLENKO [1902]

Why, oh why, does Savva Morozov[1] have aristocratic guests? Certainly they will cram themselves full of his food and laugh at his expense when they leave, as if he were a Yakut. I would drive those beasts out with a big stick. I have some perfume, but not much, and hardly any Eau de Cologne.

I kiss my sweetheart, my wonderful, beloved wife, and await her arrival impatiently. It is overcast today, not warm, drab, and if it weren't for thoughts of you and your visit, I think I might start drinking.

Now then, let me embrace my little German lady.

Your
Ant.

To VLADIMIR KOROLENKO

April 19, 1902, Yalta

Dear Vladimir Galaktionovich,

My wife arrived from St. Petersburg with a 102.2 temperature, quite weak and in considerable pain; she cannot walk, and had to be carried off the boat. . . . Now I think she is somewhat better.

I am not going to give Tolstoy the protest. When I began talking to him about Gorki and the Academy,[1a] he mumbled something about not considering himself an academician and buried his head in his book. I gave Gorki one copy and read him your letter. For some reason or other I don't think the Academy will hold a meeting on the twenty-fifth of May, as all the academicians will already have left town by the beginning of the month. I also think they won't vote for Gorki a second time and that he'll be blackballed. I want awfully to see you and talk things over. Can't you come to Yalta? I'll be here until the fifteenth of May. I would go to your place in Poltava, but my wife is sick, and will probably be bedridden here for an-

1 Savva Morozov was a wealthy merchant, a liberal and cultured man and an early backer of the Moscow Art Theatre.

1a Gorki had been elected to the Academy, but the Czar disapproved, and had the election declared null and void. Chekhov and Korolenko wrote a declaration of principles and both resigned from the Academy.

other three weeks. Or shall we see each other after the fifteenth of May in Moscow, on the Volga, or abroad? Write.

I give you a cordial handclasp and send my very best wishes. Keep well.

Yours,

A. Chekhov

My wife sends her greetings.

To MARIA CHEKHOVA

June 2, 1902, Moscow

Dear Masha,

We are again in a predicament. The night before Trinity, at 10 o'clock, Olga felt sharp pains in her abdomen (more painful than those she had in Yalta), then followed groans, shrieks, sobbing; the doctors had all gone to their summer homes (the night before a holiday), all our friends had also departed. . . . Thank goodness, Vishnevski appeared at midnight and began dashing around for a doctor. Olga was in torments all night, and this morning the doctor came; it has been decided to put her in Strauch's hospital. Overnight she became hollow-cheeked and thin. . . .

It is now uncertain what I will be doing, when I shall arrive and when I shall be leaving Moscow. Everything has been turned upside down.

Anna Ivanovna[1] has an expression on her face as though she were to blame for some reason. She was on the hunt for doctors all night.

I shall write later. In the meantime, keep well. Compliments to Mama.

Your Antoine

Olga's illness is the kind that will probably continue for a couple of years.[2]

---

[1] Anna Ivanovna was Olga Knipper's mother.

[2] Olga Chekhova had a miscarriage. Chekhov's postscript, "Olga's illness is the kind that will probably continue for a couple of years," tells us nothing.

To KONSTANTIN STANISLAVSKI

July 18, 1902, Lubimovka[1]

Dear Konstantin Sergeyevich,

Dr. Strauch came here today and found everything in order. He forbade Olga one thing only—driving over bad highways and excessive movement in general, but to my great satisfaction he has permitted her to take part in rehearsals without reservation; she can start her theatre work even as early as the tenth of August. She has been forbidden to travel to Yalta. I am going there alone in August, will return the middle of September and then will remain in Moscow until December.

I like it very much in Lubimovka. April and May were bad months but luck is with me now, as if to make up for all I had gone through; there is so much quiet, health, warmth and pleasure that I just can't get over it. The weather is fine and the river is fine, and indoors we eat and sleep like bishops. I send you thousands of thanks, straight from the bottom of my heart. It is a long time since I have spent such a summer. I go fishing every day, five times a day, and the fishing is not bad (yesterday we had a perch chowder). Sitting on the riverbank is too agreeable a pastime to write about. To put it briefly, everything is very fine. Except for one thing: I am idling and haven't been doing any work. I haven't yet begun the play, am only thinking it over. I will probably not start work before the end of August.

. . . Be well and gay, gather up your strength and energy. I press your hand.

Yours,
A. Chekhov

To MAXIM GORKI

July 29, 1902, Lubimovka

Dear Alexei Maximovich,

I have read your play,[1a] which is new and good beyond any doubt. Act II is very good, the very best, the most powerful, and

1 Chekhov borrowed the Stanislavski's summer cottage.
1a *The Lower Depths.*

in reading it, especially the end, I almost leaped with joy. The mood is a gloomy, painful one; its novelty will cause the audience to walk out of the theatre and at the least you can say goodbye to your reputation as an optimist. My wife is going to play Vasilisa, the lewd and vile-tempered female; Vishnevski walks around the house acting like a Tatar—he is sure that part will be his. Alas, it is not possible to give Artem the part of Luka, as he will be repeating himself and tire the audience; on the other hand he will play the policeman splendidly, that is really his part; Samarova will do the roommate. The part of the actor, whom you hit off most successfully, offers a magnificent opportunity and should be given to an experienced actor, say Stanislavski. Kachalov will play the Baron.

You have disposed of the most interesting characters by Act IV (except the actor), so you'd better watch out lest something happen on that account. This act can prove boresome and unnecessary, especially if only the mediocre characterizations remain after the exit of the vigorous and interesting actors. The death of the actor is terrible; it's as though you gave the spectator a box on the ear for no good reason, and without preparing him for the blow. It isn't sufficiently clear, either, how the Baron happened to find himself in the flophouse, and why he is a baron.

I am leaving for Yalta around the tenth of August (my wife is remaining in Moscow), then that same month I am returning to Moscow to stay until December, if nothing particular occurs. I will be seeing "Small Folk" and attending the rehearsals of the new play. Can't you manage to break away from Arzamas and come to Moscow if only for a week? I heard that you will be allowed to come to Moscow, that people are interceding for you. . . .

I am living in Lubimovka, Stanislavski's summer cottage, and do nothing but fish from morning to night. The stream here is delightfully deep, with plenty of fish. I have become so lazy I even feel disgusted with myself. . . .

L. Andreyev's "A Dilemma" is a pretentious thing, unintelligible and obviously of no use, but it is performed with talent. Andreyev has no simplicity and his talent reminds one of the singing of an artificial nightingale. . . .

Whatever happens, we'll see each other at the end of August. Keep well and happy, don't get lonesome. . . .

Your

A. Chekhov

To VLADIMIR KOROLENKO

August 25, 1902, Yalta

Dear Vladimir Galaktionovich,

Where are you? At home? At any rate, I am directing this letter to Poltava. This is what I wrote to the Academy.[1]

Your Imperial Highness,

In December of last year I received notification of the election of A. M. Peshkov as an honorary academician; I lost no time in getting in contact with Mr. Peshkov, who was then in the Crimea, was the first to bring him the news of his election and the first to congratulate him. After a lapse of some time, an announcement appeared in the newspapers stating that in view of the investigation of Mr. Peshkov under Article 1035, the election was considered invalid; it was definitely indicated that this announcement emanated from the Academy of Sciences. Since I am an honorary academician, this announcement in part came from myself as well. Thus, I was congratulating him heartily and, at the same time, was one of those who were involved in considering his election invalid—and I was unable to reconcile my conscience to this contradiction. A knowledge of the contents of Article 1035 explained nothing. After lengthy reflection I was able to arrive at only one decision, extremely distressing and grievous to me, namely, most humbly to request

[1] This was the letter of resignation to the Academy. Peshkov was, of course, Gorki's real name.

Your Imperial Highness to accept my resignation of the title of honorary academician.

There you have it. It's a long-winded composition, drafted on a very hot day; I couldn't, and probably can't do any better.

Visiting you was out of the question. My wife and I wanted to travel along the Volga and the Don, but she fell seriously ill in Moscow again, and we were both in such torments that we couldn't even consider a trip. . . .

I wish you the best of everything, and extend a cordial handclasp. Keep well and happy.

> Yours,
> A. Chekhov

To OLGA KNIPPER

September 6, 1902, Yalta

My little crocodile, my unusual wife,

This is why I didn't get to Moscow despite my promise. Hardly had I got to Yalta when my physical barometer started falling, I began coughing fiendishly and lost my appetite entirely. It was no time either for trips or writing. In addition, as if on purpose, there was no rain, a perilous, heat-laden drought that parched one's very soul. As is my custom I wanted to take some Hunyadi Janos water, but the Yalta brand was the artificial variety, and for two days after taking it I had palpitations of the heart.

You see what a dull husband you've got! Today I feel much better, but there is still no rain and it doesn't look as if there will ever be any. I would leave for Moscow, but am afraid of the journey, afraid of Sevastopol, where I would have to remain half a day. And don't you come here. I am ill at ease asking you to visit this sultry, dusty desert; besides, there isn't any special necessity, as I am already better and will soon be arriving in Moscow.

One hundred rubles for two and a half acres is an absurd,

ridiculous price. Please, my sweet one, stop looking at summer cottages, we won't buy one anyhow. We can wait for some special opportunity, that would be the best of all, or else we can hire a cottage every summer. . . .

In case you want to come here, bring my cuspidor (the blue one, I forgot it), the pince-nez; don't take along any shirts, but the jersey underwear, the Jaeger stuff.

Suvorin stayed here two days, told me all sorts of things, a great deal that was new and interesting, and left yesterday. One of Nemirovich's admirers by the name of Fomin came to see me; he delivers public lectures on "The Three Sisters" and "Three of Us" (by Chekhov and Gorki). He is an honest, high-minded, but obviously not very bright little gentleman. I filled him with a lot of ponderous remarks, saying I did not consider myself a dramatist, that the only one such in present-day Russia was Naidenov and that [Nemirovich's] "In My Dreams" (a play he likes very much) was a middle-class piece and so forth and so on. Whereupon he left.

I am writing to your own Moscow address, since, if I am to believe your last letter, you have already moved to town. And a good thing.

I kiss the mother of my future family and embrace her. . . .

Your A.

To OLGA KNIPPER

September 18, 1902, Yalta

My exquisite little missis,

I have a real event to relate: we had rain last night. . . . My health has improved immensely, at least I am eating a lot and coughing less; I am not drinking cream because the local product upsets my stomach and is extremely cloying. To put it briefly, don't worry, everything is all right, and even though things are not at their best, at least they are not worse than usual.

Today I am sad, for Zola has died. It was so sudden and

untimely, so to speak. I wasn't particularly devoted to him as a writer, but on the other hand, during these last years, with all the clamor of the Dreyfus affair, I esteemed him highly as a man.

And so we shall soon be seeing each other, my little bug. I am going to stay until you drive me out. I'll manage to bore you, you may rest easy on that score. If you discuss Naidenov's play with him, assure him he has great gifts—no matter what the play is. I am not writing him, as I shall soon be talking with him—you can tell him that. . . .

Don't get into the dumps, it doesn't suit your style of looks. Be a gay little girl, my sweetie. I kiss both your hands, your forehead, cheeks, shoulders. . . .

Your A.

. . . Mother sends her greetings and keeps on complaining you don't write her.

To ADOLF MARX[1]

October 23, 1902, Moscow

Dear Adolf Fedorovich,

. . . As to Mr. Ettinger's manuscript, his "Thoughts and Ideas" are put together in an absolutely childish fashion, so that it would be impossible to discuss his book seriously. In addition, all these "thoughts and ideas" are not mine, but those of my characters; for instance, if some character in a story or play of mine asserts that he must kill or steal, it certainly does not signify that Mr. Ettinger has the right to characterize me as an advocate of murder or theft.

I am returning Mr. Ettinger's manuscript. Permit me to wish you all the best, and to remain,

Yours sincerely,
A. Chekhov

[1] Marx wanted to know if Ettinger's manuscript was worth publishing.

To LEOPOLD SULERJITSKI

November 5, 1902, Moscow

The new theatre is very fine; spacious, bright, no cheap, glaring luxury. The acting remains as ever, i.e., good; there are no new plays, and the only one they did stage did not meet with success. Meierhold is not missed; Kachalov substitutes for him in "The Three Sisters" and turns in a magnificent performance; the rest of their repertory ("Lonely Lives," for instance) has not gone on yet. The absence of Sanin, who is enjoying success in St. Petersburg, is keenly felt. Box office prices are the same as last year's. They give a superb performance of "Uncle Vanya."

My mother is in St. Petersburg, my sister isn't painting, my wife is well, Vishnevski visits us daily. Last night my wife went to hear Olenina d'Alheim, who is reputed to be an extraordinary singer. I am not allowed anywhere and am kept at home for fear that I may catch cold. I will probably not go abroad, but will return to Yalta in December. . . . You know you ought to buy yourself a small plot of ground not far from Moscow and cultivate it, keep busy with the orchard and truck garden and write short stories during the winter. You can buy land or rent it for sixty to ninety years, but it is most important to have it as close as possible to Moscow. . . . Are you treating sick people? It won't do. The best thing is to send the person to a doctor. Let me have the name of the article you are writing. May the heavenly angels guard you.

Yours,
A. Chekhov

To OLGA KNIPPER

December 20, 1902, Yalta

My sweet love,

I had a letter today from Alexeyev along these lines: "Gorki's play[1] and the theatre have had a tremendous success. Olga

[1] *The Lower Depths.*

Leonardovna gleamed like a shining light before an exacting audience." Rejoice, my sweet. Your husband is very pleased and will drink to your health today, if only Masha brings some beer with her.

I am currently having a lot of trouble with my teeth. I don't know when all this stupid business will come to an end. Yesterday I had a letter from you that was practically unsealed (again!) and today is a sad day for me, since Arseni brought nothing from you from the post office. And today's weather is dismal: warm and quiet, but not even a hint of spring. I sat out on the balcony, basking in the sun and thinking of you, and Fomka, and crocodiles, and the lining of my jacket, which is in shreds. I thought how much you needed to have a little boy to take up your time, to fill your life. You will have a baby son or daughter, my beloved, believe me, but you must just wait and get back to normal after your illness. I am not lying to you, nor am I concealing a single word of what the doctors have told me, cross my heart.

Misha sent some herrings. . . . There is absolutely nothing else to write about, or at least it doesn't seem so, life goes on obscurely and rather emptily. I am coughing. I sleep well, but dream all night long, as is fitting for an idle fellow.

Write me everything in detail, my child, so as to make me feel that I belong not to Yalta, but to the north, that this mournful and empty life has not yet engulfed me. I am hoping to get to Moscow not later than the first of March, i.e., two months from now, but I do not know whether I will do so or not. God keep you, my good little wife, my little red-haired kitten. Just imagine me holding you in my arms and carrying you around the room a couple of hours, kissing and embracing you. . . .

I will write tomorrow. Sleep in peace, my blessed joy, eat properly and think of your husband.

Your A.

To ALEXEI SUVORIN

December 22, 1902, Yalta

. . . Today the news came that Gorki's play "The Lower Depths" had an enormous success and was magnificently performed. I am rarely in the Art Theatre, but it seems to me that you have overestimated Stanislavski's role as producer.[1] The theatre is of the most usual sort, and their business is carried on in the most usual way, as it is everywhere, except that the actors are cultivated, very decent people; as a matter of fact they do not gleam with talent but they work hard, love what they do and learn their parts. If much of their repertory has not enjoyed success it is because the play is not suitable or the actors haven't enough of what it takes. Stanislavski certainly is not to blame. You write that he is chasing all the gifted people off the stage of the Art Theatre, but actually during all the five years of its existence not a single person with any pretension to talent has left. . . .

You write, "You are such an amiable person, why have you thrust yourself now into this acting and new-literature circle?" I have thrust myself into Yalta, into this little provincial country town, and that is the root of all the evils besetting me. Regretfully, the new-literature circle considers me an outsider, and old-fashioned; its relations toward me are warm but practically official, and as for the acting circle, that consists only of the letters of my wife, an actress, and nothing more. . . .

Merry Christmas and Happy New Year, and I wish you good health. . . . Many thanks for the letter, which was very interesting.

Yours,

A. Chekhov

[1] The Russians, like most Europeans, use the word "producer" to mean the man who directs the play. They use "director" to mean the general head of the theatre, a kind of manager for the acting company and the theatre itself.

To SHOLOM ALEICHEM

June 19, 1903, Naro Fominskoye

Dear Solomon Naumovich,

Generally speaking, I am not writing nowadays, or rather I write very little, so I can only give you a conditional promise: I will be very glad to write a story for you if illness does not interfere. As to my already published works, they are at your entire disposal, and a translation into Yiddish to be published in a collection[1] for the benefit of the Kishinev victims[2] would afford me heartfelt pleasure.

With sincere respect and devotion,

A. Chekhov

I got the letter yesterday, June 18th.

To KONSTANTIN STANISLAVSKI

July 28, 1903, Yalta

Dear Konstantin Sergeyevich,

I am so very, very sorry you are not in Yalta now; the weather here is extraordinarily fine, enchanting; it couldn't be any better. . . .

My play[1] is not done and is moving ahead a little stiffly, a state of affairs I attribute to my laziness, the marvelous weather and the difficulty of the subject. I will write you when I finish, or better yet will wire. Your rôle, it seems, has come off not badly, though I won't set myself up as a judge, because generally speaking I can hardly form an estimate of a play merely by reading it.

Olga is well and bathes in the sea every day; she fusses over me. My sister is also in good health and the two of them thank you for your greetings and send theirs. Yesterday I saw Mik-

[1] The collection referred to was printed in Warsaw and included one of Chekhov's stories, "Grim People."

[2] This was the pogrom in the Ukraine that shocked the Western world.

[1] Chekhov was at work on *The Cherry Orchard.*

hailovski-Garin, the engineer and writer, who is building the Crimean railway; he says he is going to write a play.

I am well. . . . I press your hand cordially, wish you health and all the best.

Yours,
A. Chekhov

I won't read my play to you because I don't know how to; but I'll give it to you for reading, providing I can get it ready, of course.

To KONSTANTIN STANISLAVSKI

October 30, 1903, Yalta

Dear Konstantin Sergeyevich,

Thank you very much for the letter and for the telegram. Letters are always very precious to me because, one, I am here all alone, and two, I sent the play off three weeks ago and your letter came only yesterday; if it were not for my wife, I would have been entirely in the dark and would have imagined any old thing that might have crept into my head. When I worked on the part of Lopakhin, I thought it might be for you. If for some reason it doesn't appeal to you, take Gayev. Lopakhin, of course, is only a merchant, but he is a decent person in every sense, should conduct himself with complete decorum, like a cultivated man, without pettiness or trickery, and it did seem to me that you would be brilliant in this part, which is central for the play. (If you do decide to play Gayev, let Vishnevski play Lopakhin. He won't make an artistic Lopakhin but still he won't be a petty one. Lujski would be a cold-blooded foreigner in this part and Leonidov would play it like a little kulak. You mustn't lose sight of the fact that Varya, an earnest, devout young girl, is in love with Lopakhin; she wouldn't love a little kulak.)

I want so much to go to Moscow but I don't know how I can

get away from here. It is turning cold and I hardly ever leave the house; I am not used to fresh air and am coughing. I do not fear Moscow, or the trip itself, but I am afraid of having to stay in Sevastopol from two to eight, and in the most tedious company.

Write me what rôle you are taking for yourself. My wife wrote that Moskvin wants to play Epikhodov. Why not, it would be a very good idea, and the play would gain from it.

My deepest compliments and regards to Maria Petrovna, and may I wish her and you all the best. Keep well and gay.

You know, I haven't yet seen "The Lower Depths" or "Julius Caesar." I would so much like to see them.

Yours,
A. Chekhov

To VLADIMIR NEMIROVICH-DANCHENKO
November 2, 1903, Yalta

My dear Vladimir Ivanovich,

Two letters from you in one day, thanks a lot! I don't drink beer, the last time I drank any was in July; and I cannot eat honey, as it gives me a stomach ache. Now as to the play.

1. Anya can be played by any actress you'd like, even an utter unknown, if only she is young and looks like a young girl, and talks in a young, resonant voice. This rôle is not one of the important ones.

2. Varya's part is more on the serious side, if only Maria Petrovna would take it. If she doesn't the part will turn out rather flat and coarse, and I would have to do it over and soften it. M. P. won't repeat herself because, firstly, she is a gifted actress, and secondly, because Varya does not resemble Sonya or Natasha; she is a figure in a black dress, a little nun-like creature, somewhat simple-minded, plaintive and so forth and so on.

3. Gayev and Lopakhin—have Stanislavski try these parts

and make his choice. If he takes Lopakhin and feels at home in the part, the play is bound to be a success. Certainly if Lopakhin is a pallid figure, played by a pallid actor, both the part and the play will fail.

4. Pishchik—the part for Gribunin. God have mercy on you if you assign the part to Vishnevski.

5. Charlotta—a big part. It would of course be impossible to give the part to Pomyalova; Muratova might be good, perhaps, but not funny. This is the part for Mme. Knipper.

6. Epikhodov—if Moskvin wants the part let him have it. He'll be a superb Epikhodov. . . .

7. Firs—the role for Artem.

8. Dunyasha—for Khalutina.

9. Yasha. If it is the Alexandrov you wrote about, the one that is assistant to your producer, let him have it. Moskvin would make a splendid Yasha. And I haven't anything against Leonidov for the part.

10. The passer-by—Gromov.

11. The stationmaster who reads "The Sinner" in Act III should have a bass voice.

Charlotta speaks with a good accent, not broken Russian, except that once in a while she gives a soft sound to a consonant at the end of a word rather than the hard sound that is proper, and she mixes masculine and feminine adjectives. Pishchik is an old Russian fellow broken down with gout, old age and satiety, plump, dressed in a long Russian coat (à la Simov) and boots without heels. Lopahkin wears a white vest and tan shoes, flails his arms when he is in motion, takes long strides, is lost in thought when he moves about and walks in a straight line. He doesn't cut his hair short and so he frequently tosses his head back; in reflection he strokes his beard back and forth, i.e., from his neck to his lips. I think Trofimov is clearly sketched. Varya wears a black dress and wide belt.

I have been intending to write "The Cherry Orchard" these past three years and for three years have been telling you to hire an actress who could play a part like Lubov Andreyevna. This long waiting game never pays.

I have got into the stupidest position: I am here alone and don't know why. But you are unjust in saying that despite your work it is "Stanislavski's theatre." You are the one that people speak about and write about while they do nothing but criticize Stanislavski for his performance of Brutus. If you leave the theatre, so will I. Gorki is younger than we and has his own life to lead. As to the Nizhni-Novgorod theatre, this is only an episode in his life; Gorki will try it, sniff at it and cast it aside. I may say in this connection that people's theatres and people's literature are plain foolishness, something to sweeten up the people. Gogol shouldn't be pulled down to the people, but the people raised to Gogol's level.

I would like so much to visit the Hermitage Restaurant, eat some sturgeon and drink a bottle of wine. Once I drank a bottle of champagne solo and didn't get drunk, then I had some cognac and didn't get drunk either.

I'll write you again and in the meantime send my humble greetings and thanks. Was it Lujski's father that died? I read about it in the paper today.

Why does Maria Petrovna insist on playing Anya? And why does Maria Fyodorovna think she is too aristocratic to play Varya? Isn't she playing in "The Lower Depths," after all? Well, the devil take them. I embrace you, keep well.

> Yours,
>
> A. Chekhov

To ALEXANDER VISHNEVSKI

> *November 7, 1903, Yalta*

Dear Alexander Leonidovich,

I got your letter and finally am getting around to thanking you. Since I am coming to Moscow soon, please set aside one seat for me for "Pillars of Society." I want to have a look at this amazing Norwegian play and will even pay for the privilege. Ibsen is my favorite author, you know.

You didn't write how you were getting along, and how your health is. Are you exhausted? I stay put, cough a lot and run to the toilet, if you will pardon the expression, five times a day minimum. One of nature's tricks.

When you dine with us in Moscow, please don't laugh.

I press your hand and send you a thousand heartiest greetings. I begged so earnestly in my letters that you not be given a part in "The Cherry Orchard"—now I see my request has been honored.

Yours,
A. Chekhov

To KONSTANTIN STANISLAVSKI

November 23, 1903, Yalta

Dear Konstantin Sergeyevich,

Haymaking usually takes place from about the twentieth to the twenty-fifth of June, during which time it seems the corn crake and the frogs are over their summer music and are silent. Only the oriole can be heard. There is no cemetery—there had once been one, but two or three gravestones leaning in disorder are all that remain. A bridge—that is a very good idea. If you can get the train into the action without noise, without so much as a single sound—go ahead. I am not against using the same scenery in Acts III and IV as long as entrances and exits can be conveniently managed.

I am impatiently waiting for the day and hour when my wife will permit me to come to Moscow. Devil take it, I am beginning to suspect her of being foxy with me!

The weather here is quite warm, remarkable weather, but when one recalls Moscow and the Sandunov baths all this delight seems stale and unprofitable.

I sit in my study and keep looking at the telephone. I get my telegrams by telephone and am expecting every minute to be summoned at last to Moscow.

I press your hand heartily and am everlastingly grateful for your letter. Keep well and happy.

Yours,

A. Chekhov

To MARIA CHEKHOVA

June 6, 1904, Berlin

Dear Masha,

I am writing you from Berlin, where I have been for the last twenty-four hours. Moscow got awfully cold after you left; there was snow and I probably caught cold on account of it, had rheumatic pains in my arms and legs, couldn't sleep, got terribly thin, had morphine injections, took thousands of assorted medicines and gratefully recall only heroin, which Altshuller had once prescribed for me. At departure time I picked up new strength, my appetite came back, I started dosing myself with arsenic, and so on and so forth, and finally left for abroad on Thursday, very skinny, with very thin, spindling legs. I had a really good, pleasant journey. Here in Berlin we have taken a comfortable room in the very best hotel and are enjoying our stay thoroughly; it's been a long time since I've eaten as well, with as much appetite. The bread here is marvelous and I eat too much of it, the coffee is excellent and as for the dinners, they are beyond words. People who haven't been abroad don't know what good bread means. There isn't any decent tea here (we brought along our own), no appetizers, but on the other hand all the rest is superb, despite its being cheaper than at home. I've already put on weight and today even took quite a long drive to the Tiergarten, although it was cold. And so you can tell Mama and everyone interested that I am getting better, or even that I am already better, my legs no longer ache, I don't have diarrhea, am beginning to fill out, am on my feet all day, and don't lie down. Tomorrow I am having a visit from the local celebrity—Prof. Ewald, a specialist in intestinal ailments; Dr. Taube wrote him of me.

I drank some wonderful beer yesterday. . . .

Do keep well and in good spirits, and may the heavenly angels guard you. Give my greetings to Mama and tell her everything is fine now. I'll leave for Yalta in August. Regards also to Grandma, Arseni and Nastya. . . . Let me kiss you.

Your

A. Chekhov

We forgot to take along our dressing gowns.

To MARIA CHEKHOVA

June 8, 1904, Berlin

Dear Masha,

Today we leave Berlin for our prolonged residence on the Swiss border, where it will probably be very boresome and very hot. My address is: Herrn Anton Tschechow, Badenweiler, Germany. As that is the way they spell my name on my documents here, it must be the way it should be written in German.

It is somewhat cold in Berlin, but nice. The worst thing here, the thing that intrudes upon your vision piercingly, are the outfits of the local ladies. There is a horrible lack of taste, nowhere do they dress as abominably, with complete absence of taste. I haven't seen a single handsome woman and not one who isn't trimmed up with some variety of absurd braid. Now I understand why taste is grafted so slowly and painfully upon the Moscow Germans. On the other hand, life in Berlin is most comfortable, the meals are delicious, the prices not high, the horses are well fed, the dogs, which are harnessed to little carts, are also well fed, and the streets are clean and orderly. . . .

My legs don't ache any more, I am eating splendidly, sleep well and dash around Berlin, but my one trouble is shortness of breath. I bought myself a summer suit today, Jaeger caps, etc., etc., This stuff is much cheaper than it is in Moscow. . . .

Regards to Mama and Vanya. Have a good time and don't get downhearted if you can avoid it. I press your hand warmly and kiss you.

Your Anton

To MARIA CHEKHOVA

June 12, 1904, Badenweiler

Dear Masha,

. . . Villa Friederike, like all the local houses and villas, is a private house situated in a luxuriant garden, exposed to the sun, which shines upon me and keeps me warm until seven in the evening (after that hour I stay indoors). We take both room and board here. For fourteen or sixteen marks a day we have a double room flooded with sunlight, with a washstand, beds, etc., etc., a desk, and the most important thing—marvelous water which is like seltzer. The general impression is one of a big garden, with tree-covered mountains in the background, few people, very little movement on the streets, the garden and the flowers beautifully tended; but today for no good reason we had rain, and I must sit indoors, and it seems to me that another few days like this and I will start thinking of how I can get away.

I continue eating butter in enormous quantities—and without effect. I can't stand milk. The local doctor, Schwöhrer (married to a girl from Moscow named Zhivo), has turned out to be proficient and pleasant.

From here we may perhaps take the sea route to Yalta by way of Trieste, or some other port. I am gaining health here in leaps and bounds. At least I have learned the right way to keep myself well fed. I am absolutely forbidden coffee; they say it has a laxative effect. I am already beginning to eat an occasional egg. God, how frightfully the German women dress!

I am living on the ground floor. If you could only have some idea of the sunshine we have here! It doesn't burn, but caresses. I have a comfortable armchair in which I can sit or lie down.

I will buy you a watch without fail, I haven't forgotten. How is Mama's health? How are her spirits? Write me. Give her my regards. Olga is going to the dentist here, a very good one.

Well, keep healthy and merry. I'll write you again in a few days.

I bought a lot of this paper in Berlin, and envelopes as well. I kiss you and press your hand.

Your A.

To MARIA CHEKHOVA

June 16, 1904, Badenweiler

Dear Masha,

I had your first postcard today, thanks a lot. I am living among the Germans and have already become accustomed to my room and my regime but just cannot ever get used to German peace and quiet. There's not a sound in the house or outside it, except for a band in the garden at 7 in the morning and at noon, expensive, but no talent in the playing. You feel there isn't a drop of talent in anything, not a drop of taste, but on the other hand there is order and honesty, and to spare. Our Russian life is much more talented, and as for the Italian or the French, they are beyond comparison.

My health has improved and when I walk I no longer feel aware of my illness, and just walk around calmly; my shortness of breath has abated, nothing aches, but my illness has left me painfully thin, and my legs are skinnier than they have ever been. The German doctors have turned my life upside down. At 7 A.M. I have tea in bed, and it must definitely be in bed, for some reason or other; at 7:30 a German who is a sort of masseur comes in and rubs me with water, which is not so bad; then I have to lie down for a while, after which I get up and drink acorn cocoa and with it eat an enormous quantity of

[323]

butter. At 10 o'clock oatmeal, thin, unusually delicious and aromatic, not at all like our Russian stuff. Fresh air and basking in the sun. Reading the newspapers. Dinner at one in the afternoon, at which I can't help myself to all the courses, but eat only those that Olga chooses for me on orders from the German doctor. Cocoa again at 4 o'clock. Supper at 7. Before going to bed I have a cup of strawberry tea to make me sleep. There is a lot of quackery in all this, but a lot that is actually good, the oatmeal, for instance. I'm going to take some of their oatmeal with me.

Olga has just left for Switzerland, to have her teeth fixed in Basle. She will be home at 5 this afternoon.

I want terribly to go to Italy. I'm very glad Vanya is with you and give him my regards. Give them to Mama, too. . . .

I am glad everything is going well at home. I will remain here another three weeks probably, then spend a short time in Italy, and on to Yalta, perhaps by the sea route.

Write oftener. Tell Vanya to write, too. Keep well and happy. I kiss you.

Your A.

To MARIA CHEKHOVA[1]

June 28, 1904, Badenweiler

Dear Masha,

A fierce heat wave has come upon us and caught me unawares, as I have only my winter suits with me. I am stifling and am considering leaving here. But where to go? I would like to visit Como in Italy but everybody there has run away on account of the heat. All southern Europe is hot. I would like to take the steamer from Trieste to Odessa but don't know how feasible this is during June and July. Would you mind perhaps inquiring from Georgie what kind of boats they have on that run?

---

[1] This is the last letter Chekhov wrote. He died four days later in Badenweiler, on July 2, 1904.

Have they comfortable accommodations? Do they make long stops, is the food good, etc., etc.? This would be an invaluable trip for me, but only if the ship were a good one. George[2] would do me a great favor if he would cable me *at my expense*. The cable should take this form: "Badenweiler Tschechow. Bien. 16. Vendredi." These words would mean: bien—the steamer is all right. Sixteen—number of days the trip takes, Vendredi—the day the steamer leaves Trieste. Of course I am only giving the form of the cable, and if the steamer leaves on a Thursday it certainly won't do to write Vendredi.

It won't be a calamity if the trip is a somewhat hot one, as I will be wearing a light flannel suit. I might as well confess I am rather afraid of making it by train. The coaches are suffocating in this kind of weather, especially with my shortness of breath, which the least little nothing makes worse. Besides, there are no sleeping cars from Vienna right through to Odessa, so it would be a restless trip. Then too, the train gets one home faster than necessary and I haven't yet had my fill of traveling.

It is very hot, enough to make you strip. I just don't know what to do. Olga went to Freiburg to order my flannel suit—there are no tailors or shoemakers in Badenweiler. She took the suit Duchard made for me as a sample.

I am eating really delicious food, but not much of it as my stomach is always getting out of order. I daren't eat the butter here. Apparently my stomach has been hopelessly spoiled and it is hardly possible to set it to rights by any means short of fasting, i.e. to stop eating—and that's that. As for the shortness of breath, there is only one remedy—not to move.

You don't see a single decently dressed German woman, the lack of taste is depressing.

Keep well and happy, regards to Mama, Vanya, George, Auntie and all the rest. Write. I kiss you and press your hand.

Your

A.

2 Chekhov's cousin George worked for a steamship line.

INDEX